Understanding ASEAN

Understanding ASEAN

edited by
Alison Broinowski

St. Martin's Press
AIIA

New York

© Alison Broinowski: 1982; Chapter 1 © Wang Gungwu: 1982; Chapter 2 ©
Roger Irvine: 1982; Chapter 3 © David Irvine: 1982; Chapter 4 © Amado
Castro: 1982; Chapter 5 © Michael Richardson: 1982; Chapter 6 © Allan Gyngell:
1982; Chapter 7 © Frank Frost: 1982; Chapter 8 © Alan Rix: 1982; Chapter 9
© Ho Kwon Ping: 1982; Chapter 10 © Robyn Lim: 1982.

St. Martin's Press, Inc., 175 Fifth Avenue, New York, NY 10010
in association with
The Australian Institute of International Affairs
Printed in Hong Kong
First published in the United States of America in 1982

ISBN 0−312−83076−9

Library of Congress Cataloging in Publication Data
Main entry under title:

Understanding ASEAN.

Bibliography: p.
Includes index.
Contents: Introduction, ASEAN between tradition and modernity / Wang
Gungwu − The formative years of ASEAN, 1967-1975 / Roger Irvine − Making
haste less slowly, ASEAN from 1975 / David Irvine − [etc.]
1. ASEAN − Addresses, essays, lectures. 2. Asia, Southeastern − Economic
integration − Addresses, essays, lectures. 3. Asia, Southeastern − Foreign
economic relations − Addresses, essays, lectures.

I. Broinowski, Alison.
HC441.u5   337.1'59   81-9036
ISBN 0-312-83076-9   AACR2

Contents

List of Figures and Tables

Map of Southeast Asia Showing ASEAN Countries

Editor's Foreword

From ASEAN's earliest days, it has had its share of admirers and detractors. The Association has aroused suspicion, antagonism, resentment, respect and fulsome praise, but most generally, curiosity. Observers of Southeast Asian affairs in government, universities, in business and in the Press continue to question the nature and purpose of ASEAN: why it was formed, what ASEAN gives its members which they would not otherwise have, what effects it has on its neighbours and how they should deal with it, what direction ASEAN will take in the future, and even whether it has a future.

More particular questions also arise: will ASEAN achieve a Zone of Peace? To what extent does regional co-operation override national competition in ASEAN? How will the ASEAN countries reconcile export-led growth with the need to expand their industrial and agricultural production for domestic consumption? Is ASEAN set to follow the newly industrialising countries of East Asia, and to emulate Singapore, ASEAN's most atypical member? What happens to ASEAN when the present leaders change? Will ASEAN become a common market? How will ASEAN cope with Vietnam, the Soviet Union, China, the United States, and with Japan? Will ASEAN develop a common foreign policy?

For people dealing with these questions, the need for a convenient source of information on ASEAN, on both general and specialised levels, has become obvious. This book is an attempt to meet that need by addressing the questions in a factual, objective way. It does not aim to arouse controversy or to make sensational revelations: we leave that to others.

In planning the book, I have deliberately crossed disciplines and national boundaries to bring together contributors who are officials, academics and journalists, with a common interest in Southeast Asian affairs: some are nationals of ASEAN countries, while all the others live or have lived in the region. All write here in a private capacity, and from publicly available sources. Since the organisations with which we are professionally associated have not intervened in any way in our project, we do not intend that they should be implicated in any of the views we put forward.

We sought to adopt a consensus approach, discussing the issues among ourselves, reading and commenting on each others' drafts, and trying to arrive at views which could be reflected in the final chapter. Inevitably, differences exist between us on some points, and I have preferred to let these remain to stimulate further inquiry, rather than take them out of the text to achieve unanimity.

Earlier accounts of ASEAN have been written by economists, by foreign relations specialists, by investment consultants and by governments: we are indebted to their detailed work. Others have approached ASEAN from fixed ideological positions which we have tried to avoid. In keeping with the widening impact of ASEAN, and growing interest in it, our intention has been to match that range in our coverage of ASEAN affairs. We have paid close attention to the original blueprint for ASEAN economic co-operation drawn up by a United Nations team in the early 1970s, because it remains relevant as a basis for many of the decisions ASEAN is now making, and because most other studies have neglected it.

As well as tracing the antecedents, development and structure of ASEAN and its co-operative efforts both economic and political, internal and external, we have tried throughout to take account of the Association in terms of its five countries and to give due weight to the differences between them. Chapter 9, which deals in detail with the difficulties facing some of the individual countries, provides a perspective on ASEAN which contrasts with the measured optimism of the rest of the book. It is a view supported by some reports of the Asian Development Bank, IBRD and ILO, and its inclusion in any realistic assessment of ASEAN is essential. We have selected ASEAN's relations with Japan and with Australia for special scrutiny, since they demonstrate similarities and differences in ASEAN's approaches to the dialogue countries, as well as in the responses to ASEAN of the two countries themselves. If this way of dealing with the subject succeeds in covering the full range of ASEAN's affairs without sacrificing depth, and if it answers some questions while stimulating others, it will have served its purpose.

I acknowledge with appreciation the support of the Australian Institute of International Affairs, and particularly of its Director, Mr R. L. Harry. Dr Carlyle A. Thayer, Dr Ross Garnaut, Dr Nancy Viviani, Dr John Funston and Dr Peter King read parts of the manuscript and made useful suggestions, and Professor J. A. C. Mackie and Dr Milton Osborne gave me valuable advice in the preparatory stages. Professor Estrella Solidum's work on ASEAN and defence, while it does not appear as a chapter, provided an important point of reference, and will I hope find its proper place in a larger study. I was particularly fortunate, just before completion of the manuscript, in having the opportunity to discuss it with the Secretary-General of ASEAN, Ambassador Narciso G. Reyes, who was present at ASEAN's birth and whose knowledge of ASEAN from the inside has few rivals. Finally, David Irvine's contributions to the book included many hours of hard work beyond those he gave to his own chapter, and I am grateful for them.

ALISON BROINOWSKI
Canberra, December 1980

Notes on the Contributors

ALISON BROINOWSKI is an officer of the Australian Department of Foreign Affairs, who has also worked as a novelist and journalist. She served in Manila from 1975 to 1978.

Dr AMADO CASTRO was Director of the Economic Bureau of the ASEAN Central Secretariat in Jakarta from 1977 to 1980. He is Professor of Economics, University of the Philippines.

Dr FRANK FROST is a foreign affairs specialist in the Legislative Research Service of the Parliamentary Library in Canberra. He received his PhD from the University of Sydney in 1976 for a thesis on 'The Operations of the Australian Army in South Vietnam, 1966–1971: Political and Military Problems'. He has written and published extensively on Southeast Asian affairs.

ALLAN GYNGELL is an Australian foreign service officer who has served in Rangoon and Singapore. From 1978 to 1980 he was a national assessments officer for the ASEAN countries in the Office of National Assessments, Canberra. He is at present on the staff of the Australian Embassy in Washington.

HO KWON PING is economics editor on the staff of the *Far Eastern Economic Review*, Hong Kong. He has written, lectured and broadcast extensively on ASEAN affairs.

DAVID IRVINE is an officer of the Australian Department of Foreign Affairs and served in Jakarta from 1976 to 1979.

ROGER IRVINE was until 1981 an analyst in the Joint Intelligence Organization, Department of Defence, Canberra, concurrently undertaking postgraduate research on ASEAN in the International Relations Department of the Australian National University. He is at present on the staff of the Australian Embassy in Washington.

Dr ROBYN LIM is a Lecturer in the Department of General Studies, University of New South Wales. She holds a PhD in International Relations from the Australian National University and has published mainly on Philippine domestic and foreign policy. Her most recent publication is 'Australia and ASEAN', in *Southeast Asian Affairs* (ISEAS, Singapore, 1980). She is at present a visiting lecturer in Australian Studies at Tokyo University.

MICHAEL RICHARDSON has worked for the past ten years as the Southeast Asia correspondent of the Melbourne *Age*, based in Singapore. He was a major contributor to *The Boat People* (Penguin Books, 1980).

Dr ALAN RIX received his degree from the Australian National University in political science, specialising in Japanese foreign aid. He worked there for two years on the Australia–Japan Economic Research Project, and is at present on a two-year assignment to the Japan Secretariat, Canberra. He is the author of *Japan's Economic Aid: Policy Making and Politics* (Croom Helm, 1980).

Professor WANG GUNGWU was Director of the Research School of Pacific Studies, Australian National University, 1975–80. He has been Professor of Far Eastern History at ANU since 1968, having previously been Professor of History in the University of Malaya. He is President of the Australian Humanities Academy (since 1980), and from 1978 to 1980 was President of the Asian Studies Association of Australia. He has written and broadcast extensively on Southeast Asian affairs. His latest book is *Community and Nation: Essays on Southeast Asia and the Chinese* (Heinemann, 1981).

Abbreviations

AAECP	ASEAN–Australian Economic Cooperation Programme
ADB	Asian Development Bank
ASA	Association of Southeast Asia
ASEAN	Association of Southeast Asian Nations
ASEAN–CCI	ASEAN Chambers of Commerce and Industry
ASPAC	Asian and Pacific Council
COMECON	Council for Mutual Economic Aid
CPP	Communist Party of the Philippines
CPT	Communist Party of Thailand
EC	European Community (ies)
ECAFE	(United Nations) Economic Commission for Asia and the Far East
EEC	European Economic Community
ESCAP	Economic and Social Commission for Asia and the Pacific
IBRD	International Bank for Reconstruction and Development (World Bank)
ICAP	International Civil Aviation Policy (Australian)
ILO	International Labour Organisation
IMF	International Monetary Fund
MNLF	Moro National Liberation Front
NPA	New People's Army (Philippine)
SCCAN	Special Co-ordinating Committee of ASEAN Nations

SEAMEO	Southeast Asian Ministers of Education Organisation
SEATO	Southeast Asia Treaty Organisation
UNCTAD	United Nations Conference on Trade and Development
UNDP	United Nations Development Programme
UNESCO	United Nations Educational Scientific and Cultural Organisation
ZOPFAN	Zone of Peace, Freedom and Neutrality
ZOPIGN	Zone of Peace, Independence and Genuine Neutrality

1

Introduction: ASEAN between Tradition and Modernity

Wang Gungwu

The papers in this volume underline an obvious point. ASEAN is a thoroughly modern phenomenon, a product of new kinds of external pressures and no less novel internal ones. As the volume already describes how ASEAN came about and how it is now stronger than most people expected only ten years ago, I need say no more here except to echo the warning note that such success does not mean that ASEAN has come to stay. Also, there is enough speculation about whether it is merely a step towards some larger regional grouping comprising all nine states of Southeast Asia, or towards an even larger one comprising most of the countries of the Pacific. Even if this happened, ASEAN may still survive as a small tight bloc within any kind of larger grouping.

The fact that ASEAN is modern does not guarantee its durability. What is interesting is how the quest for modernity sits with the desire to preserve or revive long-established traditions of language, religion and politics, and how the relationships between the two enhance or diminish this kind of regionalism. In particular, when traditions that had kept much of the region fragmented and divided are still largely alive, how far can the modernising élites of each country transform these traditions so that they support ASEAN and not weaken it? The short history of ASEAN has demonstrated that external pressures, whether strategic, economic or ideological, have helped the élites bring the five countries closer together. The strength of these pressures has enabled each of the élite groups to stress modernity over tradition and thus promote ASEAN as necessary for the survival of each member nation.

And we have every reason to believe that these pressures will remain strong. Under such conditions one may ask how relevant questions of modernity and tradition *within* each country are for the future of regionalism.

The quality of the modernising élites may indicate the long-term commitment to modernity of each country. By the development criteria widely employed today, it is obvious that Singapore heads the list, with the Philippines and Malaysia closely behind. Indonesia and Thailand use similar rhetoric but are constrained by more traditional concerns. For example, by far the most modern and the least sensitive to any kind of local tradition are the ruling élites of Singapore. They have become so because of the need for efficiency for the grim purpose of survival, and this efficiency feeds on that of the most developed regions of the world, in North America, Western Europe and Japan. Left to itself, Singapore would prefer not to be confined by regional priorities, but its leaders recognise that it will not be left to itself and, certainly for the time being, ASEAN is necessary and fortunately can also serve as a modernising force.

Filipino and Malaysian élites are no less modern in spirit than those in Singapore but different traditions prevail in their respective countries. For the Philippines, the only meaningful traditions are relatively new and are rooted in Spanish Catholicism and Malay-world Islam. These two have pulled in quite different directions and the strongly Americanised modern élites have countered them by an early commitment to internationalism which has survived intact. For the modern Filipino élites, almost any supra-national grouping is worth considering. They look to a pluralistic world and value their freedom to decide which kind of grouping to join. ASEAN is one of the organisations the Philippines needs and is best qualified to join. In contrast, Malaysian modernisers have to contend with traditions that have been highly politicised and represent powerful forces beyond the region. The existence of Chinese and Indian traditions among the large minorities threaten local traditions. In this case, ASEAN regionalism actually helps to contain the divisive forces that plague the country. It also strengthens the claims of *bumiputraism* to be able to link with the indigenous peoples across the Straits of Malacca and Johore as well as into southern Thailand and southern Philippines. In this case, Malay-world Islamic traditions could be made to work in support of the regional organisation rather than against it. The Malaysian modernising élites have long been aware of this and it is no accident that they have showed great keenness for ASEAN from the start.

As for Indonesia and Thailand, different cultural factors have limited the commitment to modernity of their respective élites. For one thing their modern élites are smaller in proportion to total population than those of the other three countries. For another, a large proportion of them are military men and, although many of them are modern in outlook, especially about military technology, and may become unconscious agents of modernisation, they are largely committed to traditional ways. ASEAN regionalism, however, represents in itself a departure from historic and conventional responses. It certainly is a challenge to both countries: to Thailand because it draws the Thais away from close traditional ties with Burma, Laos and Cambodia, and to Indonesia because it is still engaged in building a single nation out of the multi-ethnic and multi-cultural components of what is almost itself a regional organisation.

In suggesting that the more modern the élites the more support there is for ASEAN, I have assumed that the traditional divisions in the region work against ASEAN. There is one obvious exception. I have already mentioned the underlying Malay-world Islam that encourages Malaysian support for ASEAN. But, of course, we must also consider how this same encouragement may pose problems for ASEAN unity. Militant Muslim groups looking outwards from their respective countries and, even more likely, looking towards the Islamic world outside could disrupt the internal stability of each of the five countries as well as the relations among them. Libyan money, Palestinian politics, Iranian revolutionary rhetoric and deviant pan-Islamic fanaticism of various sorts may form the strongest challenge to the kind of modernisation that ASEAN supports and is supported by. The point, however, is that ASEAN itself serves as a counter to that kind of traditional revivalism. A regional pluralism

which includes Buddhism, Christianity and Javanese syn-
cretism as well as a modern secular and scientific spirit should
provide protection from one kind of narrow religiosity.

This leads me to say that, while the other traditions do
not necessarily assist the development of regional unity, they
are each in themselves not strong enough to obstruct it. Gone
are the days when pious kings, self-proclaimed messiahs and
ambitious warriors could disrupt weakly structured alliances
and seek to build new empires. In fact, it is easier now to see
how traditions could be used to support the modernisation
process and even how such traditions could be manipulated
to legitimise the work of the new élites. Indeed, the stability
of each country still depends on how these élites keep
traditions viable and assimilate such symbols to national,
and now regional, purposes. In short, there are now many
new tests of a country's vitality that require its leaders to
grasp not only the speed of modern changes but also the
simultaneous renewal of traditional values. And clearly, the
mobilisation and modification of these values can help
ASEAN in the long run.

Having suggested that traditional forces within ASEAN
are in themselves unlikely to disrupt the organisation, let me
turn to two other questions concerning tradition. Firstly,
what if the process of transforming traditions should end
in disaster because the modernising élites are insensitive,
incompetent, corrupt or a combination of all three? Secondly,
what effect would the surviving traditions of ASEAN's neighbours, or the lack of them, have on ASEAN's future?

If the élites fail in their attempt to make traditions serve a
common goal of modernisation, then each separate set of
traditions in each ASEAN country could play an important
role that may be hard to predict. For example, if the Marcos
government alienates the Church in the Philippines or
if the Indonesian military loses the confidence of a highly
politicised Islamic movement, ASEAN would find itself
burdened by the internal instability of two of its members.
This could in turn affect the traditional forces mobilised by
the other members and also distract the organisation from
its regional goals; or — and this may be the more serious
result — the failure to control revived traditions could lead

ASEAN countries to support one another and even join forces to suppress what they cannot manipulate.

More immediate is the question of Thailand. Where the military is itself still a traditional force seeking to modernise slowly and it proves to be both corrupt and incompetent, what would ASEAN's responsibilities be? To help the Thai élites no matter whether they are right or wrong? To offer fraternal advice and hope for the best? The test here would be ASEAN's capacity to assist in the modernisation of the region as a whole. ASEAN can guarantee that none of its members would take advantage of the failures of one of them. It can fight to protect Thailand from its non-ASEAN neighbours. But what it still has to demonstrate is the ability of its élites to share their modernisation experiences and learn to recognise the common need to cope with traditions which they themselves have stimulated to a new life. This is specially difficult because regionalism has come early to countries where the nation-building process is still far from complete. To admit a common need where internal matters are concerned calls for a political maturity which it would be unreasonable to expect for some time. Yet the fast-moving events in the region may force the ASEAN élites to learn to do so very quickly.

The remaining question concerns the traditions of ASEAN's neighbours in Southeast Asia. The obvious set of traditions is that of Thailand's Buddhist neighbours and the obvious speculation covers relations with Burma, Laos and Kampuchea. This ignores the ethnicity of Lao cousins within Thailand and the Shan cousins in Burma, but this is probably less important than that the Buddhist neighbours are now all socialists in one form or another. It is too early to say which of the three elements, or combination thereof, of ethnicity, Buddhism and socialism will eventually dominate ASEAN's future relations with the larger Southeast Asian region. For the moment, Buddhist traditions seem hardly an issue, except possibly the remarkable fact that Buddhist states have been prone to the socialist way. For Thailand, and for ASEAN as well, this is a far from comfortable fact.

The final distinctive 'Great Tradition' in Southeast Asia is that of Vietnam with its historical links with China, both socialist and pre-socialist. The present hostility between Vietnam and China is unusual, despite what the Vietnamese leaders say today. Nevertheless, the urge to see Vietnam as part of Southeast Asia is both genuine and legitimate on the part of both Vietnam and the ASEAN group. What is important is that the Vietnamese élites seek protection against China and have played down those elements in their tradition which owe their origins to China. By so doing, they have eliminated tradition as an active factor in their search for a Southeast Asian identity. Indeed, they would see themselves as modernised and, compared with ASEAN élites, more advanced ones at that. They, more than the Burmese élites, offer the answer to ASEAN's brand of middle-class modernisation oriented towards Western capitalism.

It is this very modernity that Vietnam espouses which, I believe, will determine the way ASEAN, if it is to survive, will become an ever more efficient medium of modernisation in Southeast Asia. The rivalry between the two varieties of modernity which started more than thirty years ago in Europe has now settled upon the region and taken on some indigenous colouring. Indeed, it could be said that ASEAN had taken the initiative against socialist modernity in the 1960s. The existence of ASEAN on the one hand and the hostility of China on the other thoroughly justifies, in Vietnamese eyes, Vietnam's plans for something that might become an Indo-Chinese Federation. Vietnam's only safe alternative would be to be part of a larger ASEAN aimed at China that included all the countries of Southeast Asia. As long as there is little prospect of that occurring, Vietnam would not wish to negotiate over any matters concerning such a 'federation'. Without Laos and Kampuchea firmly attached to its cause, it would feel wholly isolated. If these two countries were to become part of a larger ASEAN, Vietnam would be forced to consider applying for membership or face eventual dominance by China.

The road seems clear for Vietnam and probably also for Laos and Kampuchea. The quest for socialist modernity together is the goal. There does not seem to be any traditional force to stand in the way of that goal. In contrast, the members of ASEAN are more sure of what they are not than what they are and what they ought to become. Only by joining together have they begun to admit to themselves that reviving traditions is not enough, that nationalism is not enough and that regionalism is not simply a right-sounding slogan. It has been hard work for its élites to bring ASEAN to the present stage of growth and it might be even harder work in the years to come to progress beyond this, but it represents a kind of modernity its members can all live with. If this modernity demands that traditions be slowly modified and subordinated to the new regional vision, it may be a price the ASEAN states would be willing to pay.

2

The Formative Years of ASEAN: 1967–1975

Roger Irvine

In early August 1967 the Foreign Ministers of Indonesia, the Philippines, Singapore and Thailand, and the Deputy Prime Minister of Malaysia, met in Thailand to discuss the formation of a new Southeast Asian regional organisation. After three days of talks at the seaside resort of Bangsaen and in Bangkok they signed on 8 August 1967 a Declaration establishing 'the Association of Southeast Asian Nations' (ASEAN).

Antecedents

ASEAN was not of course the first regional co-operative venture in which Southeast Asian nations had participated. Previous attempts at regional co-operation can be dated from the beginning of the post-Second World War period, when a number of Asian countries secured their independence. But for the most part these attempts also included countries outside Southeast Asia and apart from some ventures aimed primarily at encouraging economic co-operation, which usually depended heavily on support from major Western countries, such co-operative efforts were relatively short-lived. Nevertheless they laid some of the intellectual foundations for later attempts to institutionalise forms of regional co-operation in Southeast Asia. Particularly important in this respect was the Afro–Asian Conference hosted by Indonesia in Bandung in April 1955, which provided a forum for self-assertion by the newly independent Third World countries in Asia and Africa and for their claim to a voice in deciding the conduct of world affairs. Generally, however, Southeast Asian attempts at regional co-operation prior to the 1960s were hindered by the preoccupation of most countries with the pressing post-independence tasks of adapting to the severance of colonial links, establishing and consolidating indigenous political and economic institutions and achieving national integration.

The early 1960s saw the emergence of two regional groupings that, for the first time, were confined to Southeast Asian states and that were created at regional initiative. The first of these was the Association of Southeast Asia (ASA), formed at a meeting in Bangkok on 31 July 1961 and comprising Malaya, the Philippines and Thailand as founding members. The initial proposal for such an association was agreed upon during a visit by the Malayan Prime Minister, Tunku Abdul Rahman, to the Philippines in January 1959 as the guest of President Garcia. ASA was handicapped by its limited membership and by accusations that it was a pro-Western, anti-communist group whose motivations were primarily political. ASA's stated objectives in fact emphasised co-operation in the economic, social, cultural, scientific and administrative fields. It attempted to keep a low profile politically. The practical and modest approach that it adopted led its members to regard it as a valuable beginning to regional co-operative efforts. However, ASA's activities were disrupted during the latter part of 1963 following the steady deterioration in relations between Malaya and the Philippines over the latter's claim in June 1962 to North Borneo, which — renamed Sabah — became part of the Malaysian federation in September 1963.

Approximately coinciding with this interruption of ASA's activities the Philippines was developing proposals for a 'Greater Malay Confederation', later dubbed by Indonesia's Foreign Minister Subandrio 'Maphilindo', combining the first syllables of the names of the three proposed member countries — Malaya, the Philippines and Indonesia. Maphilindo was established during tripartite discussions in Manila in July/August 1963 attended by the heads of government of the three countries. These discussions centred upon their respective differences over the establishment of Malaysia. The Maphilindo proposal promoted by President Macapagal was essentially supplementary to these negotiations and appears to have been accepted by Indonesia and Malaya mainly as a concession to the Philippines and as a means to paper over the serious remaining differences between the three countries. Given these circumstances of its founding it is not surprising that Maphilindo did not become a vital organisation for regional co-operation. Furthermore, Maphilindo's emphasis on the common Malay origins of its members limited its appeal to other Southeast Asian countries.

Formation

Developments in the region in 1965 and 1966 paved the way for the formation of ASEAN. The abortive *coup* of 1 October 1965 in Indonesia led to the political demise of President Sukarno, whose pursuit of 'Confrontation' in opposition to the formation of Malaysia since early 1963 had seriously disrupted relations with neighbouring countries. President Marcos's election in November 1965 resulted in the soft-pedalling of the Sabah claim by the Philippines. The subsequent improvement in relations with Malaysia enabled the revival of ASA in March 1966. Late in 1965 and through the early months of 1966 discussions took place between Malaysian and Indonesian officials with the objective of bringing Confrontation to an end. These discussions led to formal talks on 29 May to 1 June 1966 between Malaysia's Deputy Prime Minister, Tun Abdul Razak, and Indonesia's Foreign Minister, Adam Malik. The talks were hosted in Bangkok by Foreign Minister Thanat Khoman who had for some time previously been playing a mediatory role in seeking solutions to Confrontation and the Philippine claim to Sabah. Comments by Malik at the conclusion of this meeting indicated that a new regional grouping had been discussed. Malik remained at the forefront of subsequent diplomatic endeavours to establish such a grouping, with active support from Thanat. In August 1966 Malaysia and Indonesia concluded an agreement that formally ended Confrontation.[1]

These developments brought to a close a period during

the late 1950s and the first half of the 1960s when the prospective members of ASEAN had been mutually engaged in a number of highly acrimonious and destabilising disputes. In the cases of Indonesia, Malaysia, the Philippines and Singapore these disputes were for much of this period the dominant preoccupations of their respective foreign policies. Indonesia's Confrontation policy and the Philippine claim to Sabah have already been mentioned. Even prior to Confrontation, Indonesia's relations with its northern neighbours had been subject to frequent strains. After the formation of Malaysia, Malayan and Singaporean leaders fell out over their different approaches to the management of communal and economic policies in the new federation. These differences led to Singapore's separation from Malaysia in August 1965. Continued friction marked relations between the two countries in subsequent years. Thailand had generally good relations during this period with its future fellow-members of ASEAN, although frictions with Malaysia over border problems occasionally surfaced.

Given this turbulent regional environment, it was all the more notable that attempts had continued to be made, in the form of ASA and Maphilindo, to provide a more co-operative basis for intra-regional relationships. The resolution of most of the major disputes by the end of 1966 offered the opportunity to put those attempts on a much sounder basis through the establishment of a new and more broadly based grouping. Although Malik was unsuccessful in attempts to attract countries such as Burma and Cambodia to join ASEAN, membership was declared to be open to all states in the Southeast Asian region that subscribed to ASEAN's aims, principles and purposes.

Objectives

The most difficult initial task facing prospective members of ASEAN was to decide just what these aims, principles and purposes were to be. A largely unstated but important underlying objective was clearly to establish a framework for peaceful intra-regional relationships between member states and to attempt to contain those disruptive disputes that had in the past distracted attention away from internal tasks. In particular, the new Association offered the prospect of drawing Indonesia into peaceful and co-operative relations with its neighbours within a forum that would provide some scope for it to play a leadership role and to secure at least tacit acceptance of its status as the first among equals. In addition, participation in ASEAN had for Indonesia the advantage of confirming its peaceful intentions and restoring its international respectability at a time when it was in dire need of economic assistance from major Western countries and from international financial institutions.

But the new Association also required a set of formal principles and objectives to underscore and define a positive programme of action for the future. As a result of meetings with Malik and Indonesian officials, Thanat Khoman is believed to have circulated late in 1966 a 'Draft Joint Declaration' proposing the establishment of a 'Southeast Asian Association for Regional Cooperation (SEAARC)'.[2] The draft formed the basis of the ASEAN Declaration signed at the conclusion of ASEAN's inaugural meeting. Both documents, and especially Thanat's initial draft, drew heavily in their preambular statement of principles on the Manila Agreements of July/August, 1963 that had, *inter alia*, endorsed the concept of Maphilindo. Press reports at the time of the inaugural meeting indicate that it was this preambular statement of principles that attracted the most controversy during negotiations. In particular, Thanat in his draft adopted from the Manila Agreements the formulation that

> foreign bases are temporary in nature and should not be used directly or indirectly to subvert the national independence of Asian countries, and...arrangements of collective defence should not be used to serve the particular interest of any of the big powers . . .

The Philippines apparently saw these statements as inconsistent with its desire to maintain its defence relationship with the US and as critical of the presence of US bases in the country. Indonesia urged that the statements be included, apparently arguing that it would be vulnerable to domestic criticism if some such reference was not made. The formulation agreed upon in the ASEAN Declaration stated that

> foreign bases are temporary and remain only with the expressed concurrence of the countries concerned and are not intended to be used directly or indirectly to subvert the national independence and freedom of states in the area . . .

This statement is rather more defensive of the presence of foreign bases. Malik remarked following the meeting that Indonesia left it to the judgement of the countries concerned how long bases were to remain.[3] The statement concerning collective defence arrangements that served the interest of big powers was conspicuous by its absence.

That part of the ASEAN Declaration that listed ASEAN's aims and purposes was apparently much less controversial. In this respect, and in defining the structure of the new organisation, ASEAN drew very heavily on the precedent set by ASA. From its revival in March 1966 ASA had been quite active. Its members were in fact initially reluctant to see its demise. Both ASA and ASEAN assigned top priority in their listing of aims and purposes to co-operation in the economic, social and cultural fields. Of these, economic co-operation was clearly considered to be the most important.

Apart from the intrinsic benefits anticipated from the pursuit of economic co-operation among ASEAN members, a second major reason was given to explain the priority given to it. This was that economic co-operation not only paved the way for co-operation in other areas but was indeed an essential precondition for the achievement of objectives in these other area. This view was succinctly expressed by Malaysia's Tun Ismail in his assertion that it was 'axiomatic that economic co-operation is often the most durable foundation upon which political and cultural co-operation can be built'.[4] This argument probably exercised a good deal of suasion in the minds of ASEAN's founders given the very high if not top priority that each country assigned in their national programmes to economic development. But especially taking into consideration the fact that the ambitions of ASEAN members in the field of economic co-operation were initially very modest, it is perhaps rather more likely that the key factor behind the emphasis on economic co-operation was that co-operation in this field, and even more so in the social and cultural fields, was relatively uncontroversial compared to co-operation in political or security matters.

Though political considerations were played down in the ASEAN Declaration there are good grounds for the view that they were of primary importance in the minds of most of the delegations attending ASEAN's inaugural meeting, even though on a number of specific issues not all prospective members would have seen eye to eye. Although the principles that are outlined in the preamble to the ASEAN Declaration are very broadly stated, they suggest at least the rudiments of a common political programme for the organisation. More important is the acknowledgement that from the beginning political matters were discussed by ASEAN delegates in private sessions. The description of these discussions as 'informal' appears to have been purely presentational. In this context it is worth citing remarks made in October 1974 by Adam Malik. Malik recalled the basic motivations that had led to the establishment of ASEAN as follows:

> Although from the outset ASEAN was conceived as an organisation for economic, social and cultural co-operation, and although considerations in these fields were no doubt central, it was the fact that there was a convergence in the political outlook of the five prospective member-nations ...which provided the main stimulus to join together in ASEAN...There was early recognition that meaningful progress could only be achieved by giving first priority to the task of overall and rapid economic development. It was also realised that, to this end, policies should be consciously geared towards safeguarding this priority objective, not only in purely economic terms but simultaneously also to secure the essential conditions of peace and stability, both domestically and internationally in the surrounding region.[5]

ASEAN's political overtones led to some speculation that it was intended to serve as yet another anti-communist grouping and in particular that it was designed to counter, even if only indirectly, the allegedly expansionist ambitions of the People's Republic of China which since 1966 had been in the throes of the Cultural Revolution. Lin Piao's call in September 1965 for 'People's War' had been taken up with enthusiasm by China. A number of other contemporary developments could also be construed to provide an anti-communist rationale for ASEAN. US involvement in the Vietnam War was rapidly escalating. June 1966 had seen the formation in Seoul of the Asian and Pacific Council (ASPAC), which included as members Malaysia, the Philippines and Thailand. The joint communiqué endorsed efforts 'to safeguard their national independence and integrity against any Communist aggression'. In October 1966 the Philippines hosted a conference of allies of South Vietnam, which was attended by Thailand. July 1967 also saw an announcement by Britain of its intention to withdraw its forces from east of Suez by the mid-1970s.

Thanat Khoman stated his view at the Fourth ASA Ministerial Meeting in late August 1967 that regional groupings such as ASA, ASPAC and ASEAN would assist to counter 'the revived germs of an old disease — imperialism — which are still being cultured in a large area of mainland Asia and are threatening to spread into neighbouring lands'. Similarly, at ASEAN's inaugural meeting, Philippine Foreign Secretary Narciso Ramos had declared that 'the time has come for a truly concerted struggle against the forces which are arrayed against our very survival in these uncertain and critical times'. Though the source of the threat was alluded to only indirectly, these remarks indicate that for at least some ASEAN members, anti-communism was an important element in their support for the Association's formation. Both China and the USSR were quick to make the accusation that ASEAN was essentially an anti-communist grouping.

It is difficult, however, to sustain the contention that ASEAN was intended to be a specifically and purposefully anti-communist grouping. The fact that one searches in vain in the official statements of ASEAN for explicitly anti-communist views seems not so much due to an excess of discretion as to an apparent consensus amongst ASEAN members that the Association, if not necessarily its individual members, would be best advised to espouse the principles of non-alignment and self-reliance.

Indonesia played a particularly important role in encouraging the espousal of non-alignment within ASEAN. Though President Suharto's New Order marked a major departure from the foreign policy orientation of his predecessor, there was an important degree of continuity in the basic principles underlying Indonesia's approach to international affairs, including continued attachment to an 'independent and active' foreign policy. In other ASEAN countries also, the principles of non-alignment were, to a greater or lesser extent, exercising an increasing allure by the time of ASEAN's formation. A foreign policy posture that was less subservient to the interests of the major Western powers was emerging to some degree in each of them. Growing scepticism about the value of major power security guarantees was supplemented, especially in the case of Indonesia, by expressions of more deep-seated distrust of major power intervention in the region in any form. Addressing a student group in Jakarta in December 1966 Adam Malik, in explaining why he had initiated moves towards a new regional grouping, reportedly stressed the need for

a strong bulwark against imperialist manipulations as well as a decisive stabilising factor in this part of the world. . . ending once and for all foreign influence, domination, and intervention. . .stemming the 'yellow' as well as the 'white' imperialism in South East Asia.[6]

In the same vein, Tun Razak observed at ASEAN's inaugural meeting:

For many centuries most of us have been dominated by colonial powers either directly or indirectly and even today we are not entirely free from being exposed to the struggle for domination by outside powers. Unless therefore we are all conscious of our responsibility to shape our common destiny and to prevent external intervention and interference, our region will continue to be fraught with danger and tension.

Moreover, the ASEAN declaration itself contained the assertion, adapted from the Manila Agreement, that

> the countries of Southeast Asia have a primary responsibility for strengthening the economic and social stability of the region and ensuring their peaceful and progressive national development, and. . .they are determined to ensure their stability and security from external interference in any form or manifestation in order to preserve their national identities in accordance with the ideals and aspirations of their peoples.

It is clear that ASEAN represented a break from the approach that had characterised SEATO and ASPAC. The prevailing view among ASEAN members appeared to be that greater emphasis should be placed on collective self-reliance in dealing with regional problems. Regionalism in this form seemed to acquire for ASEAN members an emotional or psychological dimension comparable to that associated with nationalism and which appeared to exercise considerable appeal to the small group of élites involved in ASEAN's formation.

One further question that arose concerning ASEAN's objectives was whether its members favoured the Association becoming a vehicle for military co-operation. At the time of ASEAN's formation it was usually asserted by spokesmen such as Malik and Razak that ASEAN would not involve itself in military or defence co-operation. However, there appeared on occasion to be some ambiguity about this and particularly about whether such co-operation might be taken up at a suitable time in the future. For example, Tun Razak is reported to have said following the inaugural meeting that it was possible for ASEAN to have defence arrangements 'once we have become good friends with a common interest and destiny'. He reportedly found it 'difficult to say whether there will be a defence arrangement now'.[7] In the early months of 1968 there were several reports that ASEAN leaders favoured some form of military co-operation in ASEAN, short of a formal military alliance. In March 1968 Suharto is reported to have said that ASEAN was aimed at, among other things, establishing peace and stability in

Southeast Asia, and to have observed: 'From this standpoint, there is a possibility that ASEAN may arrive at establishing military cooperation.'[8] Such reported remarks prompted considerable Press speculation that ASEAN's 'militarisation' was imminent, which occasioned several denials from ASEAN countries that this was the case and the issue of 'clarifications'. Very possibly several of the reports can be attributed to unwarranted amplification of comments by ASEAN spokesmen that merely acknowledged ASEAN's security significance without advocating specific forms of military co-operation.

In any case, by the time of ASEAN's Second Ministerial Meeting in Jakarta on 6–8 August 1968 it was evident that opinion had firmed among ASEAN leaders that the prospect of military co-operation in ASEAN should be de-emphasised. Rajaratnam stated at the meeting that during the preceding year ASEAN members

> had been able to clarify their ideas in regard to what ASEAN could and could not do. One significant clarification that had emerged was that ASEAN was an organisation to promote economic, social and cultural cooperation between member countries. This should dispose of the early misunderstanding that ASEAN had military implications.

Rajaratnam repeated the view that the essential basis for the attainment of both political and security goals lay in the pursuit of economic development. There also appeared to be general endorsement of the notion that an ASEAN military pact would be of little utility, especially given the fact that ASEAN members would be too weak, either individually or collectively, to form a credible military alliance, and the consideration that such a pact might be more likely to invite hostilities than deter aggression. Thanat Khoman advocated that security would be best served by a concept of 'collective political defence'.[9] In subsequent years ASEAN members pursued security co-operation on a bilateral basis, outside the formal framework of ASEAN.

Teething Problems

ASEAN's initial progress was not auspicious. Just a little over one year from ASEAN's establishment the organisation's activities were suspended for a period of nearly eight months due to the deterioration of relations between Malaysia and the Philippines over the 'Corregidor affair' and a revival of the Sabah dispute. For a much longer period ASEAN's co-operative efforts were hampered to a lesser degree by the strained relations between the two countries.

The Corregidor incident erupted in March 1968. Although there was and still is considerable uncertainty about exactly what happened, it appeared that the incident involved a special military force of Muslim recruits that was being trained on Corregidor Island, near Manila, allegedly with a view to being infiltrated into Sabah. The Malaysian Government announced other evidence of an infiltration attempt and lodged a formal protest. Relations were further aggravated when senior officials met in Bangkok in June and July 1968 for further discussions on the Sabah claim. The discussions were fruitless, serving only to exacerbate existing frictions. At the Second ASEAN Ministerial Meeting, Tun Razak and Narciso Ramos agreed upon a 'cooling-off period', apparently without any consensus as to what this meant. Relations reached a new low, with the passage in the Philippine Congress in September 1968 of a resolution delineating Philippine territorial waters that included the provision that this legislation would be 'without prejudice to the delineation of base lines of the territorial sea around the territory of Sabah . . .over which the. . .Philippines had acquired dominion and sovereignty'.[10]

Matters were not assisted by a Philippine directive to its diplomats attending international conferences to record a reservation concerning Malaysia's competence to represent Sabah. When such a reservation was made at a meeting of the ASEAN Permanent Committee on Commerce and Industry held from 30 September to 5 October 1968, the Malaysian delegation replied that until the reservation was retracted Malaysia would not attend any further ASEAN meetings.[11] This led to a hiatus in ASEAN meetings until late May 1969. Malaysian and Philippine diplomatic representatives were withdrawn from each other's capitals in late November 1968.

Another major incident in inter-ASEAN relations was sparked in October 1968 by the hanging in Singapore of two Indonesian marines who had been found guilty of acts of sabotage and murder during the Confrontation period, leading to an angry public reaction in Indonesia and some relatively mild Government reprisals. The Indonesian Government, however, expressed its desire to maintain good relations with Singapore and in the following months bilateral relations resumed their previous steadily improving course.

The effect of these developments on the architects of ASEAN must have been depressing. The continued existence of ASEAN had appeared at times to be in grave doubt. It is of some significance, however, that members did not appear at any stage to consider that the experiment should be concluded. Instead, the view seemed to be upheld that regional co-operation was an imperative that could be abandoned only at peril. Indonesia and Thailand in particular appear to have played an important role in holding ASEAN together, but even the major disputants, Malaysia and the Philippines, stopped short of dismissing the utility of ASEAN. Some argued plausibly that the Association had been a moderating influence that had prevented the Sabah dispute from escalating further.

Reactivation

Despite Malaysian irritation over Philippine Press comment concerning the 13 May 1969 racial riots in Kuala Lumpur, ASEAN meetings resumed later that month. The Third Ministerial Meeting was postponed from August to December 1969 apparently to avoid possible disruption during campaigning for the November 1969 Philippine elections. At that meeting the Malaysian Prime Minister announced the normalisation of diplomatic relations with the Philippines, stating that this showed 'the great value we place on ASEAN'. The period since May leading up to the Ministerial Meeting had seen a number of meetings of ASEAN committees resulting in ninety-eight recommendations proposing co-operation between ASEAN countries in various fields which were approved by the Ministerial Meeting. The ministers also signed an agreement on the establishment of an ASEAN Fund to finance joint projects and an agreement for the promotion of co-operation in the mass media and in cultural activities. As part of efforts to promote tourism, 1971 was designated 'Visit ASEAN Year'.

In the period between the Second and Third Ministerial Meetings when the ASEAN Standing Committee had supposedly been located in Kuala Lumpur there had been only two meetings of the Standing Committee and only one meeting of the Secretaries-General of the five ASEAN National Secretariats. In the period between the Third and Fourth Ministerial Meetings, when the Standing Committee was located in Manila, there were six meetings of the Standing Committee and four meetings of the Secretaries-General. There were seventeen Committee meetings of officials and experts on particular areas of co-operation compared to eight such meetings in the previous period. These meetings resulted in the presentation of 121 recommendations to the Fourth Ministerial Meeting held in Manila on 12–13 March 1971. An ASEAN Pavilion was set up at the 1971 Jakarta International Trade Fair. The ministers signed in Manila an agreement on Commercial Rights of Non-Scheduled Air Services.

ASEAN spokesmen acknowledged that in concrete terms these achievements were modest. They apparently did not, however, feel the need to be excessively apologetic on this account. Rajaratnam commented at the Fourth Ministerial Meeting:

> I for one feel reassured that ASEAN has not attempted any great leap forward. . .I know that such an attempt at this juncture of ASEAN's history would also prove to be the last leap forward. Instead, ASEAN has quite correctly chosen to move forward through a series of small steps . . .this no doubt is a tedious way of moving forward but it is a surer and more reliable way of promoting regional co-operation.

Malaysia's Deputy Prime Minister, Tun Ismail, acknowledged that ASEAN projects that were being implemented 'represent but co-operation based on the lowest common factor' and that they were 'not likely to startle the senses nor stir the imagination' but he asserted that:

> The constant contact and communication between our officials has helped to develop a habit of co-operation and a sense of solidarity which will in turn help us when we move forward towards wider areas of co-operation. . .

Such wider co-operation was indeed under consideration and had been envisaged in broad terms from ASEAN's inception. President Marcos in his opening address to the Fourth Ministerial Meeting proposed as an ultimate goal the establishment of an ASEAN Common Market and urged that steps be taken at an early stage to set up a limited free trade area on a selective commodity basis and to establish a payments union within the ASEAN region. Thanat Khoman urged that ASEAN had 'passed its organisational stage' and that it should proceed to consider and implement concrete measures and projects that would bring direct and tangible benefits.

The most concrete manifestation of ASEAN's interest in wider co-operation in the economic field was its association with a study being undertaken by a United Nations team. The joint communiqué issued following ASEAN's Second Ministerial Meeting had welcomed 'the offer of services made by ECAFE to carry out an economic survey'. In 1969, ECAFE (the United Nations Economic Commission for Asia and the Far East) in conjunction with other UN agencies drew up a 'Memorandum of Understanding on Assistance to the Association of Southeast Asian Nations on Economic Co-operation' whose purpose was to establish a project to assist ASEAN in identifying opportunities for closer economic co-operation. At the Third Ministerial Meeting Adam Malik noted with pleasure that ECAFE had appointed a team to carry out an ASEAN study. The Fourth Ministerial Meeting reviewed a report of the UN Study team entitled 'A Preliminary Assessment of Co-operation Possibilities and Policy Instruments for ASEAN', and directed 'that the sectoral studies be pursued'. Details of how this directive was carried out appear in the next two chapters.

Neutralisation

In the meantime, major developments had been occurring in the international and regional environment that considerably enhanced the value that members placed on ASEAN as a vehicle for political co-operation. The first of a series of dramatic changes in major power relationships affecting the region occurred with the announcement in January 1968 of an accelerated withdrawal of British forces east of Suez, the new target being the end of 1971. The Tet offensive staged by North Vietnam and the National Liberation Front of South Vietnam later that month and in February 1968 marked a turn-about in US attitudes towards involvement in the war and led in July 1969 to the announcement by President Nixon of the 'Guam Doctrine', which signalled that in the future the US would place much greater reliance on indigenous forces to cope with security problems. The Ninth Congress of the Chinese Communist Party in April 1969 marked the beginning of a new phase in the foreign policy of the People's Republic, bringing an end to the period of turmoil and xenophobia during the Cultural Revolution. The era of 'ping-pong diplomacy' led in due course to the startling announcement in July 1971 that President Nixon would visit Peking and to the admittance in October 1971 of China to the United Nations. The Soviet profile in Southeast Asia was also moving into sharper relief. Diplomatic relations with Malaysia had been established in March 1967 and with Singapore in June 1968. The first deployment of Soviet naval vessels to the Indian Ocean occurred in March 1968. In June 1969, following border clashes with China on the Ussuri River, Secretary-General Brezhnev presented his proposal for an Asian collective security system. Japan also was having a greater impact on the region as a consequence of its rapidly expanding economic presence (see Chapters 3 and 8).

These developments led to a perception that the old bipolar structure of major power relationships affecting the region had given way to a new 'multipolarity' in which as many as four major powers — the US, the USSR, China and Japan — would now have an important influence upon events in Southeast Asia. This new situation was viewed by ASEAN members with a mixture of hope and apprehension. Growing *détente* between the US and the USSR was not considered to have necessarily enhanced the security of smaller countries — indeed it was seen by some to present new dangers. But an important part of opinion among ASEAN leaders also considered that the new developments presented an opportunity and a challenge to shape a new pattern of international relationships in the region that would seek to assign a greater role in the management of regional affairs to the countries of the region and to exclude the disruptive effects of major power intervention and competition. Such an outlook took a concrete and specific form in Malaysia's proposal for the neutralisation of Southeast Asia.

Neutralisation of Southeast Asia had first been proposed by Tun Ismail, as a backbencher, in January 1968 with an eye to the changed circumstances that would follow withdrawal of British forces. As he later remarked, 'the idea was not seriously taken up by the Government'. Tunku Abdul Rahman stated at the time:

> This is something which is worth giving thought to, but nevertheless it is something that is difficult of achieving without working hard and conscientiously for it. . .We will begin to sound other nations as and when we are able to do so.[12]

The proposal was taken up again in early 1970 when Tun Razak and Tun Ismail increasingly came to assume control of Malaysia's affairs during the period of emergency rule following the May 1969 riots. In April 1970 the Permanent Secretary of Malaysia's Ministry of Foreign Affairs, Tan Sri Ghazali Shafie, stated at the Preparatory Non-aligned Conference in Dar-es-Salaam that

> It is Malaysia's hope that non-aligned countries will be able to endorse the neutralisation of not only the Indo-China area but of the entire region of Southeast Asia, guaranteed

by the three major powers, the People's Republic of China, the Soviet Union and the United States, against any form of external interference, threat or pressure.[13]

Shortly before becoming Prime Minister in September 1970, Tun Razak repeated this call at the Lusaka Non-aligned Conference. Support for the proposal was sought in other forums including the United Nations, the Commonwealth and ASEAN. Razak personally explained the proposal to Indonesia and Thailand in December 1970. It was presented to the Fourth ASEAN Ministerial Meeting in March 1971 by Tun Ismail in the following terms:

It is with Vietnam in mind together with the withdrawal of the American and British from Southeast Asia that my government is advocating a policy of neutralisation from Southeast Asia to be guaranteed by the big powers, viz. the US, the USSR and the People's Republic of China. The policy is meant to be a proclamation that this region of ours is no longer to be regarded as an area to be divided into spheres of influence of the big powers.

Further details of the proposal were given during 1971 in several speeches and articles by Tun Razak, Tun Ismail and Tan Sri Ghazali. In a speech in July Tun Razak argued that the reason that Southeast Asia had not been at peace during the previous two decades had been 'essentially because of the involvement of major powers in our affairs'. He concluded:

It is clear from this therefore that peace and security can only be safeguarded by a policy of neutralisation which will ensure that this region will no longer be a theatre of conflict for the competing interests of the major powers. This requires first of all that the States in the region should work to bring about the conditions which are necessary for the realisation of the neutralisation proposed and show that a neutralised Southeast Asia meets the basic legitimate interests of the great powers themselves.

Razak further explained that Malaysia saw the proposal as a

'long-term solution' and stressed that: 'While we look ahead we should not lose sight of our own immediate dangers and preoccupations. We would be guilty of a gross dereliction of duty if we did not take all necessary precautions for our defence.' In this context he asserted that the Five-Power Defence Arrangements, involving Malaysia, Singapore, the United Kingdom, Australia and New Zealand, which had been formalised in London in April 1970, were 'in no way incompatible with our neutralisation proposal or our non-aligned policy'. He said that the Arrangements were 'for the purpose of meeting our present defence needs' and that they were 'entirely defensive in nature'.[14]

In an article published in October 1971 Tan Sri Ghazali sought to dispel the notion that the neutralisation proposal was 'premised upon a euphoric view of the world and the natural tendencies of states in the international arena'. He argued that Malaysia's own experiences indicated that it 'does not need any lesson from anyone about the realities of the power-struggle'. He stated that the proposal was, on the contrary,'based on the long view of the developing mood on the regional as well as the international stage. . .This mood must be used to positive purpose or it may go wrong'. Ghazali then gave what is perhaps the most detailed public presentation of the steps that Malaysia envisaged for the implementation of the proposal:

> On the first level, the countries of Southeast Asia should get together and clearly view their present situations and agree upon the following:
>
> • individual countries in the region must respect one another's sovereignty and territorial integrity, and not participate in activities likely to directly or indirectly threaten the security of another. This is an essential requirement. Non-interference and non-aggression are basic principles which Southeast Asian countries must unequivocally accept before any further steps can be taken.
> • all foreign powers should be excluded from the region.
> • the region should not be allowed to be used as a theatre of conflict in the international power struggle.

- they should devise ways and means of, and undertake the responsibility for, ensuring peace among member states.
- they should present a collective view before the major powers on vital issues of security.
- they should promote regional co-operation.

On the next level, the major powers (the US, the USSR and China) must agree on the following:

- Southeast Asia should be an area of neutrality.
- the powers undertake to exclude countries in the region from the power struggle amongst themselves.
- the powers should devise the supervisory means of guaranteeing Southeast Asia's neutrality in the international power struggle.[15]

The broad principles underlying Malaysia's proposal were consistent with views espoused previously by members of the foreign policy élite in other ASEAN countries, and indeed with the principles outlined in the preamble to the ASEAN Declaration that have already been cited. For example, during a lecture tour in Australia in July/August 1967 Soedjatmoko of Indonesia spoke of

> the widely held vision in Indonesia of a neutral Southeast Asia working together in freedom and equality with an increasing degree of regional co-operation towards greater stability and prosperity for each of its members and for the region as a whole, guaranteed in its external security and supported in its economic growth by the Soviet Union as well as the Western powers.[16]

Similarly, in a lecture delivered in October 1969, Thanat Khoman in outlining the preparations necessary for a 'Pax Asiana' had spoken of the need for 'a tacit or explicit agreement among larger powers to refrain from interfering or intervening in the internal affairs of smaller nations with a view to upsetting the present precarious international balance'.[17] But although there may have been agreement on broad principles, when it came to matters of detail and of implementation of a neutralisation proposal ASEAN members appeared to diverge.

On 26–27 November 1971 ASEAN Foreign Ministers met in Kuala Lumpur to review recent international developments and to consider Malaysia's proposal. On 27 November the Ministers signed a Declaration that gave a cautious endorsement to Malaysia's proposal, announcing agreement 'that the neutralisation of Southeast Asia is a desirable objective and that we should explore ways and means of bringing about its realisation'. It further stated that:

> Indonesia, Malaysia, the Philippines, Singapore and Thailand are determined to exert initially necessary efforts to secure the recognition of, and respect for, Southeast Asia as a Zone of Peace, Freedom and Neutrality, free from any form or manner of interference by outside Powers.

A joint communiqué agreed that the ministers would encourage other countries of Southeast Asia to associate themselves with the Declaration and that they would establish a Committee of Senior Officials 'to study and consider what further steps should be taken'.

Thanat Khoman, who had submitted the draft upon which the Declaration was based, referred at the closing session of the meeting to 'diverging opinions and viewpoints'. The Declaration left unanswered a number of questions concerning what steps should be taken to achieve a Zone of Peace, Freedom and Neutrality and the order in which such steps should be taken. Thanat himself stressed upon his return to Bangkok that Thailand would maintain its existing defence agreements 'until a time when the prospects of peace, freedom and neutrality are completely assured'.[18] Philippine Foreign Secretary Carlos Romulo in an article published in March 1972 acknowledged that the Foreign Ministers had been able to agree 'only on the broadest plane of principle'. He considered that

> there are deep-seated attitudes to change and habits to overcome, as well as matters of more practical character. For example, we may have to re-examine traditional

alliances, and revise long-standing arrangements. This will require a transitional period, a time of experiment before final commitment is made to the Zone of Peace, Freedom and Neutrality.[19]

While Thai and Philippine reservations seemed to hinge mainly upon the implications of the concept of a Zone of Peace, Freedom and Neutrality for their alliance relationships with the United States, Indonesian and Singaporean objections appeared to be based on somewhat different perspectives to that of Malaysia concerning the most appropriate means to counteract the problems arising from major power involvement in the region. Indonesia appeared to feel that in placing emphasis upon going cap-in-hand to the major powers seeking a guarantee that they would not interfere in the affairs of the region, there was a danger of overlooking the primary task, namely the development of the 'national resilience' of each country which would through regional co-operation facilitate the growth of 'regional resilience'.

Singapore's reservations appear to have been based upon a typically hard-headed assessment of the prospects for the establishment of the proposed Zone. For example, in a lecture delivered in November 1973 Rajaratnam stated that he found

> no serious grounds for believing that the so-called *détente* means that the great powers have abandoned the traditional game of power politics and that, in the interests of peace and the brotherhood of man, they are going to leave Southeast Asians to solve the problems of Southeast Asia in their own way and in their own time.[20]

He pointed particularly to the continued strife in Vietnam. Given this climate of uncertainty Singapore expressed the view that its interests and the interests of major power equilibrium would be best served by the involvement of all major powers in the region so that the prospects for balance would be enhanced.

In view of these reservations and diverging approaches it is not surprising that the Committee of Senior Officials made slow progress in reaching agreement on further definition and modes of implementation of the concept.

Vietnam

Singapore's scepticism about the prospects for achievement of a Zone of Peace, Freedom and Neutrality while the Vietnam conflict continued and its outcome remained uncertain, was not unwarranted. Indeed, this was the issue that posed the greatest political challenge to ASEAN members during the first half of the 1970s. It was in turn chiefly responsible for the urgency that ASEAN members increasingly felt about the need for the Association to demonstrate tangible progress. By contrast, the issue of the establishment of diplomatic relations with China did not have a central place in political co-operation among ASEAN members during this period. The matter was apparently discussed at ASEAN meetings but the maximum of co-operation or co-ordination appears to have been an agreement that members who wished to embark upon the establishment of relations should keep other members informed.

The first major occasion on which ASEAN members concentrated their attention collectively on the Vietnam issue was at a meeting in Manila on 13–14 July 1972. This meeting had been called following agreement at the Fifth ASEAN Ministerial Meeting in Singapore on 13–14 April 1972 that 'a Ministerial meeting should be convened at least once a year to discuss international developments of concern to the region'. Such meetings would be 'outside the purview of ASEAN' and 'informal' in character. Rajaratnam had suggested earlier at the meeting that the time had come for ASEAN countries to 'regularise their extra-curricular activities'.

A Press statement issued at the conclusion of the July meeting stated that the meeting had decided to urge the parties in the Indo-China conflicts to intensify their efforts to achieve a settlement and that the ASEAN countries should 'explore the possibility of making concrete contribution towards the final settlement of the Indochina question'. Reports at the time indicated that ASEAN members had formulated a five-point proposal. North Vietnam reportedly rejected the proposal on the grounds that it favoured the US and South Vietnam.[21]

A second 'informal' meeting was held on 15 February 1973

in Kuala Lumpur to consider the implications of the Agreement on Ending the War and Restoring Peace in Vietnam reached by the negotiators at the Paris peace conference on 27 January 1973. The Agreement brought closer the day when ASEAN members would have to decide on what basis to conduct their future relations with Vietnam. They were also drawn together by mutual concern and uncertainty regarding the effect that the Agreement might have on the alignment of forces between North and South Vietnam. The Press statement issued at the conclusion of the meeting contained expressions of optimism. It stated that the meeting 'warmly welcomed the signing of the Cease-fire Agreement and was gratified that as a result of goodwill and co-operation by all parties the most tragic episode in recent history involving so much misery and suffering for the Vietnamese people may at last come to an end'. The meeting called for 'the development of mutual trust and understanding among the countries of the region' which would be facilitated by a meeting 'at an appropriate time in the future' of all Southeast Asian countries to constitute an 'Asian Forum'. The meeting further agreed that 'every effort should be made towards establishing and furthering contacts and promoting interlocking relationships amongst these countries' and that 'it was desirable to expand the membership of ASEAN at an appropriate time to cover all the countries in Southeast Asia'. As a final measure it was agreed that ASEAN 'should participate in whatever way possible towards the rehabilitation and reconstruction throughout Vietnam and the rest of Indochina'. ASEAN members seem to have had difficulty in agreeing upon what form of assistance could be provided. The joint communiqué of the Sixth Ministerial Meeting included the puzzling formulation that 'ASEAN participation could be jointly effected by making allowances for the preferences of the countries concerned'. North Vietnam rejected a Thai invitation for it to attend the Sixth Ministerial Meeting, pointing to Thailand's involvement in the Indo-China conflict in support of the US.

The issue of ASEAN's relations with Vietnam reached a critical point two years later with the sudden collapse of anti-communist regimes in Phnom Penh and Saigon in April

1975. ASEAN countries were caught unprepared by this turn of events. At the Eight Ministerial Meeting held shortly thereafter in Kuala Lumpur on 13–15 May 1975, opinions appeared to diverge as to the most appropriate future course. Malaysia adopted the most conciliatory response. In his opening address to the meeting Tun Razak described the new situation as presenting an unprecedented opportunity to establish peaceful relationships among Southeast Asian countries. He expressed his 'fervent hope' that the countries of Indo-China would join with others in the region 'to build a strong foundation of regional co-operation and regional peace' in Southeast Asia. He stated that the founders of ASEAN had envisaged that the Association would eventually include all countries in the Southeast Asian region. He added: 'When I look at the map of the world, I see Southeast Asia as a cohesive and coherent unit. . .Surely the moment has come for that community of Southeast Asia, which has been our dream, to be realised?' Singapore, on the other hand, took a rather more circumspect attitude. Rajaratnam agreed that ASEAN should not give the new communist regimes in Indo-China the impression that ASEAN was hostile to them, at least until they proved themselves to be hostile to a non-communist Southeast Asia. But he went on to urge that

> ASEAN should not give the impression that it is discon-certed by the emergence of communists or communist-influenced regimes in Indochina. Nor should we give the impression that we are prepared at any cost to readjust ourselves to win the favour of the Indochina states. We should not be the only one wooing the new regimes in Indochina, they should be wooing us too.

Rajaratnam emphasised the strength of the existing member-ship of ASEAN and its potential as 'a practical way of safe-guarding against the possible adverse consequences of the emergence of revolutionary Indochina'. He felt that if ASEAN were made a going concern it would not need to 'go around touting' for new members.

The Press statement issued at the conclusion of the meeting indicated that ASEAN was not prepared at that stage to take any major initiatives towards Vietnam. The ministers expressed a willingness to enter into friendly relations with the countries of Indo-China and 'to co-operate with these countries in the common task of national development' but the statement made no mention of the possibility of an expanded membership. It concentrated rather on the need to intensify co-operation among the existing members of ASEAN.

Reappraisal

This concern to achieve intensified co-operation did not arise only from the events of April 1975, however. Nor was it confined to the political sphere. As early as the Fifth Ministerial Meeting in April 1972 an effort was made to initiate a reappraisal of ASEAN's programmes and performance, particularly in regard to economic co-operation. In his opening address to the meeting Singapore's Prime Minister Lee Kuan Yew cited the low percentage of recommendations approved by previous Ministerial Meetings that had been implemented and the low level of intra-ASEAN trade. He did this, he said, not to denigrate what had been achieved but as a reminder of what more needed to be done. At this meeting Adam Malik also urged that international circumstances imposed an urgent necessity to undertake a review of ASEAN's accomplishments and shortcomings. Tun Ismail suggested that the question should be examined whether the ASEAN apparatus would be able to cope with the ambitious programmes that were planned. Philippine Under-secretary of Foreign Affairs Jose Ingles advocated a formal system of periodic review of ASEAN's strengths and weaknesses based on a cost-benefit approach and clearer priorities. He revived a proposal made by the Philippines at the Second Ministerial Meeting for the creation of a central secretariat. Singapore's Minister of State for Foreign Affairs, Rahim Ishak, called for a more pragmatic and business-like approach. The joint communiqué of the Fifth Ministerial Meeting agreed that an 'overall review' of ASEAN's organisational and procedural framework be undertaken, including consideration of the need for and desirability of establishing a central secretariat. The communiqué noted the establishment of a Special Co-ordinating Committee of ASEAN Nations (SCCAN), whose first task would be to pre-pare for a dialogue between ASEAN and the EEC. ASEAN members were also urged to study the recommendations of the United Nations study team.

SCCAN held its first meeting in June 1972 and a dialogue with the EEC commenced with a meeting in Brussels later that month. The ASEAN delegation pressed for trade con-cessions. Further steps to enhance ASEAN's role as a vehicle for collective negotiations on international economic issues were decided upon at the Sixth Ministerial Meeting held at Pattaya, Thailand, on 16–18 April 1973. A collective approach to the forthcoming multilateral trade negotiations was agreed upon. Moves were also initiated that led to discussions with Japan concerning the rapid expansion of Japan's synthetic rubber industry, which was considered to pose a threat to the natural rubber exports of ASEAN countries. The meeting also decided upon the establishment of a central secretariat and appointed a special committee to study recommendations from each country. In addition, the ministers directed that ASEAN should 'implement those recommendations of the UN study team that can be agreed upon'. In April 1974 a formal dialogue was initiated with Australia, which agreed to sponsor a programme of co-operative projects.

The joint communiqué of the Seventh ASEAN Ministerial Meeting, held in Jakarta on 7–9 May 1974, expressed satis-faction that Japan had agreed to exercise a restraining influence on synthetic rubber exports. It appeared to have been more difficult to reach agreement on intra-ASEAN co-operation. Little progress had been made in deciding the details of the proposed secretariat – the main development noted being the reaching of agreement that the secretariat should be sited in Indonesia rather than the Philippines. Prospects for more substantial progress, along the lines recommended by the UN study team, were indicated by 'the view that the three techniques of co-operation among others, trade liberal-isation, complementary agreements and package deal arrange-ments, might be useful techniques for ASEAN co-operation'. Work was said to have already begun on liberalising trade in selected food products. A further indicator of continuing reappraisal of ASEAN's achievements and a search for a more efficient apparatus was the Joint Meeting of the ASEAN Standing Committee and Secretaries-General with ASEAN Permanent Committee Chairmen in Kuala Lumpur on 22 October 1974, which was given the task of examining ways and means to streamline and co-ordinate the work of the Association.

Though it was held only two weeks after the fall of Saigon, the Eighth ASEAN Ministerial Meeting reflected the view that the time had come for ASEAN to show that it was capable of achieving tangible results. Adam Malik commented that the meeting would take up 'the urgent task of reassessing and reaffirming ASEAN's place, purposes and potentials within the spectrum of fast moving events and developments taking place in the region'. He urged that decisions regarding the recommendations of the UN study team should not be delayed. The joint communiqué recorded agreement to give a mandate to the Permanent Committees to give high priority to projects such as those in the field of trade liberalisation and industrial complementation and urged that an early study be undertaken on the possible adoption of a 'package deal' approach through allocation of industrial projects to individual ASEAN countries. The formulation of 'an ASEAN strategy for raw materials' was described as a matter of urgency. The communiqué also noted that a Draft Agreement on the establishment of an ASEAN secretariat had been considered and approved. Offers of assistance from New Zealand, Canada and the Netherlands were welcomed.

A further step forward in political co-operation was announced at the meeting in the form of agreement to accept a Draft Treaty of Amity and Co-operation for consideration by respective governments. This was hailed as an important step towards realisation of the Zone of Peace, Freedom and Neutrality. It was moreover noted with satisfaction that progress was being made by Senior Officials in working out a 'blueprint' for the Zone, although no details were publicised.

The end of the Vietnam war clearly brought ASEAN to a turning point in its development. It provided the necessary stimulus for initiatives that had been contemplated during an earlier period of reappraisal to be implemented and for co-operation to be lifted to a higher plane marked by more spectacular and tangible achievements. The preceding brief account should be sufficient, however, to dispel the notion that the earlier years of ASEAN, pre-1975, were a time of inactivity and stagnation. This was a formative period in which the members of ASEAN moved by degrees quite a long distance from the state of mutual ignorance, isolation and conflict that was in too many cases the main distinguishing feature of their inter-relationships before 1967. In its relations with extra-regional countries ASEAN had also begun to acquire increasing stature.

3

Making Haste Less Slowly: ASEAN from 1975

David Irvine

Many observers have tended to portray ASEAN as being long on words and short on performance, concentrating on the differences of opinion that must inevitably arise between regional partners rather than on their capacity to reach agreed regional positions through discussion and compromise. At best, it has frequently been argued, ASEAN's only concrete achievement in its first phase was that it survived.

On the contrary, as Roger Irvine has pointed out, survival was only part of the achievement. It may indeed have been convenient to describe ASEAN's existence between 1967 and 1975 as one of obscurity, isolation and stagnation, but this ignored the enormous progress in developing the habit of ASEAN consultation, the prudence in allowing time for the concept of regionalism to enter the strongly nationalistic thought-processes of the leaderships of the individual member countries and the successful application of that concept in minimising the effects of serious intra-regional disputes and mutual suspicions. ASEAN in those early years provided its seemingly mismatched members with a forum in which they could learn to come to terms with one another, to talk together and identify the common concerns and problems facing them both individually and as a group.

In that early period of over-optimistic and self-congratulatory ASEAN communiqués, the concept of regionalism in a world unsettled by super-power rivalry and dominated economically by a few great industrial powers had time to take root and grow.

Without these essentially political achievements, the move into ASEAN's second phase of development, with coherent economic objectives, would have been impossible. Prior to 1975, individual ASEAN leaders had been hesitant to commit themselves fully to regional economic co-operation until they had a clearer idea of whether the Association could meet their expectations. Only when they saw that it could, were they prepared to contemplate gradually making sacrifices of purely national interest for the wider regional interest. It was not until May 1974 that the ASEAN Foreign Ministers could agree that: 'ASEAN, having completed its first stage and presently entering its second stage of cooperation, should now embark on a more substantial and meaningful economic cooperation.'[1] In pursuit of that agreement, they recommended that the Ministers responsible for economic planning should seriously examine specific proposals for economic co-operation: trade liberalisation, large-scale industrial projects and industrial complementation schemes. In October 1974, Malaysian Prime Minister Tun Razak told ASEAN senior officials at a meeting convened to discuss ASEAN's future directions that it was time 'to go beyond mere form to the substance, beyond politics and projects on paper to actual action and results'.[2]

Clearly, the realisation was widespread in the second half of 1974 that the Association was ready to enter its second phase and the broad directions and instruments of enhanced ASEAN co-operation were being discussed more than twelve months prior to the political upsets in Indo-China in 1975. Perhaps the ASEAN processes might have continued their slow, somewhat indecisive progress towards meeting the new objectives, according to an ASEAN time-frame whereby patience and concern for the forms of consensus were and remain the greatest of regional virtues. However, external events − both political and economic − were to force the pace.

World oil prices were rising dramatically and economic growth was slowing down in the developed countries. As Laurence Stifel points out, the threat of worldwide protectionism was seen as a real obstacle to ASEAN development.

The proliferation of non-tariff barriers, quotas and orderly marketing arrangements is particularly troubling to the ASEAN countries which are late starters in the process of export-oriented industrialisation. . .All five countries have a vital interst in using their collective bargaining power with the developed countries to seek assurances that market access will not be restricted by the growth of addit-ional trade barriers.[3]

It is frankly admitted in ASEAN that the emergence in mid-1975 of total communist control of Indo-China — that 'other part' of Southeast Asia — was the obvious catalyst for the speeding up and implementation of a wider and more concrete ASEAN co-operation. The balance of power in the region was now unquestionably altered. The United States had withdrawn its forces from the mainland of Asia. China, the traditional bogey-man, was adopting a more amenable attitude towards the Western world and towards the countries of ASEAN.[4] Newly unified Vietnam was still an unknown factor. Would Vietnam devote its energies, and the strongest military force in the region, to fulfilling some revised version of the 'Domino Theory'? Would it take over China's role in fostering subversion and instability in the still-volatile develop-ing countries of ASEAN — a role China appeared less anxious to play? Hanoi had made no secret of its suspicion, if not outright hostility, towards ASEAN, and ASEAN leaders were genuinely concerned that the United States weaponry captured by the Vietnamese would soon find its way into the ASEAN countries to bolster the communist insurgencies still operating from within.

Or would Vietnam turn inwards to the tasks of consoli-dation and reconstruction? In each of the ASEAN capitals in late 1975 there were many who believed this would be the case, or thought it politic to give the Vietnamese leadership the benefit of the doubt. Thus, publicly, the ASEAN leaders were ready to offer the hand of friendship and co-operation to Vietnam, Laos and Cambodia. After all, ASEAN's original design had contemplated the inclusion of the Indo-Chinese states as well. Two weeks after the fall of Saigon, Tun Razak announced that ASEAN was ready to co-operate with the new Governments of Indo-China:

> Never before in the history of this region have we had the opportunity to create and establish for ourselves a new world of Southeast Asia — a world at peace and free from foreign domination and influence — a world in which the countries of the region can co-operate with one another for the common good.[5]

In private, however, suspicion about Vietnam's future intentions towards the region pervaded ASEAN's collective thinking. A common perception was that at the very least ASEAN was in political and economic — if not direct military — competition with Vietnam. The Malaysians saw their concept of a Zone of Peace, Freedom and Neutrality (ZOPFAN) as a principal means of guaranteeing the threatened stability of the region, and a series of official discussions on ZOPFAN took place in the second half of 1975. Increased military co-operation was also canvassed in some ASEAN circles as a response to the changed regional balance of power. From Jakarta came the call to place more stress on the Indonesian concept of 'national resilience', translated into a wider 'regional resilience'.

These concepts are now firmly established in the jargon of ASEAN and have become keys to understanding the fundamental objectives of the Association. President Suharto described 'national resilience' as the ability of a country to make the social and economic changes necessary for progress, and to meet all external threats while preserving the country's essential national identity.[6] Daud Yusuf, then of the Centre for Strategic and International Studies in Jakarta, described it as an inward-looking concept, based on the proposition that national security lies not in military alliances or under the military umbrella of any great power, but in self-reliance deriving from domestic factors such as economic and social development, political stability and a sense of nationalism.[7] The Indonesian view, now generally accepted within ASEAN, is that, if each member country develops its own 'national resilience', gradually a 'regional resilience' will emerge: that is, the ability of member countries to settle jointly their common problems and look after their future and well-being together.[8] The Indonesians were suggesting that ASEAN response to the changes of 1975 should be to increase the pace of economic development, both through individual country efforts and through increased regional political and economic co-operation. Raised living standards were the best defence against foreign-inspired subversion.

The common hope in ASEAN was that Hanoi would be forced to devote at least five to seven years to internal consolidation, reconstruction and pacification of the South before it would be ready to turn its attention to other countries of the region. This period would give the ASEAN countries the breathing space they needed to get their houses in order and to develop regional resilience through expanded intra-ASEAN co-operation, particularly in the economic field. Indo-China and ASEAN were in direct competition as the showcases of economic and social development for their respective ideologies. ASEAN had to be seen to succeed through its own efforts if it was to resist the perceived threat from communism. ASEAN would not adopt a confrontationalist policy towards Vietnam, but rather a policy of accommodation. To do this, it had to start from a position of strength.[9]

In their rhetoric of the previous seven years ASEAN leaders had gradually convinced themselves that joint co-operative endeavours were an obvious way for five like-minded governments to pursue common economic and political goals. With the fall of Saigon, it was time to put words into action, to define and then embark on the long-discussed industrial and economic projects. ASEAN needed concrete achievements that would prove its claim to be an effective regional organisation. They also realised that it was necessary to revise ASEAN's consultative and decision-making machinery in order to accommodate the new and urgent demands of economic co-operation. Thus, a sense of urgency and purpose, unusual in ASEAN until that time, pervaded the increased tempo of consultations after 1975. This urgency was to lead to some mistakes requiring correction when the realities of practical co-operation were better understood.

The Bali Summit

The historic ASEAN Summit Meeting in Bali on 23–4 February 1976 marked the formal commencement of ASEAN's second phase. In the flurry of meetings in the preceding eight months, aimed at defining the essential fabric and direction of ASEAN regionalism, the ASEAN leaderships were intensely conscious of the seriousness of the task of harmonising strictly national preoccupations and perceptions with the recognised need to develop common regional policies in a revitalised Association. A number of issues made this task more difficult. The unresolved dispute over Sabah between Malaysia and the Philippines hampered discussions on a mechanism for the settlement of intra-ASEAN disputes.[10] Singapore and the Philippines were promoting a more ambitious programme of economic co-operation, particularly with regard to the libralisation of trade, than Indonesia could be expected to support. There was concern at the possibility of economic exploitation by the more advanced Singaporean economy. The position of the ASEAN countries *vis-à-vis* communist Indo-China needed clarification, with some elements favouring conciliation and others looking to counter the potential threat from Indo-China (and China) through increased ASEAN security co-operation.

In the event, ASEAN leaders were able to reach compromises without destroying the spirit of unanimity. The stakes were too important, as President Suharto, the main architect of the compromises, realised. It was perhaps fortuitous that Suharto – as leader of the most populous ASEAN country, but which faced the biggest development problems – played host at the Summit and was therefore under added pressure to ensure that the well-publicised meeting was a success. The Summit produced three major documents which laid the foundations for a more active ASEAN future: the Treaty of Amity and Co-operation, the Declaration of ASEAN Concord and a joint communiqué that broke new ground for weight of content in ASEAN statements.

ECONOMIC DELIBERATIONS

On the economic side, the most important preparatory

meeting was that of the ASEAN Economic Ministers in Jakarta on 26–7 November 1975. They endorsed a series of broad proposals, largely adopted from the United Nations report on ASEAN economic co-operation, for co-operation in basic commodities, industrial projects, trade and international economic issues. The emphasis in any co-operative endeavour was that it should contribute to national and, by implication, regional economic development. They singled out food and energy as the most important foci for co-operation in basic commodities, whereby ASEAN members should assist each other in times of critical shortages and co-operate in the production of such commodities. They agreed that ASEAN should undertake large-scale industrial projects to meet the regional demand for essential products. These projects were to be selected on the basis that they utilised materials available in the region, that they contributed to food production, saved foreign exchange or created employment. It was understood that the product of the joint industrial projects should be accorded preferential treatment within ASEAN. The Economic Ministers also proposed that ASEAN should work towards the establishment of intra-regional preferential tariff arrangements, but as a longer-term objective to be negotiated on a commodity-by-commodity basis and subject to the unanimous consent of the members. Although pressing for more rapid progress in the preferential tariff area – through across-the-board percentage tariff reductions – both Singapore and the Philippines had to accept a more modest view of the prospects when measured against the tentative responses of Indonesia, Malaysia and Thailand. Only a month before the Economic Ministers' meeting, Prime Minister Lee Kuan Yew of Singapore had been optimistic that the ASEAN countries could form a free trade association, perhaps along the lines of the Latin American Free Trade Association, within seven to ten years. Lee accepted that the different levels of economic development between the ASEAN countries meant that there was little chance of a common market being developed in the immediate future, or well into the 1990s.[11] President Marcos of the Philippines agreed with Lee; the emphasis was to be on graduality.

Unanimity was more easily forthcoming on the Economic

Ministers' proposal that ASEAN countries should co-operate in seeking the reduction of trade barriers raised by third countries against the export of ASEAN raw materials and finished products. The earlier success of the ASEAN Natural Rubber Producers' Association paved the way for approaches to developed countries across a wider range of products of concern to ASEAN exporters. In effect, the ASEAN Economic Ministers were advocating that ASEAN adopt in a rather mild form the tactics of 'economic bloc' pressure to improve their market access with other regional economic groupings and major industrialised countries. This was a matter of particular importance to the ASEAN economies as their development strategies moved from unsatisfactory reliance on import substitution to an emphasis on the expansion and diversification of their exports, the processing of raw material exports and the growth of manufactured exports. These strategies increasingly brought them up against what Stifel describes as 'protectionist pressures. . .mounting in the industrialised countries because of the world recession and as a reaction against the first generation of developing countries' success in rapid and deep penetration of their markets with a narrow range of labour-intensive exports, primarily textiles, garments and shoes'.[12] The ASEAN Economic Ministers also agreed that they should adopt common positions in approaching commodity problems in the context of the Multilateral Trade Negotiations and the establishment of a New International Economic Order, particularly with regard to export stabilisation and bufferstock schemes designed to increase the export earnings of the developing countries.

The Economic Ministers recognised that their meetings should be regularised and that a machinery under their control was essential to implement economic co-operation.

POLITICAL DELIBERATIONS

Differing perceptions of Vietnamese intentions and the overall approach to communist Indo-China and China have been constant and dominant themes in ASEAN's political deliberations. Malaysia in 1975 seemed to believe that Vietnam could be reasoned into peaceful coexistence and that ASEAN should do nothing that Vietnam might interpret as antagonistic towards it.[13] For Malaysia, the solution lay in the principles of a Zone of Peace, to which the countries of Indo-China might eventually accede. Singapore remained wary of Vietnam's true intentions.[14] Many influential Indonesians still saw China as the ultimate threat to regional peace and stability, but the Indonesian leadership was also conscious of a need to be wary of Vietnam – at least until that country showed some evidence of a genuinely friendly attitude towards ASEAN. The Indonesians accepted that ASEAN should aim for peaceful coexistence with the Indo-Chinese states. However, as communist states, these were by definition committed to promoting communist subversion and supporting communist insurgencies within ASEAN. In order to deal more effectively with this potential threat, some Indonesians raised the idea of closer military co-operation between ASEAN countries.[15]

The notion of military co-operation calls to mind grand alliances and defence pacts on the scale of NATO or the Warsaw Pact. In fact, the Indonesian military circles were not suggesting a regional defence pact, but rather a milder form of co-operation involving joint land, sea and air exercises, the standardisation of weaponry, equipment and logistic procedures, and the establishment of an ASEAN military staff college. Their focus was inwards to counter-insurgency, rather than outwards to joint defence against open attack by a third country.[16] After all, bilateral military co-operation against insurgency was by then an established practice between some ASEAN members. The real issue was whether military co-operation of any kind should come under the formal aegis of ASEAN, or whether it should be left to the bilateral relations between individual countries which also happened to be members of ASEAN. Malaysia argued that ASEAN diplomatic overtures to Hanoi would be prejudiced by open discussion of a military role for ASEAN. 'It would make Hanoi see red!' one ASEAN official remarked drily. In the event, consensus was achieved against formal military co-operation within the ASEAN context. In early January 1976, the Indonesian Defence Minister, General Panggabean, announced:

Any military alliance in whatever form is definitely un-
acceptable to us. . .Such a military pact would not achieve
its goal. . .As soon as it was set up, a military pact would
immediately be countered by the conclusion of a similar
military treaty by those who would be against it. . .But
this does not mean that there is no close cooperation in
military and defence matters between members of ASEAN.
Such cooperation is definitely there; for example, between
Malaysia and Indonesia, Indonesia and the Philippines and
Malaysia and Thailand, which all deal with the communist
insurgencies on their common borders.[17]

In early February, the ASEAN Foreign Ministers confirmed
that military or security co-operation was not even to be on
the agenda for the Bali Summit.

The issue of military co-operation within ASEAN has
cropped up from time to time since 1976, but the policy has
always been reiterated that this does not fall within the
formal context of ASEAN and is a matter for bilateral arrangements between member countries. ASEAN, therefore, was
to remain an economic and socio-cultural organisation. In
addition, the Bali Summit was to establish it formally as
a political Association.

FINAL PRELIMINARIES

On 14 January, Tun Razak, Prime Minister of Malaysia and
a founding father of ASEAN, died of leukaemia in London.
His funeral in Kuala Lumpur a few days later provided ASEAN
leaders with a sad but useful occasion to consult on details
for the Summit. One decision of interest, illustrating an often
forgotten key to the nature of ASEAN, was that no third
country heads of government should be invited to attend the
Summit as observers.[18] It was felt important to avoid creating
any impression that ASEAN's formal entry into its vital
second phase might be influenced from outside the region.
It has always been one of the Association's proudest claims
that, unlike some other regional organisations, ASEAN was
neither conceived nor established with the help of external

powers. At this time, evidence of foreign influence over ASEAN could only have fortified Vietnam's fundamental distrust of it.

The informal meetings at Razak's funeral did not, however, resolve all the outstanding problems, and further meetings in Bali on the eve of the Summit were necessary for President Suharto to persuade Marcos and Lee Kuan Yew to accept the extent of economic co-operation to which the other ASEAN leaders could commit themselves, and to take into account Malaysian concerns about the provisions on the peaceful settlement of disputes in the Treaty of Amity (which seems to have led to some watering down of the original provisions).[19] As a result of these last-minute talks, very little of substance remained to be decided at the actual meeting itself.

THE MEETING PROPER

In their opening statements, the ASEAN Heads of Government demonstrated how firmly the concept of regional resilience had taken hold in ASEAN's collective thinking. Suharto's reiteration of this common theme was taken up by each of the other leaders. The new Malaysian Prime Minister, Datuk Hussein Onn, said: 'If we can progress in economic cooperation, we would have made a substantial contribution towards the maintenance of our respective national security as well as the larger regional security.'[20] President Marcos put it this way:

> The principal danger and threat against our individual states should be subversion and the economic crisis. . .Social or economic development, when utilised as an instrument of social justice, will answer these two questions, and thus the concentration on our economic problems.[21]

Prime Minister Lee Kuan Yew, also:

> The basic question is how to ensure continuing stability by stimulating economic development to resolve social

and political problems. Otherwise, increasing disaffection and discontent fuel incipient insurgencies into full-scale revolutions.[22]

And finally, Thai Prime Minister Kukrit Pramoj: 'National stability and progress is primarily based on economic and social development.'[23] Each leader stressed that solutions to regional problems had to be found in the region and not in reliance on outside help, which could never be entirely without strings. Similarly, each took pains to rule out the possibility that ASEAN might develop into a military pact. ASEAN was, as Hussein Onn stressed, to be non-ideological, non-military and non-antagonistic.

The texts of the three major Bali documents are provided in the Appendices at the end of this volume. The Treaty of Co-operation in Southeast Asia represents a major advance on the original Bangkok Declaration of 1967, the founding charter of the Association. It is a restatement of ideals, whereby the contracting parties undertake a number of general commitments in order to expand and intensify ASEAN co-operation in the economic, social, cultural, technical, scientific and administrative fields. Political co-operation on international and regional matters was now formally recognised as a basic element of co-operative regionalism, in Article 9 of the Treaty. The twin Indonesian concepts of national and regional resilience were formally enshrined in Articles 11 and 12 of the Treaty.

Articles 13–17 lay down procedures for the peaceful settlement of disputes between ASEAN members. The mechanism is not watertight, since parties to a dispute are not strictly bound to accept the mediation of other members of the 'High Council' set up to provide a forum for the settlement of such disputes. Malaysia, it seemed, wish to avoid being placed in a position where it might have to respond to a Philippines attempt to use the ASEAN machinery to settle the dispute over Sabah. (This was in spite of a clear statement by Marcos in January 1976 that the Philippines did not intend to pursue its fourteen-year claim to Sabah.) While it can be argued that this section of the Treaty lacked teeth, at least it established the principle that disagreements between ASEAN countries were to be settled wherever possible within the region and without outside interference. The principle has never properly been tested.

The ASEAN countries claim that the Treaty of Amity and Co-operation is one element of the gradual move towards the declaration of a Zone of Peace, Freedom and Neutrality in Southeast Asia. In this context, it is interesting to note that Article 18 of the Treaty specifies that it shall be open for accession by other States in Southeast Asia, another indication of the ASEAN desire at that time to extend to Vietnam the hand of closer co-operation which might at some future date go beyond mere peaceful coexistence.

Whereas the Treaty represented a formal but broadly stated commitment to the ideals of regionalism, the Declaration of ASEAN Concord had more immediate and practical implications in that it moved from ideals to a plan of action for expanded ASEAN political, economic, social and cultural co-operation. In the Declaration, the Heads of Government accepted in its entirety the programme of economic co-operation proposed by the Economic Ministers. Considerable importance was placed on the decision to develop preferential tariff arrangements and the joint ASEAN industrial projects, which came to be regarded as the symbols of ASEAN's move into its second phase. To ensure momentum was maintained, the ASEAN leaders agreed that the Economic Ministers should meet regularly, and develop the necessary machinery to formulate, co-ordinate and implement the economic co-operation proposals. Other elements of ASEAN co-operation outlined in the Declaration, although not in as specific terms as those for economic co-operation, included social development (with an emphasis on the rural sector, other low-income groups, women and youth), population programmes and narcotics control. With a view to allaying fears about incipient militarism in ASEAN, the Declaration specifically stated that there should be a 'continuation of cooperation on a non-ASEAN basis between member states in security matters in accordance with their mutual needs and interests'. Finally, the Declaration noted the signing by the ASEAN Foreign Ministers in Bali of the Agreement on the Establishment of the ASEAN Secretariat.[24] It noted also the need for a regular review of ASEAN's organisational structure in order to improve its effectiveness.

The Bali Summit was a turning point in ASEAN development, a genuine attempt to provide direction and purpose. The leaders had asserted that the solution to regional problems lay within the region and not on reliance on outside help. They had given substance to the aspirations for economic co-operation. Political co-operation had formally been accorded its obvious place in the practice of regionalism – belated recognition that political motivations had always been fundamental to ASEAN inception and continued existence. Of course, the dispassionate observer could still claim the documents lacked real substance on specifics. The more cautious or cynical might correctly insist that the final judgement should await the efforts to match subsequent performance with the rhetoric of Bali. But this was to ignore one of the characteristic strengths of ASEAN; namely, ASEAN works on the principle of consensus as to what is attainable at the time. It has tried to set realistically achievable objectives for intra-ASEAN co-operation bearing in mind the distinctive features of the individual economies, and at a pace broadly acceptable to each member. The consensus process tends to draw back the front-runners on a particular issue, while drawing the wary or conservative laggards forward.

The significance of the Bali Summit is not, however, to be found only in the documents it produced. An equal, if more subtle achievement, was psychological. That the five Heads of Government had met together for the first time, to give their imprimatur to ASEAN's second phase, was in itself important. Atmospherics are of great consequence in ASEAN's view of itself, and the ceremonies and receptions focused on the presence together of the five leaders, the congratulatory epithets and the posed five-way handshakes complemented the fulsome sense of achievement in reaching consensus on matters of some division. For ASEAN, the external appearance and the manner by which this achievement is seen to have been reached is almost as important as the achievement itself. A feeling of ASEAN unity and solidarity – even of euphoria – pervaded the tropical airs of Bali on

those two days in February 1976. There was a sense of revital-
isation, that ASEAN really was about to do what people had
been saying for years it could and should do. Here at last was
the chance for ASEAN to begin to live up to its rhetoric. Of
course, even at Bali it was recognised that the most difficult
tasks still lay ahead. Immensely complex issues of trade
liberalisation and industrial complementation could hardly be
solved at one hit. However, this sense of progress in Bali
carried over to the implementation of the Bali accords, to
which we must now turn.

The momentum engendered by the Bali Summit has been
sustained, although somewhat patchily. The Summit was
followed by a rash of meetings at official and ministerial
level that gradually developed the multi-faceted character of
the Association as we know it today. Until the end of 1978,
the economic programme occupied centre stage. ASEAN
bodies proliferated. The ASEAN private sector, which had
been officially encouraged to create its own machinery for
intra-regional commercial and industrial co-operation, began
to come more into the picture. ASEAN's dialogue relationships with selected third countries were developed, as the
important industrialised nations of the West found themselves
having to recognise both the Associations's political role
within the region and the potential its expanding economies
offered for trade and investment. This international recognition was another boost to ASEAN's self-confidence. The
organisational structure existing in 1975 was incapable of
meeting the demands arising from the post-Bali expansion
of ASEAN activities, and had to be renegotiated painstakingly
over the next two years. While economic co-operation continued to develop during 1979 and 1980, political co-operation
suddenly took over centre stage at the beginning of 1979, as
the ASEAN countries were forced to formulate joint responses
to events in Indo-China. Most of these developments are discussed in more detail in subsequent chapters, but the broad
themes should be charted here if we are to have a picture of
the structure, nature and aspirations of ASEAN as it entered
the 1980s.

Structural Reorganisation

In the formal structure laid down by the Bangkok Declaration, the supreme decision-making body in ASEAN was the Annual Ministerial Meeting, attended by the five Foreign Ministers. Between the Annual Ministerial Meetings, the ASEAN Standing Committee was responsible for the day-to-day running of all of the Association's routine or urgent activities. It formally vetted and submitted the reports and recommendations of the official ASEAN bodies for approval by the Foreign Ministers. The Chairman of the Standing Committee was the Foreign Minister of that country which would host the Annual Ministerial Meeting for that particular year. The members of the Standing Committee were the Ambassadors of the other four ASEAN countries accredited in the host capital. Below this were eleven Permanent Committees composed of senior government officials from each country. Responsible through the Standing Committee to the Annual Ministerial Meeting, their task was to recommend and implement ASEAN programmes. In addition there were two special co-ordinating committees (for relations with the EEC and for co-operation between the ASEAN central banks and monetary authorities) and a number of *ad hoc* committees set up to handle specific issues (for example, the reconstruction of Indo-China, synthetic rubber negotiations with Japan, sugar, the Multilateral Trade Negotiations, etc). Other semi-permanent sub-committees and working groups were set up from time to time to deal with individual matters as they arose. Finally, a most important element of the structure has been the establishment of national ASEAN secretariats in each country. Located within the foreign ministries, their function was to co-ordinate the national responses to ASEAN requirements. The heads of these national secretariats, initially entitled Secretaries-General but now more commonly Directors-General, met formally as a group to prepare the agenda for all Standing Committee meetings.

FIGURE 3.1   *ASEAN Organisational Structure Prior to the Bali Summit*

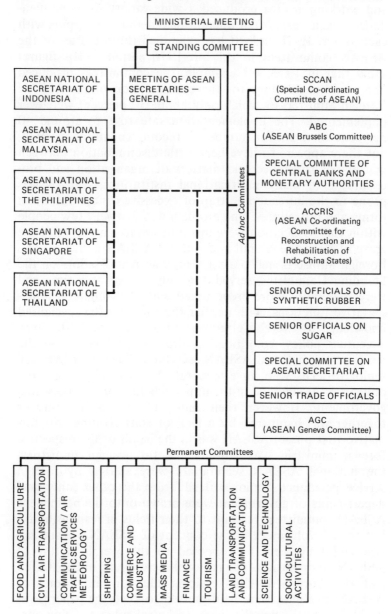

This decentralised system of committees, sub-committees and working groups produced a wide variety of recommendations each year, often uncoordinated and overlapping with each other. H. H. Indorff has examined the activities of the ASEAN committees in this pre-1976 period.[25] His figures show that in 1973, for example, the committees produced 285 recommendations for the consideration of the ASEAN Foreign Minister, of which only about 30 per cent were ever implemented. The implementation rate rose to around 40 per cent for a similar number of recommendations in 1974, but there appears to have been little discrimination between matters of substance and matters of organisation and procedure. Like many multinational institutions, ASEAN was prone to the bureaucratic trap of excessive concentration on forms and procedures. One problem was that very few people within the Association were in a position to have an effective grasp of both the overall and specific ASEAN activities. The Foreign Ministers met once a year. The Ambassadors on the Standing Committee served for only a year at a time and were frequently more preoccupied with their bilateral representative functions, with neither the time nor the specialised knowledge to exercise effective managerial oversight. Thus, executive policy co-ordination devolved primarily on the heads of the national ASEAN secretariats, a club of five very senior officials who, in effect, ran ASEAN. They were the only true 'Aseancrats' in the upper echelons of the individual governments. However, their ability to draw all the threads together was hampered by a lack of staff. During this formative first phase, ASEAN was in the hands of the respective foreign ministries. As adjuncts of the foreign ministries, the national ASEAN secretariats were staffed by foreign service personnel. Senior officials from the other functional departments of government were drawn onto the permanent ASEAN committees relevant to their fields of responsibility, but their involvement in the concept of ASEAN was specialised and they were less exposed to the overall picture of ASEAN co-operation. The national secretariats, under-staffed and over-burdened with servicing the constant round of ASEAN meetings, were hard-pressed to keep the paper flowing, let alone master the many technical subjects being considered. Clearly restructuring was necessary.

The permanent ASEAN Secretariat (hereafter referred to as the 'central Secretariat' to distinguish it from the five national secretariats) was established in Jakarta under the agreement signed by the Foreign Ministers in Bali. In June 1976, they formally appointed the Indonesian nominee, Lieutenant-General Hartono Rekso Dharsono, as its first Secretary-General. Meanwhile, the ASEAN Economic Ministers had agreed at their second meeting in Kuala Lumpur in March 1976 that new economic committees should be created under their direct control, rather than being answerable to the Standing Committee and Foreign Minsters as had been the case with all ASEAN committees until then. They recommended the abolition of the old permanent committees which had previously dealt with economic matters. These developments opened an intense debate, most of which was conducted behind closed doors, on the question of centralisation or decentralisation of the ASEAN structure, on the role of the central Secretariat and the general lines of responsibility within the formal ASEAN framework.

The functions and powers of the Secretary-General were laid down in Article III of the Bali agreement on the central Secretariat. In broad terms, these were that he should attend all major ASEAN meetings, act as a channel of communication between the various ASEAN bodies, co-ordinate and monitor all ASEAN activities and, significantly, 'initiate plans and programmes of activities for ASEAN regional cooperation in accordance with approved policy guidelines' for the consideration of member countries. The Secretary-General was to be responsible to the ASEAN Ministerial Meeting when it was in session and to the Standing Committee at all other times. He had the right to address communications directly to the individual member governments and to deal on the Secretariat's behalf with third countries.

Within these broad guidelines, however, the actual or practical functions and powers of the Secretary-General were open to wide interpretation. Dharsono, an outwardly unassuming Javanese but strongly determined to make something of his job, began his term of office with a liberal interpretation of his functions. It was quickly made clear that Dharsono was only to act on instructions from the ASEAN Standing Committee or the Annual Ministerial Meeting of Foreign Ministers. The Secretariat's staff was severely restricted in numbers, making it difficult for Dharsono to develop its activities to the extent that he and the Indonesian Government had envisaged. Nor did the Secretariat become the formal channel of communication between ASEAN and third countries, as many had expected. Instead, the old system of nominating one member as 'contact country' for ASEAN's relations with individual dialogue partners was retained for the time being. Although nothing was ever said in public, it was clear to observers of the ASEAN machinery in 1976–7 that the old-established bodies had difficulty in coming to terms with the new Secretariat and in finding a place for it in the ASEAN framework. Most members remained in favour of a decentralised ASEAN policy-formulation and decision-making structure, rather than centralising the policy-formulation and executive functions in the Secretariat.

The ASEAN Economic Ministers' Meeting was now a permanent element in the ASEAN structure. As things stood in 1976, Economic Ministers and the committees they were setting up would have to report to the Standing Committee and the Foreign Ministers on purely economic matters. This was clearly intolerable if the first priority in ASEAN's second phase was to be given to economic matters. It was also inappropriate that the Economic Ministers should have to work through a Standing Committee composed mainly of officials, albeit of ambassadorial rank. These same sorts of argument would also apply to other groups of ASEAN ministers who were expected to develop their own meetings within the ASEAN framework. The Economic Ministers therefore proposed they should be answerable only to the ASEAN Heads of Government, in effect requiring ASEAN summits to become institutionalised.

Thus, on the one hand, there was pressure from the long-established elements of the ASEAN machinery for the Standing Committee to retain its functions of policy planning, co-ordination and management, thereby limiting the central Secretariat to a more general administrative and policy support function. On the other hand, the Economic Ministers and the Indonesian Government were proposing the abolition of the Standing Committee entirely and its functions and powers transferred to a strengthened central Secretariat.[26] Under the Indonesian plan, each ASEAN country would accredit a full-time Ambassador to the central Secretariat. These Ambassadors, meeting under the chairmanship of the 'Secretary-General of ASEAN', would constitute ASEAN's senior policy planning and management body at the executive or senior officials' level. Overall, the Indonesian proposal envisaged an 'ASEAN Council of Ministers' with ultimate policy control. Such an arrangement would also nicely avoid difficulties of precedence between the various ASEAN Ministerial Meetings. Failing a Council of Ministers, it was argued that the meetings of Heads of Government should be institutionalised as the permanent apex of ASEAN's structure. The Indonesian proposal drew heavily on the analogy of the European Community's Council of Ministers and the EEC Commission. An interesting facet of the debate on the restructuring was that, possibly for the first time, opinions cut across national boundaries and were divided between functional groupings within ASEAN — between the economic and political elements.

Numerous meetings were held in 1976 and early 1977 to resolve these issues. The Economic Ministers pressed on regardless, formally agreeing in January 1977 to the establishment of their five economic committees (Trade and Tourism; Industry, Minerals and Energy; Transport and Communications; Finance and Banking; and Food, Agriculture and Forestry — each with their own sub-committees). In June 1977, the Economic Ministers formally recommended that they should be answerable only to the Heads of Government, that the Standing Committee should be abolished and that its functions be assumed by the central Secretariat. Although it was clear that the Economic Ministers must have their own committees and that the old Permanent Committees dealing with economic matters should be abolished, when restructuring was discussed at the Tenth Annual Ministerial meeting in Singapore in July 1977, General Romulo of the Philippines and Dr Upadit Pachariyangkun of Thailand argued strongly in favour of the

ASEAN Foreign Ministers remaining the principal policy-making organ of the Association. Malaysia's Tengku Rithauddeen in effect proposed that the Foreign Ministers should ignore the proposals of the Economic Ministers altogether. Only Indonesia's Adam Malik disagreed:

> With the increasing role and involvement of other ASEAN Ministers besides the Foreign Ministers and the necessity for a speedier decision-making process, it is felt that the ASEAN organisational structure has become inadequate and some of its organs even irrelevant. In view of these considerations, I strongly feel that the ASEAN Secretariat must be strengthened and that the present agreement on the Establishment of the ASEAN Secretariat needs to be reviewed.[27]

The eventual decision taken by the ASEAN Heads of Government in August 1977 was a compromise between the conflicting positions adopted by the Economic and Foreign Ministers and between Indonesia and the other four. The Foreign Ministers remained the principal co-ordinators of overall ASEAN policy in their Annual Ministerial Meeting, but other Ministerial groupings could report direct to the Heads of Government if they so wished. The assumption was that ASEAN Summit meetings would need to be held from time to time to review progress and approve any new guidelines. The Economic Ministers were given full autonomy on economic matters, but were to keep the Foreign Ministers informed of their decisions through the central Secretariat. The Standing Committee was retained, its role and functions confirmed. The old Permanent Committees were replaced by the five economic committees responsible to the Economic Ministers and four new ones responsible to the Foreign Ministers through the Standing Committee (Social Development, Culture and Information, Science and Technology, and the Budget). The central Secretariat would function as a channel of communications between the economic and political sides of ASEAN, in addition to developing its supportive role across the range of ASEAN activities. As a result of the 1977 reorganisation, the new organisational structure of ASEAN may be represented as shown in Figure 3.2.

The structure that emerged in 1977 has proved just adequate for the present level of ASEAN activity. However, Asean decision-making is still a time-consuming process dependent on a great number of committee and sub-committee meetings operating on the principles of unanimity and consensus. As the volume of ASEAN activity grows over time, and particularly if the Association evolves towards a common market or a free trade entity, the pressure for the centralisation of its bureaucratic and management structure will increase. Centralisation will almost certainly focus on the idea of a Council of Ministers and the central Secretariat taking over the executive function.

Indeed, the small central Secretariat has entered in the 1980s with perhaps the best potential for development into a key ASEAN body. In 1976–7 while its role was being debated, the central Secretariat remained more or less in limbo. In the face of lack of acceptance by the Standing Committee and the national Secretariats, Dharsono had been unable to carve out any real role for himself. After his dismissal in February 1978,[28] Dharsono's successors have been able to develop a modest level of activity for the Secretariat. Since 1978, the Secretariat has begun regularly to prepare briefing papers for ASEAN meetings and to undertake research work related to ASEAN programmes. Papers on cultural co-operation, the effects of the preferential tariff arrangements, EEC/ASEAN trade, investment relations and special commodity matters of interest to the Economic Ministers have been produced. The Secretariat worked closely with a United Nations consultant to produce a report on a scientific and technological programme for ASEAN. It has been entrusted with the management of the ASEAN Cultural Fund, although still subject to the final authority of the Standing Committee. Negotiations with Japan over the establishment of permanent ASEAN trade centre in Tokyo were conducted by Secretary-General Datuk Ali, who also undertook discussions on behalf of the Standing Committee with India and the South Pacific Commission (SPEC) to explore the possibility of their developing formal relations

FIGURE 3.2 *ASEAN Organisational Structure Since 1977*

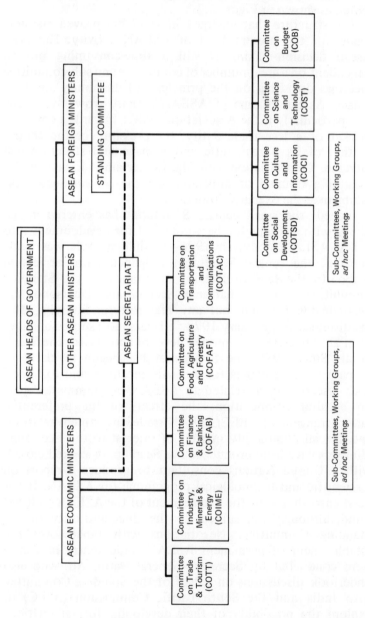

with ASEAN. The Secretariat acts as rapporteur for ASEAN Ministerial Meetings. These functions fall short of a significant role for the Secretariat at present, but the potential for future development exists and can be exploited when it is really needed.

Economic and Other Co-operation since 1976

The ASEAN Economic Ministers moved quickly after the Summit to develop concrete proposals from the broad policy guidelines laid down in the Bali Accords. Difficulties were encountered immediately. The Philippines and Singapore were keen to promote intra-ASEAN trade by means of substantial tariff reductions, whereas Indonesia and Malaysia were hesitant to agree to measures that might leave their heavily protected developing industries open to competition from the other members. Nevertheless, an agreement on Preferential Trading Arrangements (PTA) was hammered out during 1976 and initialled by the Economic Ministers at their third meeting in Manila in January 1977. It was formally signed by the Foreign Minsters a few days later and subsequently ratified by the individual member States. Tariff reductions were to be negotiated at quarterly round table sessions on a commodity-by-commodity basis. By late 1980, the Economic Ministers had approved 5,825 commodities under the PTA and by May 1981 the total had risen to 6,581. This gradualist approach to intra-regional tariff reduction is another example of the characteristic ASEAN practice of feeling its way towards greater economic co-operation, without creating problems for the less developed constituent economies. Nevertheless, the ASEAN PTA represents a firm commitment to the development of intra-ASEAN trade over the longer term.

In their keenness to institute a showcase scheme of ASEAN joint industrial projects, insufficient thought was given to whether the projects selected (Urea Fertiliser for Indonesia and Malaysia, Superphosphate for the Philippines, Soda Ash for Thailand and Diesel Engines for Singapore) might conflict with existing or proposed industries in the individual member countries. Singapore faced concerted opposition when it tried to negotiate the terms for its diesel engine plant under the ASEAN scheme, and eventually it was shelved. Instead of withdrawing from the scheme altogether, however, Singapore agreed to contribute a token 1 per cent equity to the projects of the other countries, thus enabling them to remain joint ASEAN projects and to qualify for Japanese concessionary financing. By 1980, three of the five projects originally agreed were getting under way and consideration was being given to a second generation of projects.

The stimulus for industrial complementation, as recommended in the United Nations Report, has come mainly from the private sector, organised on a regional basis as the ASEAN Chambers of Commerce and Industry (ASEAN–CCI). ASEAN–CCI working groups have produced a number of plans for industrial complementation, but ASEAN Governments have had difficulty in establishing a set of basic guidelines for the treatment of products manufactured or assembled under complementation schemes. Singapore, for example, has opposed the idea of having to give special treatment to products under the scheme, arguing that this would result only in further protectionism and even in the granting of monopoly rights within the region for an ASEAN product.[29] Prime Minister Lee Kuan Yew suggested in 1980 that a member country should be permitted to abstain from participating in the complementation scheme. 'When four agree and one does not, this can still be considered as consensus and the five-minus-one scheme can benefit the participating four without damaging the remaining one.'[30] Formal acceptance of such a fundamental change to one of ASEAN's most important guiding principles would imply some loosening of the original ideals of ASEAN cohesion. However, this need not *per se* weaken ASEAN; it would be recognition of the very different nature of the Singaporean economy compared with the other four, and might introduce a greater flexibility into ASEAN co-operation. The commitment to the broader ideals of ASEAN would remain unaltered.

Other ASEAN ventures in economic co-operation have been less ambitious. They include the establishment of a Food Reserve Scheme, an emergency oil sharing scheme, a US $100 million swap arrangement between central banks, an ASEAN Finance Corporation designed to promote intra-ASEAN trade and investment, a proposal for a regional communications satellite and plans for an ASEAN Bankers' Acceptance Market. In August 1979, the ASEAN Agricultural Ministers announced an 'ASEAN Common Agricultural Policy' which, while it bears no resemblance to its EEC namesake since it concentrates on the development rather than the protection of agriculture against foreign competition, seeks to increase ASEAN interdependence and co-operation in the production of foodstuffs.

Co-operation is being developed slowly in a number of other fields, including labour relations, social welfare programmes, information exchanges, narcotics control, civil aviation, cultural exchanges, population programmes and natural disaster relief. Co-operation in science and technology has been undertaken on a piecemeal basis. However, a report prepared jointly in 1979–80 by a UNESCO consultant on science policy, Dr Leon Peres, and the then Director of the central Secretariat's Bureau of Science and Technology, Dr Swasdi Skulthai, suggests that broad priority should be given to the joint search for solutions to common regional problems in areas such as fisheries, energy resources, the recycling of waste material, the development of manufacturing industries and integrated rural development.

An ASEAN Inter-Parliamentary Organisation (AIPO) was formed in 1978. It is not, however, a legislative body and can in no way be seen as analagous to present European Parliament.

Apart from the formal ASEAN bodies, the AIPO and private sector groups associated with the ASEAN–CCI, there is an ever-increasing number of private or non-governmental ASEAN associations actively promoting the concept of regional contact, exchange and co-operation across the broader spectrum of ASEAN society. These cover such diverse fields as tourism, orchid growing, trade unionism, film production, cardiology, women's affairs, journalism, consumer protection, the judiciary, youth affairs, paediatrics, accountancy, and so on. It is difficult to keep track of them all. They are an important element in the process of gradual 'ASEAN-isation' of the community outside the immediate government apparatus.

Third Country Dialogues

If the first ASEAN Summit in Bali had been geared to the establishment of intra-ASEAN co-operation, a dominant theme of the second Summit in Kuala Lumpur in August 1977 was the desire to expand economic co-operation with Western industrialised countries. In Kuala Lumpur, the Heads of Government reviewed and endorsed progress made in implementing the Bali decision. They made the customary cautious overtures for peaceful coexistence with the Indo-Chinese States, reaffirmed their support for the ZOPFAN concept and once again denied any intention of allowing ASEAN to become a military pact. However, real interest in Kuala Lumpur centred on the series of meetings between the ASEAN leaders and the Prime Ministers of Japan, Australia and New Zealand.

On the political side, a formal dialogue with ASEAN, and now the presence of the visiting Prime Ministers in Kuala Lumpur, represented valuable international recognition of ASEAN's viability and support for ASEAN regionalism. On the economic side, the object was to encourage the developed countries to contribute joint ASEAN development projects, both through financial assistance and the transfer of technology, and to encourage them to be more forthcoming on specific North/South issues as they affected ASEAN members. The dialogue has also been used as a means of applying co-ordinated bloc pressure on the dialogue partners in order to secure better access for ASEAN exports and to promote direct foreign investment in the region. It is in this field of third country relations that ASEAN co-operation has met important, although not unqualified, successes. The reason may perhaps be discerned in a statement made by Lee Kuan Yew in August 1978: 'It is psychologically easier to deal with ASEAN's external partners, than sort out the intra-regional arrangements between the partners themselves.'

Dialogue meetings have deliberately concentrated on economic issues, but since 1978 they have also been used as an avenue for consultations with dialogue partners on common political concerns. This was to be of particular importance in

1979 and 1980, when events in Indo-China forced the primary focus of ASEAN back onto its relations with its communist neighbours to the north.

Focus on Regional Relations: 1979—80

In September and October 1978, the Vietnamese Prime Minister, Phan Van Dong, toured the ASEAN countries pledging his Government's commitment to the principles of peace, self-determination and non-interference among countries of the region. He also gave specific assurances that Vietnam would not actively support communist subversive movements in neighbouring countries – an assurance China had never been able to give. Yet within two months Vietnam had signed a defence treaty with the Soviet Union, joined COMECON and its armed forces had invaded Kampuchea (Cambodia) in support of a new Khmer Government created in Hanoi to overthrow the pro-Chinese regime of Prime Minister Pol Pot. As many as 300,000 new Kampuchean refugees crossed into Thailand, adding to the 150,000 who had fled the Pol Pot atrocities in the previous two years. At about the same time, the flow of refugees from Vietnam itself, which had began as a trickle in early 1978, became a deluge. Vietnamese refugees arrived by the dilapidated fishing-boat load on the shores of Thailand, Malaysia and Indonesia – stretching the resources and tempers of those Governments to the limit.

Faced with the loss of Kampuchea as a buffer state between ASEAN and Vietnam, with the danger that Vietnam as a Soviet proxy now presented a serious threat to regional stability, and with the need to handle the refugee problem as humanely as possible, the ASEAN countries reacted quickly. One week after the fall of Phnom Penh to Vietnamese forces in January 1979, the ASEAN Foreign Ministers held an *ad hoc* meeting at which they publicly deplored armed intervention against the independence, sovereignty and territorial integrity of Kampuchea. They called for the withdrawal of all foreign forces from Kampuchea and urged the United Nations to take action to restore peace, security and stability in the region. In March, the ASEAN countries tabled a resolution in the United Nations Security Council which condemned both the Vietnamese invasion of Kampuchea and China's subsequent punitive 'military incursion' into Vietnam. Although their Security Council resolution was inevitably vetoed by the Soviet Union, ASEAN was to win majority support in the following September for their motion in the UN General Assembly calling for the withdrawal of all foreign forces from Kampuchea and allowing the Khmer people to decide their future free from foreign interference. They also succeeded in 1979 and 1980 in mobilising Western and Third World countries to defeat attempts by the Soviet bloc to oust the Pol Pot representatives from the UN. ASEAN had further success in bringing group pressure to bear in the international community over the refugee issue, with the result that the United Nations High Commissioner for Refugees was directly involved in the resettlement of the boat people and Western countries pledged to accept these people from the first asylum countries of ASEAN. Vietnam eventually agreed to a moratorium on the exodus and, in the second half of 1979 and 1980, the outflow of boat people was reduced to manageable proportions.

At their Annual Ministerial Meeting in Bali in June 1979, the ASEAN Foreign Ministers drew broad political and practical support from their counterparts from Australia, Japan, New Zealand, the United States and the European Community. This support from the major dialogue partners was reiterated a year later at the 1980 ASEAN Ministerial Meeting in Kuala Lumpur. Such support was further recognition of ASEAN's role as a major and viable political power grouping within the region.

Of course, the ASEAN united stand was not achieved or maintained without constant internal debate and some friction between members. Indonesia was for a time upset by Malaysia's policy of towing refugee boats out to sea again and directing them south into the Indonesian archipelago. Thailand had difficulty in convincing its ASEAN partners that the land refugees posed just as serious a problem as the boat people. Malaysia and Indonesia were known to count China the greater threat to regional security and they argued that ASEAN should take care not to alienate Vietnam, but rather attempt a solution to the region's problems through a peaceful dialogue with Hanoi. Singapore vehemently attacked Vietnamese policies. In the event, the Foreign Ministers in Bali in mid-1979 did condemn Vietnam in stronger terms than previously, but still left the door open for possible discussions with Hanoi. Foreign Minister Rajaratnam of Singapore publicly expressed his disappointment that the Bali communiqué was not strong enough — an unusual departure from ASEAN's normal practice of maintaining the appearance of tight unity. Since 1978, Thailand has attempted both soft and hard line approaches to Hanoi. For its part, Hanoi has tried to deal bilaterally with the ASEAN partners, in an apparent attempt to exploit differences between them. However, ASEAN has invariably reacted by reaffirming their common stand. Indeed, their communiqué from the Kuala Lumpur Ministerial Meeting in June 1980, issued a few days after Vietnamese military incursions into Thailand in pursuit of Khmer Rouge guerrillas, was the strongest yet in its condemnation of Vietnamese 'aggression'. It appears that a continuing feature of ASEAN is that external pressure, or attempts to divide it from the outside, invariably produce the opposite effect. The regional imperative is for external pressure to negate internal divisions and to encourage unity.

ASEAN in the 1980s

ASEAN has entered the 1980s with the concept of co-operative regionalism, embodying the principles of mutual self-help and freedom from great-power interference in regional affairs, firmly rooted. There is a genuine sense of purpose which is heightened whenever the five members feel threatened by external forces. Since 1976, they have had practical experience of some of the advantages to be derived from political and economic co-operation in confronting the pressures and threats imposed on the region. By 1980, the major Western industrial powers had recognised that ASEAN was a viable regional entity, with whom it was in their interests to come to terms. The communist countries, too, seemed grudgingly to have accepted the fact of ASEAN (China more than the others), even if they still refused to deal with it as a group and professed to see in it the beginnings of a regional military bloc acting as a proxy for the United States in Southeast Asia. Since 1976, individual members have given their political commitment to the concept of ASEAN regionalism an increasingly high priority, and have generally tried to avoid the pursuit of national policies that might split the Association. The strength of both the internal commitment and the external recognition suggests that ASEAN by 1980 was proving to be one of the most successful experiments in regional co-operation amongst Third World countries.

ASEAN machinery for political and economic co-operation has been developed to meet the objectives of the early 1980s, but it is capable of considerable refinement and evolution. Decision-making and the implementation of policies is still cumbersome and time-consuming. However, members appear to have accepted that caution and gradualism applied to economic co-operation are necessary virtues if internal tensions are to be avoided. As a result of a policy of moving only as fast as the more conservative members allow, the practical impact of the economic co-operation programme will be felt only slowly. It is unrealistic to expect that ASEAN will develop into a fully fledged common market, customs union or free trade area in the immediate future, and comparisons with the EEC are premature, and generally inappropriate. The pressure to intensify economic co-operation in the 1980s may lead to some internal strains. We can nevertheless expect ASEAN to develop further its 'economic bloc' tactics in negotiations with third countries or other international bodies.

ASEAN as a group still has to come to terms with China and the Indo-Chinese States, where mutual suspicions have so far allowed for only the most uneasy forms of coexistence. Tackling its relations with the communist world — including the Soviet Union — will remain a central issue in ASEAN in the 1980s. Indo-Chinese membership of ASEAN was unthinkable in 1980, but some accommodation between the two sides will have to be found if they are not to live in perpetual distrust and rivalry. The only likely new member of ASEAN in the early 1980s would be Brunei, when that fledgling achieves full independence towards the end of 1983.

Each of the five ASEAN countries may undergo leadership changes later in the decade, but there is nothing to suggest that the commitment to ASEAN on the part of successor governments should be any less firm. With the exception of Singapore, the individual countries will continue to face enormous development and social problems throughout the 1980s. Domestic political or economic problems in Indonesia, Thailand, the Philippines and to a lesser extent in Malaysia could become a source of heightened internal instability and tension, but it is difficult to foresee these countries formally renouncing their commitment to the practice of co-operative regionalism.

4

ASEAN Economic Co-operation[1]

Amado Castro

Whatever the political motivations behind the 1967 Bangkok Declaration, the stated aims, principles and purposes of ASEAN were primarily economic in character (see Appendix A). In fact, however, economic co-operation really only began in earnest in 1967. It has been sustained since then as a result of a conscious political commitment on the part of the ASEAN leaderships, who see economic co-operation as a principal element in their concept of regionalism. The development of this co-operation has not been easy, given the complex of differences and similarities between the five ASEAN countries and their economies.

The ASEAN Economies

Some basic economic data on the ASEAN countries are given in Tables 4.1–4.5. The five ASEAN countries have a combined population of about 240 million people living within a land area of little more than three million square kilometres. In 1978, the combined ASEAN Gross National Product amounted to about US $116,000 million, with *per capita* GNP standing at about US $480. In terms of size, the ASEAN market is roughly comparable with that of the Benelux countries or Australia and New Zealand. ASEAN must obviously take a place within the so-called 'Group of 77' less developed countries but, within that group, it ranks high when factors such as *per capita* GNP and real average economic growth rates are considered. Another comparison of interest is that the five

ASEAN countries have a bigger total GNP and foreign trade than the forty-two African countries which the European Economic Community has accorded preferential treatment under the Lomé Convention.

With the exception of the small island state of Singapore, the constituent economies of ASEAN have many characteristics common to developing countries in other parts of the world: growing populations, relatively low *per capita* GNP rates and a traditional foreign trade pattern of exporting food or raw materials based on natural resources in return for imports of capital goods, manufactures and technology. The region is rich in natural resources and unskilled labour. It supplies over 80 per cent of the world's natural rubber and abaca fibre, 70 per cent of its tin, 60 per cent of its palm oil and 50 per cent of its copra. The region is well supplied with tropical hardwood and mineral and energy resources. To name but a few, Indonesia has petroleum oil and natural gas, tin, nickel, copper, manganese, bauxite and some coal; Malaysia has oil and gas, tin, iron ore and coal; the Philippines has nickel, lead, silver chromite, gold, copper, manganese, iron ore, bauxite and some uranium; and Thailand has tin, tungsten, antimony, fluorite, lead, barite, lignite, gypsum and manganese. Traditionally these four countries have relied on the export of a few principal primary commodities. The nature and pattern of their foreign trade has been such that intra-ASEAN trade has generally been at a low level – the main trading partners of the ASEAN countries being Japan, the United States and Europe.

In the 1960s and 1970s, the five ASEAN countries experienced relatively high rates of economic growth and generally managed to assert some control over inflation (at least keeping it to manageable levels). Their growth rates for Gross Domestic Product (GDP), industrial output and foreign trade began to increase rapidly in the second half of the 1960s (see Tables 4.3–4.5). Between 1970 and 1978, average annual GDP rose by 7.8 per cent in both Indonesia and Malaysia, 6.3 per cent in the Philippines, 8.5 per cent in Singapore and 7.6 per cent in Thailand – at a time when growth rates in the developed industrial countries were slowing down. These high rates have largely been maintained since 1977, with some easing in the case of Thailand and the Philippines. While Singapore has concentrated on moving into technically sophisticated industries and services, the other four members of ASEAN have endeavoured to develop their industrial and labour-intensive manufacturing sectors, thus reducing the traditional heavy reliance on primary products. The manufacturing and other industrial sectors sustained growth rates between 1970 and 1978 of about 10 per cent per annum, with member countries seeking to expand production across a wide range of commodity groupings: textiles, clothing, leather and footwear; simple electronic equipment and assembling; furniture and household fittings; paper products; chemicals and petroleum; rubber and plastic products; pottery and glassware; metal products such as piping material, agricultural machinery, diesel engines and transport equipment; as well as a wide range of semi-processed goods. Government policies to encourage the inflow of foreign capital and technology on terms which ensure a satisfactory level of national control played an important role in this growth.

In the 1960s, the ASEAN countries generally tended to pursue import-substitution policies to promote industrialisation. In the 1970s, however, Malaysia, the Philippines and Thailand gradually moved to strategies which promoted industrialisation through export promotion, while retaining import-substitution policies in some areas. Labour-intensive manufactures for export are an obvious means of coping with growing unemployment problems produced by the high population growth of the 1950s and 1960s. Indonesia, the least economically advanced and with the largest and poorest population, still looks predominantly to import substitution to promote industrialisation – although in the late 1970s it made tentative moves towards export promotion in, for example, the textiles and clothing manufacturing sector. Singapore, whose economy is so different from the others, moved quickly through import-substitution and export-promotion strategies to the development of its manufacturing and service sectors on a skill-intensive and high-technology basis.[2] The various strategies adopted by member countries have had a direct effect on their attitudes towards foreign economic relations. Indonesia, still relying heavily on import substitution, has very high rates of tariff protection against foreign goods. The Philippines and Thailand, and to a different extent Malaysia, also have relatively high levels of protection on luxury and consumer goods to protect infant industries, with lower tariff levels on capital imports needed for industrialisation. Singapore is committed both in philosophy and practice to free trade and openness to foreign investment. These differences in strategy explain in part why, as we shall see, ASEAN has adopted a gradualist approach to trade liberalisation between the partners. At the same time, the push to expand exports has led the ASEAN countries to seek to break down protectionist barriers imposed against their manufactures by the developed industrial countries, and to press for stable export markets and fair prices for their primary products.

Japan is ASEAN's single biggest trading partner, accounting in 1978 for almost 25 per cent of ASEAN's total two-way trade. It is followed by the United States (18 per cent) and the European Economic Community (14 per cent). Only 16 per cent of total ASEAN trade in 1977 was conducted between the partners (and a large proportion of this was accounted for by trade between Singapore and Malaysia and by Singapore's *entrepôt* trade with the others). The similarities in the basic export patterns of four of the five ASEAN countries have been seen as an obvious impediment to the development of intra—ASEAN trade. However, some recent studies into the patterns of trade and investment specialisation between the member countries suggest that 'the economic structures of the ASEAN countries appear to be becoming more complementary as a result of different paths of development'.[3] Singapore is moving rapidly towards specialisation in skill-intensive, high-technology exports. Malaysia, with rising wage levels, should develop a specialisation in capital-intensive export commodities, in addition to its existing natural resource exports. Thailand and the Philippines can expect to see their labour-intensive manufactured products becoming more competitive on international markets. So too can Indonesia, which has recently begun to give greater encouragement to labour-intensive manufactured goods for export, although its economy will continue to rely heavily on primary resource products as its principal source of export income.[4] In other words, 'the potential for further expansion in intra-regional trade in manufacturing exists and hence the scope for an increase in intra-regional trade should not be underestimated'.[5]

Economic Co-operation before 1976

It was not until 1970 that the first Permanent Committees as envisaged in the Bangkok Declaration were organised. By the time of the Bali Summit, there were eleven such committees dealing with economic matters, covering such fields as Food and Agriculture, Civil Air Transportation, Communications and Air Traffic Services, Shipping, Commerce and Industry, Land Transportation and Tourism (see Figure 3.1, p. 53). A wide range of issues was discussed in these committees. In the trade area, for example, proposals discussed in 1971 included trade liberalisation, trade fairs and promotions, the harmonisation of trade statistics and industrial complementation. In 1974, agreement was reached in principle for the laying of an ASEAN submarine cable system. In line with the basic commitment of the ASEAN countries to the concept of open economies and an accent on the role of private enterprise, a federation of ASEAN Chambers of Commerce and Industry (ASEAN–CCI) was organised in 1971. It gradually developed an array of committees and working groups which were separate from but matching those of the government sector, and began preliminary consideration of schemes for private sector co-operation.

However, actual progress in the implementation of economic co-operation schemes during the first eight years of ASEAN was minimal. One reason, as earlier chapters have shown, was that these years were spent in conceptualising and organising. Another is that ASEAN's activities, including those in the economic field, were conducted under the direction of the Foreign Ministers. Ministers responsible for economic affairs were rarely directly involved in ASEAN discussions, nor did they have any mandate to deal directly with each other. They therefore knew little about, or had little interest in, the efforts to promote economic co-operation, the impetus for which was coming from the foreign ministries. Economic co-operation was treated as foreign relations and not as a question of internal affairs within an economic framework.

Nevertheless, one of the highlights of this first phase was the study on economic co-operation in ASEAN, commissioned by the Foreign Ministers at their 1969 Annual Meeting and conducted by a United Nations team. The UN team was led by Professor G. Kansu of Turkey, with Professor E. A. G. Robinson of Cambridge University as senior adviser. Taking up their work in January 1970, the experts completed their assignment in June 1972. The United Nations Report was a valuable and well-argued document that has become a form of blueprint for ASEAN's economic development strategy.[6] Many of the proposals it made were to be adopted by the ASEAN Heads of Government in Bali in 1976. It is recommended reading for all who wish to make a serious study of ASEAN.

In their Report, the UN team pointed out the need to increase productivity in ASEAN and to industrialise as part of the process of continuous adaptation to changing circumstances. However, the size of the national markets was a limiting factor and there were also limitations on the expansion of exports of manufactures to the more slowly growing developed countries. The Report argued that, if the ASEAN countries were to develop further,

they need to embark on types of production which are inevitably more capital intensive, and require larger scales of production, and thus larger markets, to make it possible to reduce costs to the levels established by mass production in the advanced countries. If individual ASEAN countries attempt to introduce such industries, the high costs related to their small internal markets are likely to involve high protection and lack of power to compete in world markets.[7]

These considerations led to a key justification for ASEAN economic co-operation, as follows:

Improvements of economic performance and increased rates of growth of national economies come principally from exploiting the advantages of large scale production and the advantages presented by the fact that different geographic areas have different and potentially complementary endowments of raw materials, skills and other resources. The potential advantages in both these respects are secured through specialisation in production, expansion of trade and enlargement of markets. Both, that is to say, depend on more trade and greater freedom of trade. Inside a very large and rich country the necessary enlargement of markets can be achieved within national boundaries. For a group of countries which are relatively small or in which income per head is low and markets small for that reason, the necessary enlargement of markets involves the crossing of national frontiers and some element of international cooperation.[8]

In other words, co-operation offered the possibility of import substitution through infant-industry development not on a national but on a regional basis through which the economies of scale could be realised.

A number of techniques for industrial development on a co-operative regional basis were suggested in the Report:

(i) *Selective Trade Liberalisation,* negotiated on an item by item basis, and applied progressively on a wider scale in a series of annual or biennial negotiations designed to enable the ASEAN countries to expand a balanced trade between themselves in the products in which they individually have advantage, and to benefit by increasing specialisation and exchange;

(ii) *A System of Complementarity Agreements* in which those engaged in private enterprise in individual industries, or small groups of related industries, in the different ASEAN countries are encouraged to work out together a scheme for the specialisation of different countries on different products of the industry concerned and their exchange between them; such agreements may cover not only existing products but also the introduction of new products, and may involve proposals for assistance in the form of tariff or other incentives; and

(iii) *A System of 'Package Deal' Agreements* negotiated between the ASEAN Governments for the establishment of new large scale projects, principally in industries which have not hitherto been introduced into the region, and their allocation for a limited period to particular ASEAN countries, together with agreements to provide the products involved the necessary tariff and other assistance to make them viable.[9]

The United Nations team also recommended co-operation in the provision of certain services: in money and clearing arrangements; financing of development and insurances facilities; co-operation in research services; co-operation in various ancillary services including shipping, tourist facilities and standards; and co-ordination of national economic plans. The team did preliminary studies of thirteen projects that seemed to offer possibilities for industrial package deals (covering nitrogenous fertiliser, phosphate fertiliser, carbon black, soda ash, caprolactam, dimethyl teraphthalate, ethylene glycol, newsprint, sheet glass, small internal combustion engines, hermetically sealed compressors, typewriters and steel billets).

In pointing out many useful directions for ASEAN co-operation, the Report also suggested a formal legal framework by which co-operation could be carried out. In practice, however, ASEAN has chosen not to be as formal in its procedures as the team envisioned.

The Bali Summit

Developments in Indo-China in 1975 convinced ASEAN of the need to stand closer together. One important ASEAN reaction to these developments could be seen in the first meeting of the ASEAN Economic and Planning Ministers in November 1975. Awakened to the need for their direct involvement, they drew up recommendations for economic co-operation based largely on the Report of the United

Nations team. It was no coincidence that the first ASEAN Summit Meeting in Bali in early 1976, held so soon after the Economic Ministers had met, dealt so much with economic matters. In the Treaty of Amity and Co-operation in Southeast Asia, the Heads of Government agreed that they should intensify economic co-operation and adopt appropriate strategies for economic development and mutual assistance.[10] In the Declaration of ASEAN Concord, they formally accepted recommendations from the UN Report passed on to them by the Economic Ministers: they agreed they should co-operate to establish large scale industrial plants, to work towards the establishment of preferential trading arrangements, and to co-operate in fields of trade in order to promote development and growth of new production and trade. They also agreed to assist each other in basic commodities, particularly with regard to food and energy, and to make joint efforts to improve their access to markets outside ASEAN by seeking reductions of tariff barriers and by developing joint approaches to international commodity problems. Under Article 5 of the Declaration of Concord, they agreed on a programme to improve the ASEAN machinery for economic co-operation, formally decreeing that Ministerial Meetings on economic matters should be held regularly.[11]

Machinery for Economic Co-operation

The grant of independence to the ASEAN Economic Ministers under Section 5 of the Declaration of ASEAN Concord empowered them to carry out economic co-operation directly. The Economic Ministers' Meetings are held at least twice-yearly and may be attended not by one Minister from each ASEAN country, but by all Ministers in the member countries who are involved in economic matters: Planning Ministers, Ministers of Trade, Industry, Finance, Agriculture, Transportation and Communications, and so on. (Ministers of Labour are not considered to be economic ministers and meet separately.) In recent years there has been a trend for Ministers in individual sectors to meet separately; the Agricultural Ministers have met twice as a special group, the Transport Ministers met separately in 1979 to discuss the ASEAN joint stand on Australia's International Civil Aviation Policy, and meetings of Industry Ministers and Energy Ministers have also been held. However, the decisions of the sectoral Ministers have to be reported to and ratified by the collegial body, the ASEAN Economic Ministers' Meeting.

As David Irvine has shown in Chapter 3, the operating structure organised by the ASEAN Economic Ministers at their Third Meeting in Manila in January 1977 was decentralised (see Figure 3.2, p. 60). Five economic committees were set up and each ASEAN country was assigned to host one of them. The host country designates the chairman, provides the technical secretariat and convenes the meetings. Indonesia hosts the Committee on Food, Agriculture and Forestry (COFAF); Malaysia the Committee on Transportation and Communications (COTAC); the Philippines the Committee on Industry, Minerals and Energy (COIME); Singapore the Committee on Trade and Tourism (COTT); and Thailand the Committee on Finance and Banking (COFAB). These economic committees, meeting at least twice a year, are served by sub-committees, expert groups, *ad hoc* working groups or other subsidiary bodies. For example, COFAF has co-ordinating groups in Livestock, Food Handling and Forestry, hosted respectively by Indonesia, the Philippines and Thailand. COTT has a sub-committee on Tourism. COTAC has sub-committees on Land Transportation, Shipping and Ports, Civil Aviation and Related Services, and Posts and Telecommunications. COIME has had meetings of special expert groups on minerals, on the automotive industry, on pulp and paper industries and on the specific ASEAN industrial projects (see below).

The ASEAN Secretariat is not directly involved in the work of the economic committees. Its role is that of monitoring, co-ordinating and assisting co-operation. It facilitates communications with non-ASEAN countries and organisations, conducts research and explains ASEAN co-operation to the outside world. It also endeavours to foster relations between the various ministerial groups in ASEAN, which are co-equal in status but independent of each other. Reports of the meetings of the Economic Ministers and their committees are transmitted to the ASEAN Secretariat, which in turn passes them to the ASEAN Standing Committee and the Foreign Ministers. The Standing Committee may comment only upon the political aspects of the reports.

In addition to the government sector structure of ASEAN co-operation, there is also a private sector structure centred on the ASEAN Chambers of Commerce and Industry (ASEAN–CCI). The annual ASEAN–CCI meeting rotates around the ASEAN capitals. Its executive body is an ASEAN–CCI Council consisting of two representatives from each country. The President of the ASEAN–CCI has a two-year term, as does the Secretary-General who comes from the same country. Its subsidiary bodies are structured to match the official ASEAN committees and since 1976 there has been an established pattern of communication between these official and private sector bodies. The ASEAN–CCI Working Group on Industrial Complementation has organised industry clubs to identify possible avenues for complementation in specific fields. By the beginning of 1980 there were thirteen such clubs grouping together entrepreneurs from the same manufacturing sector and covering a variety of fields: automotive, electrical and electronic, food processing, iron and steel, paper and pulp, agricultural machinery, ceramics, rubber-based products, glass, cement, plywood and chemical manufacturing. The ASEAN–CCI structure is illustrated in Figure 4.1.

ASEAN Preferential Trading Arrangements

An important means of developing ASEAN economic co-operation is through an increase of intra-ASEAN trade, which has the great advantage of reducing ASEAN's over-reliance on the developed countries.[12] The United Nations Report acknowledged that, during the 1970s, the ASEAN countries would not yet be prepared to accept very close and complete integration in the form of a free trade area, a customs union or a common market.[13] However, it recommended that ASEAN Governments should declare as a long-

FIGURE 4.1   *Structure of ASEAN–CCI*

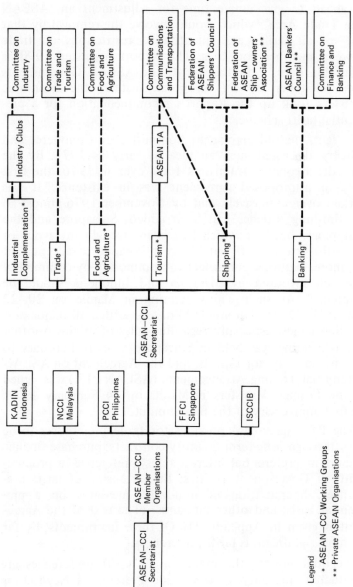

Legend
* ASEAN–CCI Working Groups
** Private ASEAN Organisations

term objective their intention to create by a date sufficiently far ahead to give ample time for adjustment an 'ASEAN Free Trade Area', which would involve the removal by that time of all tariffs and quantitative restrictions on trade between member countries. The Report suggested 1990 as a suitable date.[14] In the event, the ASEAN Governments have not taken up this proposal. Instead, the Economic Ministers took up the Report's recommendation for a preferential tariff scheme.

In fact, the old Permanent Committee on Commerce and Industry discussed such an idea as early as 1971. By the time the Economic Ministers took over in 1976, the first draft of a proposed agreement was in existence. It was worked over extensively and by November 1976 almost all the finishing touches had been added. Singapore and the Philippines, both of which had been strongly in favour of across-the-board tariff cuts, were persuaded to accept that the more cautious and selective commodity-by-commodity approach favoured by Malaysia and Indonesia should be adopted.[15] At their Third Meeting in Manila on 20–22 January 1977, the Economic Ministers settled all major outstanding issues, especially regarding rules of origin. Another special meeting was held in Singapore in early February to clear up some minor aspects, and the Agreement on ASEAN Preferential Trading Arrangements (ASEAN PTA) was signed by the Foreign Ministers in Manila on 24 February 1977, the first anniversary of the Bali Summit.

The PTA agreement provides for trade preferences to be given through long-term quantity contracts; purchase finance support at preferential interest rates; preference in procurement by Government entities; the extension of tariff preferences; liberalisation of non-tariff measures on a preferential basis; and other measures. (The text of the Agreement is given in Appendix D). Of these instruments, by far the most significant is tariff preferences.

Negotiations for the extension of tariff preferences are conducted quarterly in the Trade Preferences Negotiating Group of the Committee on Trade and Tourism (COTT). The proposals are then considered by the COTT itself, which then makes the final recommendations to the Economic

Ministers. Recommendations approved by the Ministers become effective on dates set by them, approximately ninety days after approval so as to enable the participating countries to accomplish the necessary national implementation procedures. Preferences are granted by either of two means: through negotiated offers or voluntary offers. Negotiated preferences are arrived at, GATT-style, by negotiating teams from two countries, but their agreements are multilateralised among the five partners. Voluntary offers are granted unilaterally by the individual countries and all apply to all the trading partners. The first series of offers accepted in June 1977 led to the initial list of seventy-one commodities under the PTA. It was then agreed that each country should offer a minimum of fifty items at each quarterly negotiating session. This was later raised to 150 preferences (either negotiated or voluntary) — 750 preferences a quarter or 3,000 a year. At about the same time, however, the basis for the classification of commodities was broadened from the original four-digit system to a seven-digit classification, which had the effect of reducing the significance of items offered.

By the end of 1980, the ASEAN Economic Ministers had approved 5,825 preferences under the PTA. By May 1981, the total was 6,581. In addition, they agreed in April of that year that all items traded with an import value of less than $50,000 in base year 1978 would be accorded a 20 per cent preference under the ASEAN PTA. It was claimed that this added another 6,000 items at one stroke to the PTA. Some economists have pointed to the change to a seven-digit classification, the limited extent of percentage tariff reductions actually given (usually only 10 per cent on normal rates that can exceed 100 per cent and the sometimes insignificant nature of the items offered, and they are therefore withholding their judgement on the eventual qualitative impact of the PTA on intra-ASEAN trade.[16] However, it must never be forgotten that ASEAN has quite deliberately adopted a gradualist approach to trade liberalisation within the region, at a pace acceptable to all members. The resolve to continue down the path of preferential trade is firm, and tariff cuts are being deepened from 10 per cent to 20—25 per cent on items already listed.

ASEAN Industrial Projects

The ASEAN Heads of Government adopted the recommendation in the United Nations Report for so-called
'package deal' arrangements. The idea was to establish large
industrial plants in one country to produce the region's
requirements for a given product, in order to realise economies of scale: a sort of regional import substitution plan. To
ensure acceptance of such a pooling of regional demand, each
ASEAN country was to have one such large industrial project.
A feature of the original concept was that each ASEAN
member would give adequate market support to the products
of the industrial plants of the other countries through, for
example, guaranteed purchases and tariff preferences.

The ASEAN industrial projects are large plants involving
investments of $250–350 million. They are to be owned
jointly by the five ASEAN member countries, with the host
country taking up 60 per cent of the equity and the other
four subscribing the remaining 40 per cent. Although the
formal requirement is only that the government own at
least one-third of the country's subscription, with the private
sector (local and foreign) allowed to subscribe the rest, it
is expected that all or most of the subscription will be made
by the governments. The allocation of the first generation
of projects was not a political agreement as has sometimes
been alleged, although naturally the pooling of demands and
joint ownership called for political will. It was important that
each project should be viable by world standards. By 1980,
three ASEAN industrial projects had been definitely accepted
by the Economic Ministers and another was undergoing feasibility studies. Those accepted were the ASEAN Urea Project
in Indonesia, the ASEAN Urea Project in Malaysia and the
ASEAN Rock Salt–Soda Ash Project in Thailand. The original Philippine project for a phosphatic fertiliser project was
found to be unviable and instead a compound fertiliser
project was considered. However, the Philippines was faced
with time pressures in implementing this project and proposed instead to set up an integrated pulp and paper project.
At the Economic Ministers' Second Meeting in 1980, a
further substitution was proposed by the Philippines, this

time a copper fabrication plant. Its feasibility would still have to be tested. As for Singapore's diesel engine plant under the ASEAN scheme, the proposal was not accepted by the other ASEAN countries and no substitute has been proposed.

Industrial Complementation

The third form of co-operation suggested by the United Nations team was a system of industrial complementation arrangements. Whereas the guiding principle of the joint ASEAN industrial projects was to develop a form of ASEAN complementation by means of one industrial plant in the one country to meet ASEAN requirements for the one product, the other facet of industrial complementation was based on the idea of each country producing specific components to produce a single ASEAN manufactured product. ASEAN would be able to take advantage of the larger regional market for components and products and so promote viable and efficient regional industries, promote intra-ASEAN trade in manufactures and assist the less industrialised economies to catch up. Also, whereas the ASEAN industrial projects were to be implemented largely by governments, it was intended that industrial complementation should be carried out largely by the private business sector.

Industrial complementation has been the responsibility of a Working Group of the ASEAN–CCI in consultation with the government sector committee, COIME. The first guidelines for ASEAN industrial complementation were adopted at the Eighth Economic Ministers' Meeting in May 1978 and passed to the private sector Working Group. They included provision for the lowering of intra-ASEAN trade barriers and other forms of government facilitation. After a lengthy process of refinement and discussion, agreement in principle on the first ASEAN complementation project was reached by the Economic Ministers in April 1980. This was a scheme proposed by the ASEAN Automotive Federation (AAF), one of the industry clubs of the ASEAN–CCI's Working Group on Industrial Complementation. The project finally adopted was not, in fact, for the manufacture of one type of vehicle, but included body panels from the Philippines, 80–135-horsepower diesel engines from Indonesia, spokes, nipples and drive chains for motor cycles and timing chains for cars from Malaysia, and heavier body panels for commercial vehicles from Thailand. In ASEAN, unlike in the Andean Pact countries, there is no master plan to produce an 'ASEAN car' in the foreseeable future. The members of the AAF realise that a wide variety of vehicles is produced in the region by the existing automotive manufacturers, which are affiliated with the great multinational automotive manufacturers from outside the region. Rather, the thrust is to identify components which can be produced without too many costly variations and in sufficient quantities to be economic. Among such possibilities for the future are included headlights, electric motors, steering components, rear axles and shock absorbers.

Under the original AAF proposal, Singapore was to have manufactured universal joints for cars and commercial vehicles. But Singapore, with its small domestic market and moving to less labour-intensive and higher technology component manufacture for the European, Japanese and American markets, saw no advantage for itself in developing a domestically oriented automotive industry. Moreover, Singapore objected to the idea of applying trade preferences, monopoly rights, or protection to products manufactured under complementation schemes. Singapore's objections were such that Prime Minister Lee Kuan Yew asked the ASEAN Economic Ministers in April 1980 for a redefinition of 'ASEAN consensus' and suggested that a member country might be permitted to abstain from participation in the complementation projects. This compromise was accepted and Singapore remained only nominally involved in the scheme, as it did with the industrial projects. Of course, it was not only automotive complementation or Singapore's free trade stance that prompted the Singaporeans to make this suggestion. They had been moving in that direction for at least two years. Singapore had found it difficult to agree to the programme of ASEAN industrial projects, especially since its proposed diesel engine project had encountered such problems.

The ASEAN–CCI is pressing ahead with other proposals to

COIME for complementation projects, including a security paper mill, a magnesium plant and a mini-tractor factory. Over time, and now that basic guidelines have been agreed, it is hoped that each of the industry clubs will come forward with further complementation proposals, gradually expanding the web of ASEAN industrial complementation.

Other Elements of ASEAN Economic Co-operation

Progress in the above three 'showcase' areas has been slow and steady rather than spectacular. However, there are many other forms of economic co-operation. For example, under the auspices of the Committee on Transport and Communications, the joint endeavours include arrangements for recognising driving licences, issuing commemorative stamps and use of the Indonesian Palapa communications satellite for domestic communications in the other ASEAN countries. A system of submarine cables linking the five countries will be substantially completed by 1982. It is not generally realised that this submarine cable network will cost more than any one of the current ASEAN industrial projects.

The ASEAN Council on Petroleum (ASCOPE), established in 1975, brings together the five national petroleum authorities to promote co-operation in the development of petroleum resources and their efficient utilisation through joint endeavours, training and the exchange of information. Throughout the 1970s, as OPEC oil prices have risen, energy has become a matter of increasing concern within ASEAN. In the Declaration of ASEAN Concord, member countries pledged to give priority to each others' energy needs in critical circumstances, as well as to intensify energy production. From this emerged an emergency oil sharing scheme whereby the producer countries of ASEAN have agreed to do what they can to assist the oil consumer members in times of acute shortages. (Along similar lines is the ASEAN agreement on the establishment of an emergency Food Security Reserve.) ASEAN Energy Ministers held their first meeting in Bali in September 1980 and discussed practical measures for increased co-operation in energy. They agreed on the need to lessen their dependence on imported oil by developing indigenous energy sources, improving information exchanges, under-taking research and development of alternative sources of energy and by devising a policy for regional oil and gas exploration and development. Other ideas discussed include the establishment of an ASEAN regional power grid linking all members but the Philippines. Co-operation in the energy field is an important element of most of ASEAN's 'dialogues' with Western developed countries.[17]

Co-operation is developing steadily in the monetary and banking field. ASEAN's central banks and monetary authori-ties concluded an agreement in 1977 on a US $100 million swap arrangement to assist any member in bridging temporary liquidity problems. In 1978 the amount was increased to US $200 million. An ASEAN Bankers' Council, associated with the ASEAN–CCI Working Group on Banking, was responsible in 1978 for the establishment of an ASEAN Finance Corporation to facilitate trade and investment within the region. Discussions on an ASEAN Bankers' Accep-tance Market were also well advanced in 1980. Other private sector initiatives under discussion include an ASEAN Clearing Union, an ASEAN Development Bank and an ASEAN Export Credit Insurance Scheme.[18]

Many examples of official or private sector co-operation proposals or actual programmes can be cited – in agriculture, food handling, shipping, joint ventures, trade exchanges, joint purchasing and financial co-operation. Of course, this does not amount to any significant integration of the five economies at this stage. Such a goal lies well into the future, but progress is steady and promising.

Future of ASEAN Economic Co-operation

There has been a tendency outside ASEAN official circles to overestimate the problems confronting ASEAN economic co-operation. Of course, problems exist: there are major historical, cultural, legal and ethnic differences between the members; never before have they had much of a history of exchange and close inter-relationships; their disparate economies are at different stages of development; to some extent their foreign trade is competitive rather than complementary; and so on. With regard to the problems caused by social or historical differences, members recognise their existence and take them into account in their dealings with each other – to the point where a sense of 'ASEAN regional identity' is now a fact. Furthermore, many of the obstacles to economic co-operation can be overcome provided there is at the highest levels the political will in favour of such co-operation. This has been strong since the Bali Summit of 1976.

As to the purely economic bases for scepticism, closer examination suggests that the prospects for economic integration are not nearly so bleak as has been claimed. Some degree of complementarity exists between the five economies; not all, for example, produce the same sorts of mineral. Some countries are exporters of oil and gas, others are net consumers of energy. Singapore – always seen as the odd man out – can perform an important function as a distribution, financial and service centre for the region. As we have seen, earlier, there is some evidence that the economic development patterns in each of the member countries are likely to increase complementarity between the ASEAN economies. Another factor which should not be forgotten by those who have felt the effect of the OPEC oil suppliers' cartel is that even where ASEAN members trade in the same product, they need not necessarily compete against each other to the buyer's benefit. Rather they can combine to regulate the trade in that commodity, for example, through the Association of Natural Rubber Producers or the International Tin Agreement.

It is true that intra-ASEAN trade has undergone no sudden increase as a result of the ASEAN PTA – as if expectations of immediate results were ever realistic. It is also true that the initial PTA system was inadequate and many of the concessions offered were largely cosmetic. However, by 1979, the Economic Ministers had realised the need to increase the number of commodities given preferences and to deepen the tariff cut. Even with these changes, the effect of the ASEAN PTA on regional trade will still be gradual but, over time, the cumulative effect should become marked.

Many avenues for industrial complementation clearly

exist: for example, in the automotive parts, glassware, processed foods and chemical industries. Industrial complementation can also be an important means of import substitution for capital goods, enabling the ASEAN countries to meet their demand for capital goods to be used to promote development from within the region itself. The success of complementation depends on the ability of governments to provide the necessary facilities and the entrepreneurial drive and initiative of the ASEAN private sector. The ASEAN economies are largely oriented towards private enterprise and the ASEAN private sector has so far shown a genuine willingness to initiate or consider proposals for regional economic co-operation.

Another stimulus to industrial and economic development comes from outside the region, in the exchanges with third countries. ASEAN welcomes foreign investment as supplementing local resources. ASEAN has held investment or industrial co-operation conferences with Australia and with the European Community. Investment missions have come to deal with ASEAN as a collective entity from the United States, Canada, Japan, New Zealand and individual European countries. ASEAN–US, ASEAN–Australia and ASEAN–EEC Business Councils have been formed and among their first projects is the identification of possible joint venture areas and industrial complementation schemes involving businessmen from both within and without the region. At the Government level, the first ASEAN–EEC Ministerial level meeting dealing with economic and business matters was held in Manila in late 1980 to flesh out arrangements for co-operation envisaged in the ASEAN–EEC Co-operation Agreement signed in Kuala Lumpur in March 1980.

Of course, many obstacles to ASEAN economic co-operation and possible future integration remain. The ASEAN countries recognise that slow but steady forward movement based on consensus is the only way. Time and effort are required to hammer out co-operative agreements. Different ways of doing business and dissimilar legal and administrative systems are hurdles to be overcome. Partly because of these sorts of difficulty, the ASEAN structure is decentralised and ASEAN economic co-operation is carried out with a minimum of formal legal and legislative structure.

Decisions made by the Economic Ministers at their biannual meetings are accepted and implemented even though only official minutes record such decisions — treaties or legal agreements are rarely required. For example, industrial complementation is being pursued simply on the basis of the decisions and agreed guidelines of the Economic Ministers, and without the formal legislation or agreements outlined in the Report of the United Nations team. This is in contrast with the method of the Andean Pact countries.

As intra-ASEAN economic activity expands, the confidence of governments and business in regional co-operation will grow. At their meeting in Bangkok in September 1980, the ASEAN Economic Ministers agreed that it was time for a new phase of economic regionalism to begin. The 1980s should see ASEAN making progress — at its own pace — towards that objective.

5

ASEAN and Indo-Chinese Refugees

Michael Richardson

The communist victories over US-backed governments in Kampuchea (formerly Cambodia), Vietnam and Laos in 1975 generated a series of disruptive mass migrations from, and within, Indo-China. From 1 April 1975 to 31 July 1979, more than 1.2 million people were variously reported to have been displaced from the three countries of Indo-China (sources of statistics are shown below in parentheses after figures):

250,000 (Peking)   From Vietnam to China. The overwhelming majority crossing Vietnam's northern border into China were of Chinese descent. The Vietnamese called them 'Hoa'.

321,400 (Hanoi)   From· Kampuchea to Vietnam which told the office of the United Nations High Commissioner for Refugees (UNHCR) the total was made up of: 125,600 Khmers, 25,500 ethnic Chinese residents of Kampuchea and 170,300 members of the Vietnamese minority in Kampuchea.

135,000 (US)   From Vietnam to the US as part of the American evacuation of Saigon in April 1975.

605,600 (mainly UNHCR) From Laos, Vietnam and Kampuchea. Most entered temporary camps in ASEAN countries and Hong Kong pending permanent resettlement – principally in North America, Australia and Europe. Of this exodus, Thailand received by far the largest number of displaced persons: 245,600.

TOTAL 1,312,000 (Including 280,000 'boat people' – those who left by sea – from Vietnam.)

Southeast Asia's refugee problems were heavily influenced by politics. Relations between Indo-China and its non-communist neighbours in ASEAN in the first couple of years after 1975 were marked by wariness and mutual suspicion. However by the end of 1977 there was a perceptible change in Vietnamese policy towards ASEAN members coupled with a toning down of critical propaganda in the official Vietnamese media. By mid-1978 it had become clear that Vietnam had launched a major diplomatic offensive to improve its relations not only with ASEAN, but also with Japan and the West, including the US.

In the space of less than eighteen months, the attitude of Vietnam and its ally in Laos towards ASEAN had changed from one of truculent criticism to one of coexistence and co-operation. The question the five ASEAN members – Indonesia, Malaysia, the Philippines, Singapore and Thailand – asked themselves was: why?

It could be partly explained by a natural easing of post-war tensions between the communist and non-communist halves of Southeast Asia in the three years after 1975. But obviously other factors were at work as well. One was that ASEAN had proved it was a united front which had to be taken into account in regional affairs. In dealing with pressing external problems, ASEAN members had shown they could, and would, consult and co-ordinate their responses.

But the main factor underlying Vietnam's intensified interest in improving relations with ASEAN, the US, Japan, Western Europe, Australia and New Zealand was a profoundly important shift in alignments within the communist community. Former allies in the second round of the Indo-China war against US 'imperialism' had fallen out. In the absence of a common external threat, conflicting national interests and mutual antagonism stretching back for centuries into history between Kampuchea and Vietnam on the one hand, and China and Vietnam on the other, had reasserted themselves. By late 1977 the ultra-nationalistic Khmer Rouge communists in Kampuchea were engaged in a vicious border war with Vietnam. The radical regime in Phnom Penh accused its much larger and more powerful neighbour in the east of seeking to control and eventually annex Kampuchea. It claimed Hanoi was intent on herding Kampuchea into an Indo-Chinese Federation with Laos and Vietnam, in which Vietnam would be the paramount power. Hanoi denied it had any such designs, asserting that in attacking border provinces in southern Vietnam, Khmer Rouge forces were trying to recover territory lost when, or before, the French colonial administration in Indo-China drew the existing frontier between the two countries. Hanoi said Kampuchea persistently refused to negotiate a settlement to the dispute. It also charged China with giving arms and other support to Kampuchea in order to encourage Khmer Rouge cross-border attacks and weaken Vietnam. Hanoi's relations with Peking were coming under increasing strain. Darkening this double threat to the stability of Southeast Asia was the shadow of Sino—Soviet rivalry, with Moscow supporting Vietnam and Peking buttressing Kampuchea.

In this situation it seemed logical that Vietnam would try to secure its flanks by ensuring the friendship, or at least the neutrality, of ASEAN countries. ASEAN was also being wooed assiduously by China and Kampuchea. Even the Soviet Union had changed its formerly hostile tune and joined the line of communist suitors that came tapping at ASEAN's door in 1978.

ASEAN's chief concern was to avoid taking sides in, or being drawn into, the Sino—Soviet, Sino—Vietnamese or Kampuchea—Vietnam disputes. This was not easy and it became impossible at the end of 1978. Two developments intruded which fanned anew old ASEAN suspicions about Vietnam's intentions towards its neighbours in Southeast Asia and severely tested ASEAN's policy of neutrality in the great communist power struggle.

One of these developments was the invasion of Kampuchea, spearheaded by Vietnam's army and airforce. It began on 25 December 1978 and led quickly to the occupation of Phnom Penh by pro-Vietnamese forces on 7 January 1979. Shortly afterwards, a new administration was installed claiming to be the legitimate government of the country in place of the ousted Khmer Rouge regime.

The second development profoundly affecting ASEAN's relations with Vietnam was the mass outflow of refugees from Indo-China. ASEAN officials, particularly those responsible for national security, were not slow to see a connection between the invasion of Kampuchea and the refugee exodus. After all, it was argued, about 90 per cent of the 201,000 refugees who had crossed into Thailand from Indo-China were from Laos. The bulk of those displaced were Hmong-Hill people, often called the Meo, who had traditionally resisted lowland Lao authority and who were trained, armed and paid in large numbers by the American Central Intelligence Agency (CIA) in the sixties and early seventies to fight both the Vietnamese and Pathet Lao in Laos .After 1975, remaining resistance by the Meo and other hill tribes in Laos was systematically crushed by Vietnamese-led forces. The remnants fled with their families into northern and northeast Thailand.

With Vietnamese troops fighting the Khmer Rouge in Western Kampuchea adjacent to the porous, 800-kilometre border with Thailand, ASEAN officials feared that a similar massive wave of Kampuchean war refugees would come flooding into Thailand joining some 20,000 who had managed to escape the tyranny of the Khmer Rouge regime by the end of 1978. This concern was well founded. In the first six months of 1979, about 100,000 people, some of them Khmer Rouge soldiers and their families, crossed into Thailand from Kampuchea. Nearly all were pushed back across the frontier. But as the end of the year approached, Thai authorities feared that up to a million more might come swarming over the border to escape fighting and famine in their tortured homeland. This was a prospect that Thailand, already burdened in mid-1979 with a backlog of some 150,000 earlier refugees from Indo-China, faced with foreboding.

In late 1978, ASEAN officials also feared that diversion of scarce resources to the war effort in Kampuchea would put added strain on Vietnam's threadbare economy and aggravate severe hardships affecting its population. They were worried that China would apply strong-arm pressure on Vietnam as a reprisal for Hanoi's drastic move against Peking's ally in Kampuchea, and that Vietnam would move closer to the Soviet Union. The Cassandras were right on both counts. Vietnam's action and China's reaction (the latter culminated in a 'punishing' four-week incursion by Chinese forces into northern Vietnam in February—March 1979) spurred an even greater number of discontented and harassed people, especially ethnic Chinese, to leave Vietnam by boat and head for ASEAN countries and Hong Kong.

Some seepage of economically discontented and politically disaffected citizens from a South Vietnam under communist control and undergoing a gradual socialist transformation in straitened circumstances was inevitable.

But hopes that Hanoi was embarking on a course of Yugoslav-style socialism proved to be misplaced. It is known that there was extensive debate at the top levels of the country's leadership, and that the hardliners outweighed the moderates. The outcome of this debate was dramatically underscored by the clamp-down on private trade and business in South Vietnam in March—April 1978 and by various follow-up measures. This important sector of the economy was dominated by Vietnam's Chinese minority.

Until then the refugee outflow from Vietnam was about what could realistically have been expected. The total number of boat people arriving mainly in ASEAN countries during the second half of 1975 and the years 1976 and 1977 was somewhere between 21,000 and 26,000 depending on which statistics are used. There were just under 400 arrivals in 1975 (that is after the panic wave of departures associated with the American evacuation when about 135,000 people left the South in April—May); about 5,000 in 1976 and between 15,500 and 20,500 in 1977. In the first phase, the overwhelming majority of those leaving did so secretly, and were ethnic Vietnamese from South Vietnam.

What marked the second phase of the refugee exodus from Vietnam was its very large scale, its increasingly organised and officially sanctioned nature, the inclusion of the North as well as the South as a source of the outflow, and the pre-dominantly Chinese composition of the mass movement to China, the ASEAN countries and Hong Kong. This exodus reached a peak of intensity between March 1978 and June 1979. Nearly a quarter of a million men, women and children left by boat and reached nearby non-communist countries in Asia. In the last ten months of 1978, some 82,000 arrived in ASEAN countries, Hong Kong and Macau; in the first six months of 1979, the numbers swelled to 167,000. At the same time, another massive wave of departures was under way, mainly by land, to China.

Because of the military, security, political and other impli-cations of the Indo-China crisis, ASEAN Foreign Ministers decided to hold a special meeting in Bangkok on 12–13 January 1979. The choice of venue was deliberate. Of the five ASEAN states, Thailand was closest to Kampuchea and the country that would be most severely buffeted by the shock waves from the Vietnamese invasion and the fall of Phnom Penh.

After extended sessions behind closed doors and much debate over the most appropriate wording to adopt, the Foreign Ministers came out with a statement that 'strongly deplored the armed intervention against the independence, sovereignty and territorial integrity of Kampuchea'.

With the Kampuchea conflict looming in the background, ASEAN Foreign Ministers in their January 1979 Bangkok meeting also took up the problem of 'refugees and displaced persons or illegal immigrants from Indochina'. The use of the phrases 'displaced persons' or 'illegal immigrants', rather than 'refugees', was a device employed by ASEAN members – particularly Thailand and Malaysia – to placate elements at home hostile to the influx of increasing numbers of aliens from Indo-China, and to leave open the option of denying them entry.

ASEAN Ministers had dealt with the refugee problem at earlier meetings but had not made a feature of it, as they did in Bangkok, by issuing a separate joint statement on the matter. In the earlier statements, there was no mention of the root causes or even the individual source countries of the exodus. In retrospect, it seems that ASEAN reacted to the surging tide of humanity from Indo-China in lame fashion. Three factors appear to have played a part.

The first was that this tide impacted with differing force on each of the five ASEAN members. By the end of 1978, UNHCR figures showed that of the 202,000 refugees flooding into Thailand since 1975 from Indo-China — all of whom had come overland from next-door Laos and Kampuchea — 138,000 were still in temporary camps awaiting resettlement or repatriation. In addition, since 1975 Thailand had allowed entry to 13,500 boat people from Vietnam. On the other hand, Thailand's four ASEAN partners had to live with only one aspect of the Indo-Chinese refugee problem — the men, women and children arriving by sea from Vietnam. Each of the four was differently affected by the end of 1978. Malaysia was far the heaviest sufferer with cumulative arrivals totalling more than 70,000. Of this number, 63,000 came in 1978 alone. The Philippines' combined tally of boat people was less than 4,500; Indonesia's was under 4,000 and Singapore's barely 2,300.

A second factor underlying the lame response from ASEAN over the refugee problem was a desire on the part of most members to avoid creating contentious issues in the still bruised but improving relationship with Vietnam. Trying to reach a *modus vivendi* with Hanoi was a feature of ASEAN diplomacy in 1978. Members wanted to prevent a hardening of attitudes. If pushed to extremes, such a polarisation could lead to a second era of cold-war confrontation in Asia, with China aligned on the side of the US, Australia, New Zealand, ASEAN and other non-communist countries against Indo-Chinese governments oriented towards the Soviet bloc.

A third factor restraining ASEAN over the refugee issue was the existence of fundamentally different perceptions of Vietnam, China and their respective roles in the region. These differences occurred not just between ASEAN member states, but within individual ASEAN governments as well. At least in the initial stages of the Vietnamese invasion of Kampuchea, observers believed that influential elements in

Indonesia, Malaysia and to some extent in the Philippines as well were all inclined to welcome the prospect of a united communist Indo-China at peace with itself and strongly influenced by Vietnam, as a bulwark against southward extension of undesirable influence from China in the longer term. This sort of thinking was prevalent in Indonesia where anti-China feelings ran deep, particularly among rightist leaders of the majority Muslim community and in the country's powerful military hierarchy.

By the end of 1978, all five ASEAN members had diplomatic relations of varying degrees of warmth with Vietnam. But relations with China were more tentative. Malaysia, Thailand and the Philippines had exchanged Ambassadors with Peking. Singapore was waiting until after Indonesia had moved. Indonesia suspended diplomatic ties with China in 1967 following an attempted *coup d'état* led by left-wing and communist forces in October 1965, which plunged the country into violent civil conflict. The army-backed government which took over in the wake of this trouble implicated China in the *coup* and noted with anger that when the pro-Peking Indonesia Communist Party (PKI) was crushed, some of its leaders found sanctuary in Peking.

At the end of 1978, Indonesia felt far less suspicious about Vietnam than about China. Peking's senior Vice-Premier, Deng Xiaoping, had just finished a tour of three ASEAN countries – Thailand, Malaysia and Singapore. He had refused to withdraw Chinese support (admittedly token but it could always be stepped up) for communist insurgencies in non-communist Southeast Asia, claiming that government-to-government relations and party-to-party relations were separate matters. By contrast, Vietnam's Premier Dong, on a similar tour a few weeks earlier, had disowned the insurgents (although cynical observers noted at the time that since the outlawed communist movements were predominantly Peking-oriented, Vietnam had few links to withdraw). Deng had also failed to reassure Malaysia and other ASEAN countries, such as Indonesia, with substantial Chinese minorities whose allegiance was in doubt, that China would not intervene to protect their rights or influence their behaviour.

This mistrust of China reinforced another trend in official

Indonesian thinking: the view that the sprawling archipelago Republic – by virtue of its size as the fifth most populous country in the world, its potential wealth, its strategic location overlooking the maritime crossroads between the Indian and Pacific Oceans, its influence in international affairs, and its 220,000-man armed forces – was the natural leader of ASEAN, *primus inter pares*. From this kind of thinking, it was only a short step to the view that in the longer-term in Southeast Asia there were two logical poles of mutually balancing influence – Vietnam's and Indonesia's.

At the Special Meeting of ASEAN Foreign Ministers in Bangkok in January 1979, Thailand's Prime Minister at the time, General Kriangsak Chamanand, called for a firm collective response to Vietnam's actions in Kampuchea. The tone of the statement on Kampuchea was carried over into the joint statement on the refugee problem which ASEAN saw as interconnected with Vietnam's military adventures. The five Foreign Ministers warned that the increasing flow of Indo-Chinese refugees into the ASEAN area was 'causing severe economic, social, political and security problems particularly to those countries bearing the main brunt of the influx, such as Thailand and Malaysia'. They repeated earlier calls for the UNHCR and the International Community to do more to alleviate the burden, and added that countries resettling refugees should give guarantees to ASEAN States that all displaced Indo-Chinese in temporary camps would be removed. Then, for the first time, ASEAN suggested that Vietnam was a source of the refugee problem. The statement said that if the exodus from Indo-China, which had already reached 'alarming proportions', continued it would seriously affect regional stability. It said that the Ministers 'stressed that the Government of Vietnam, which has pledged to promote regional peace and stability, and other countries of origin should take appropriate measures to tackle the problem at source'.

As the ASEAN country nearest to the eye of the storm in Indo-China, Thailand felt the need for firm verbal support from its four ASEAN partners. Mutual antagonism between Thailand and Vietnam – the two largest States in Mainland Southeast Asia – stretched back for centuries. Rivalry had been most often expressed in competition over Cambodia. With the removal of the anti-Vietnamese Khmer Rouge regime in Kampuchea, there was no longer a buffer between them. That situation was unprecedented although the Thais had learned to live with Laos where the presence of up to 40,000 Vietnamese troops helped the Lao communists to maintain control after 1975.

Thailand's suspicions of Vietnam had been sharpened by its recent termination of a protracted and frustrating series of negotiations with Hanoi over repatriation of an estimated 60,000 to 70,000 Vietnamese refugees who had come to Thailand before 1975, most of them in the late 1940s and early 1950s to escape the fighting between the French and the communist-dominated Vietminh in the first Indo-China war. They were concentrated in northeastern Thailand in provinces close to Laos. Thai authorities – fighting communist insurgents in the northeast, some of whom were thought to lean towards Hanoi – saw the Vietnamese refugee communities as potential if not actual fifth columnists, just as Vietnam regarded its Chinese minority as a threat to national security. The military Government in Bangkok was also worried that Vietnam might be tempted to push across the border into Thailand from Western Kampuchea or Laos in pursuit of Laotian irredentist claims to a number of neighbouring pro-vinces in Thailand, or to settle old scores – one of them Thai support for the American war effort in Vietnam.

While Indonesia was extremely suspicious of China, Thailand had fewer inhibitions about moving closer to Peking. Of all the ASEAN States with ethnic Chinese minorities, it had been the most successful in absorbing them into the mainstream of its national life. China was seen in Bangkok as a potential protector against Vietnam. Thai leaders greeted the news of China's military incursion into Vietnam's north-ern border provinces in February–March 1979 with con-siderable relief and they privately welcomed public warnings from Peking that Vietnam would not be able to strike with impunity at Thailand.

ASEAN finally came out with a joint statement naming Vietnam as a source of the refugee problem in January 1979, largely due to pressure from its two most seriously affected members – Thailand and Malaysia – and its least affected member – Singapore.

Singapore's attitude towards both Vietnam and the refugee problem was hard-nosed and tough-minded. It consistently turned away boat people from Vietnam unless they were guaranteed rapid resettlement. The Island-State justified this stand on the grounds that it was overcrowded and would become a magnet for refugees if it relaxed the strict policy on entries. 'You've got to grow callouses on your heart or you just bleed to death,' Prime Minister Lee Kuan Yew said in one interview. In a speech on 17 February 1979, the then Foreign Minister Sinnathamby Rajaratnam stated an argument which other ASEAN governments took increasingly seriously as the year advanced and the numbers of boat people arriving in Southeast Asian waters reached torrential proportions. He said:

The flow of boat people poses the non-communist world, including the ASEAN countries, with a moral dilema. We could respond on humanitarian and moral grounds by accepting and resettling these desperate people. But by doing so we would not only be encouraging those responsible to force even more refugees to flee but also unwittingly demonstrate that a policy of inhumanity (the Vietnamese Government's) does pay dividends. Not only that, but those countries which give way to their humanitarian instincts would saddle themselves with unmanageable political, social and economic problems that the sudden absorption of hundreds of thousands of alien peoples must inevitably bring in its wake.

While suspecting China's long-term intentions towards Southeast Asia, Singapore was more wary of the Vietnamese and Soviet threat because it was judged to be more immediate. Singapore wanted to see ASEAN give Thailand adequate assurances of support in the face of the Indo-China crisis. This would encourage the US, Japan and other non-communist countries to swing behind Thailand and prevent Bangkok from becoming excessively dependent on China for assistance. Singapore also wanted ASEAN to start speaking out in forthright terms about what it saw as the basic causes of the boat refugee flood, thus putting international pressures on Vietnam to change its policies so that people would not feel impelled to leave by the backdoor sea route.

Malaysia was the ASEAN country most seriously affected by the deluge of boat people from Vietnam. The majority of refugees headed straight for the northeast coast of Peninsular Malaysia for several reasons. It was the closest landfall to southern Vietnam in non-communist Southeast Asia. The night beacons formed by natural gas burning from near the top of several oil wells more than 100 kilometres off the Malaysian coast provided a homing point and eased the problems of navigation. And by heading for Malaysia, refugees had a better chance of avoiding attacks by pirates in the Gulf of Thailand. Up until late 1978, refugees wanting to land in Malaysia and enter a UNHCR-supervised camp pending resettlement overseas could usually do so without too much difficulty. Malaysian fishermen and villagers quite often helped the newcomers, sometimes for a fee but on other occasions from spontaneous generosity or compassion.

However the tidal wave dimensions of the refugee inflow turned Malaysia's mood to one of widespread hostility. At the end of 1978, UNHCR figures showed there was a total of just under 50,000 refugees in Malaysian camps. By the end of 1979, another 50,000 had arrived. People were coming into the camps at a far faster rate than Western countries were prepared, at that stage, to resettle them. So in mid-year, the backlog of refugees in Malaysia had mounted to 75,000.

The influx – and domestic reactions to it – generated serious undercurrents of political and communal tension in Malaysia, where Islam is the State religion and where a delicate balance between Chinese of immigrant stock and Malays, who regard themselves as the principal indigenous group, had been shattered by ugly race riots in Kuala Lumpur in 1969. The country's multiracial, multi-religious fabric had to be stitched together again with care. The population is now (1980) about 14 million with the overwhelming majority living in Peninsular Malaysia.

But the flood of so many non-Muslim aliens from Vietnam

— more than half of whom were of Chinese descent — created a backlash in conservative Malay communities along the northeast coast of Peninsular Malaysia. By late 1978, some Malay villagers were stoning incoming boats and the men, women and children on them. There were allegations in the *kampongs* (villages) that Malaysia would never be able to get rid of all the Chinese and Vietnamese refugees. The Government was accused of allowing a form of backdoor immigration, mainly Chinese, to occur. The Government itself tended to encourage this kind of alarmism by referring to the boat people as 'illegal immigrants'. Critics within the ruling Malay Party, as well as the opposition *Partai Islam*, charged that the Government was not taking firm enough action to stem the refugee tide. Several ministers made statements which, while they may have been intended to placate domestic opposition, served to provoke extremist feelings. In Kuala Trengganu in December 1978, a senior Malaysian police officer was hospitalised with a jagged gash in his head after being hit by a rock while helping supervise the landing of a boat load of more than two hundred Indo-Chinese who beached their craft near the entrance of the town's harbour. The rock was hurled from a crowd of several thousand people who had gathered on the beach. Stones were thrown at Vietnamese as they huddled on the sand guarded by police. Malaysian soldiers and police — most of them Malays — found themselves in the invidious position of having to protect Indo-Chinese from Malay villagers who wanted them ejected from the country.

Along the northeast coast of Peninsular Malaysia, Malays claimed that the refugees were being given privileged treatment; that their presence in such large numbers was driving up the cost of living; that they had a corrupting influence on fishermen, villagers, merchants and officials tempted to profit by black-marketeering or in other contacts with the refugees; that they occupied scarce hospital beds that should have been available to Malaysians. It did not matter that most of these claims were either exaggerated or untrue. They were widely believed.

Malaysian authorities reacted by locating the main UNHCR-run camps for displaced Indo-Chinese on uninhabited off-shore islands well away from the local population. In November

1978, a task force under the command of an army general was formed to co-ordinate Malaysian military and civilian efforts to control the refugee problem. At about the same time, navy ships began regular patrols in off-shore waters, a chain of refugee watch towers manned by soldiers was established in areas where boats often landed, and increasing numbers of boats were turned away or towed out to sea. This culminated in June 1979 when Malaysia's Deputy Prime Minister, Dr Mahathir bin Mohamad, was widely reported as saying that more than 65,000 boat people in camps under the protection of the UNHCR would be shipped out to sea again if the nations of the West, where the boat people wanted to go, did not resettle them more quickly. Mahathir was quoted as saying that 'shoot-on-sight' legislation would be enacted so that security force patrols could drive off all boats attempting to land. An official statement of policy issued subsequently by the Prime Minister, Datuk Hussein Onn, toned down the more draconian of these threats. But whether Mahathir intended it or not, warnings attributed to him and flashed around the world by the media jolted the slow-moving international community into more effective action to tackle the boat refugee crisis.

The Malaysian authorities expressed concern at the security implications of the refugee inflow from Vietnam, as well as its socio-political impact. This concern was echoed by other ASEAN members. In May 1979 a Thai Supreme Command spokesman was reported to have said that Vietnamese espionage and subversion agents made up an estimated 10 per cent of all refugees from Indo-China entering Thailand. Malaysia's Home Affairs Minister, Tan Sri Ghazali Shafie, declared in a speech in November 1978:

> One could well suspect that the ejection of overseas Chinese and even Vietnam citizens of Chinese origin from Ho Minh City (formerly Saigon) might be motivated by the desire of Hanoi to remove the 'Wooden Dragon', not just Chinese merchants of Cholon, but Peking-oriented communists.

Like its ASEAN partners, Malaysia was troubled by a pro-

Peking communist guerrilla movement. In Malaysia's case, the membership of that movement, and the base of its support, was almost exclusively ethnic Chinese.

The Malaysian Government was acutely aware of the volatile repercussions of mass boat refugee arrivals from southern Vietnam. It had no difficulty identifying the source of the problem. But it was hesitant over who was to blame: Vietnam, China or the US. As late as July 1979, Home Affairs Minister Ghazali said that every time China 'rattles its sword or swings its cane', the ethnic Chinese in Vietnam panicked and fled the country.

ASEAN Foreign Ministers held their regular annual meeting for 1979 on the Indonesian resort island of Bali. Their mood was sombre and late on 30 June, at the end of three days of mainly private talks, they issued a joint communiqué. It dealt with the two related issues that dominated the gatherings: the Indo-Chinese refugee crisis and the armed conflicts centred on Indo-China. The Ministers explicitly condemned 'interference by Vietnam and other foreign forces' in the internal affairs of Kampuchea — the 'other foreign forces' being an obvious swipe at Vietnam's ally, the Soviet Union. They blamed Vietnam for 'the unending exodus' of Indo-Chinese refugees and 'strongly deplored' the fact that Hanoi had not taken effective measures to stop the outflow. They said Vietnam had 'a decisive role to play in resolving the problem at source'. They also expressed 'serious concern over the incessant influx of Kampuchean illegal immigrants into Thailand arising out of the armed intervention and military operations in Kampuchea'. They said the 'deluge' of displaced Indo-Chinese had caused severe political, socio-economic and security problems in ASEAN countries and would have 'a destabilising effect' on the region. ASEAN members had a right to repatriate stranded refugees and the Indo-Chinese States must accept them back. The Foreign Ministers said they supported a proposal for convening an international conference on Indo-Chinese refugees under the auspices of the UN Secretary-General in Geneva on 20–21 July 1979. Provided the conference tackled all aspects of the problem, including a solution at source and a more responsive resettlement programme, it would help solve the crisis.

Less than six months after their special meeting in Bangkok which apportioned no public blame for the great exodus from Indo-China, ASEAN Foreign Ministers had collectively placed Vietnam in the dock. There were a number of reasons for the hardening of ASEAN's position, which was preceded by a lot of tersely worded private debate.

The five member governments were still divided in their diagnosis of the root causes of the outflow from Vietnam (that is, whether it was due to policies of the Vietnamese, Chinese or American governments, to other factors or to a combination of pressures). But they had become convinced that Vietnamese authorities had the power to control the rate of exodus and could only be prevailed upon to do so through pressure from international opinion and the community of nations. In January, after talks with the UNHCR, Hanoi had announced agreement in principle to expand the channel for legal emigration from Vietnam, a move which raised hopes that many people taking the risky sea passage out of Vietnam to transit camps in ASEAN countries and Hong Kong would apply instead to fly direct to the places where they wanted to settle – the countries of North America, Australasia and Western Europe. In subsequent contacts with Hanoi and its emissaries, ASEAN felt the Vietnamese were deliberately stalling, playing for time. Meanwhile the outflow of boat people reached record levels – 75,000 flooded into ASEAN countries and Hong Kong in June alone. Indonesia was now starting to feel the pressure. The number of boat people in temporary camps there leapt from about 12,000 in April to 40,000 in June. Most had sailed to the Anambas Islands after being pushed away or towed out from Malaysia, a practice which caused considerable irritation in Jakarta.

Another factor prompting ASEAN to toughen its stand towards Vietnam over refugees was Singapore's activism. Both Malaysia's Foreign Minister Tengku Ahmad Rithaudeen and the Philippine Foreign Minister General Carlos Romulo (who was not present at the Special Meeting in Bangkok in January) had arrived in Bali with firm mandates. Romulo declared at a Press conference after his plane touched down: 'Hanoi is the pivot and we can solve this problem only if Hanoi realises the enormity of the crime against human beings.' But it was Singapore's Foreign Minister Sinnathamby Rajaratnam who was most outspoken. In a dramatic speech to the opening session of the meeting, he proposed that the five ASEAN Governments should side with anti-Vietnamese forces in Kampuchea. He later told the Press he believed ASEAN and friendly non-communist governments should provide arms and material support to the resistance in Kampuchea, just as the Soviet Union was giving aid to Vietnam. In his speech he branded Vietnam as an expansionist power with ambitions to dominate the whole of Southeast Asia. He claimed that Hanoi was deliberately expelling hundreds of thousands of refugees from Vietnam and Kampuchea to 'destabilise, disrupt and cause turmoil and dissension in ASEAN States'. Vietnam's objective was to inflame a 'massive anti-China movement' in the region.

Approximately two-thirds of the 280,000 boat people who left their homeland between mid-1975 and mid-1979 are believed to have done so with the approval of Hanoi and its agents — principally officials of the country's internal security police organisation. Only about one-third of departures were arranged secretly. They were the illegal ones. Starting in about the last week of June 1979, the Government-sponsored departure network that most people, especially the Chinese, used was suspended, with the result that the outflow tapered off sharply. Hanoi's move was apparently designed to contain mounting international criticism of Vietnamese actions in advance of the Geneva Conference, the non-aligned summit in Havana in early September and the UN General Assembly session opening later that month.

By late September 1979, the reduction in the number of boat people leaving Vietnam had provided a welcome breathing space for countries of first asylum in the region and resettlement countries outside the region. The Geneva Conference — where Vietnam was sharply criticised by many countries including some, like Sweden, which had traditionally been sympathetic to Hanoi — ended with an announcement from UN Secretary-General Kurt Waldheim that the Vietnamese Delegation had promised to do its best to stifle the boat refugee exodus and co-operate with the UNHCR in arranging an orderly and safe departure scheme for people to leave the country.

The Geneva Conference also achieved its aim of doubling the number of resettlement places on offer for refugees seeking permanent asylum in third countries, from 125,000 available in May to 260,000. In the months following the July meeting, the pace of resettlement from congested and insanitary camps in Asia was accelerated. From a peak of more than 50,000 in June 1979, arrivals of boat people from Vietnam fell to 17,839 in July to 2,745 in December. In the same period, the monthly resettlement rate of boat people averaged around 15,000, substantially exceeding the numbers entering camps. By the end of 1979, Malaysia's camp population had fallen to just over 34,000. The other ASEAN country most heavily burdened by boat refugees, Indonesia, had 32,224 people from Vietnam in camps. By June 1980, there were only about 10,000 boat people in Indonesia and 22,000 in Malaysia. (Figures for international resettlement and international aid for refugees appear at the end of this chapter).

Intra-ASEAN co-operation over refugees also helped to reduce the strain of the boat people. In 1979 both Indonesia and the Philippines offered to make special processing centres available to accommodate several tens of thousands of Indo-Chinese approved for third-country resettlement but not due to depart for some time because of bureaucratic delays in receiving nations, chiefly the United States.

The opening of these camps on Indonesia's Galang Island and the Philippines' Bataan Peninsula at Morong west of Manila, towards the end of 1979, allowed some of the surplus refugees from first asylum camps in Thailand and Malaysia to be moved to these half-way houses.

Intensified UNHCR efforts to protect Vietnamese boat refugees from attacks by pirates in 1980 and growing Press publicity about the horrific things happening to many refugees at sea helped sustain international sympathy for the plight of the boat people. According to American officials, assaults by pirates in the Gulf of Thailand had cost more than one hundred lives in the eighteen months to May 1980. Robbery, beatings, murder and rape occurred regularly. Several dozen young refugee women had been abducted. Some were found later in southern Thailand. Others were listed as missing.

UNHCR officials said piracy in the Gulf of Thailand first became a serious problem in 1978 as the number of refugees leaving southern Vietnam in small boats grew. The pirates were looking for gold, jewellery and other valuables. With more marauders operating and the flow of refugees dwindling from the second half of 1979, attacks became more violent and pirates began striking at Thai and Malaysian fishing boats as well as refugee craft. They used Thai vessels and operated from bases in Thailand. A UNHCR survey compiled early in 1980 found that about half the boats arriving at Malaysia's biggest island camp for refugees, Pulau Bidong, reported being attacked at least once by pirates on their voyage from Vietnam. The survey investigated two hundred piracy cases and pin-pointed four main areas where attacks took place. UNHCR officials said that, as a result, these areas off southern Thailand and the northeast coast of Peninsular Malaysia were being more frequently policed by the navies of the two countries. Some of the pirate craft had struck inside Thai and Malaysian territorial waters and for the first time Thai authorities started court prosecutions against Thai nationals accused of molesting refugees at sea, while Malaysia announced in April 1980 that it had arrested a Thai boat suspected of piracy. However, despite these and other international efforts to reduce the severity of piracy in the gulf of Thailand and the South China Sea, Western officials doubted that they would have much impact on the problem.

The level of boat refugee arrivals in 1980 rose slowly from 2,690 in January to about 10,000 in June. However UNHCR and Western officials in ASEAN countries said they had no firm evidence that the steadily growing exodus was due to a Vietnamese Government decision to reopen semi-official escape channels closed twelve months earlier following wide-spread international condemnation. They said boat refugees leaving southern Vietnam were bribing low-level Vietnamese officials to look the other way, but there was no sign that Hanoi had given its blessing. Most of the refugees said they had to escape secretly, risking capture by security patrols and heavy punishments. The increasing outflow was attributed to the calm weather prevailing in the South China Sea from March to October and to economic hardship, discrimination and repression in Vietnam.

Thailand had long felt that inadequate attention was being paid by the international community to what was numerically a bigger problem for a single country than that posed by the more dramatic exodus of boat refugees from Vietnam. This was, of course, the phenomenon of 'land' refugees in Thailand – displaced persons, nearly all from adjacent Laos and Kampuchea, who arrived by crossing the land frontier or the Mekong River border. In the second half of 1979, as the outflow from Vietnam tapered off and famine and fighting in Kampuchea sent tens of thousands of refugees towards Thailand in search of food and safe haven, the focus of international concern swung towards the land refugees. UNHCR figures put the number in Thailand at the end of 1979 at 65,393, in addition to 11,928 boat people from Vietnam in Thai camps. But several hundred thousand Kampucheans dependent on international food and medical supplies were camped along or close to the ill-defined Thai– Kampuchean boundary and by mid-1980 the shifting border zone population was put at about 600,000. The close prox- imity of Vietnamese-led forces and the control over many of the refugees exercised by the Khmer Rouge or various anti-communist and anti-Vietnamese Kampuchean factions, some of whom were little more than warlords profiteering from aid supplies and control of a thriving cross-border trade, created a potentially explosive situation. A joint scheme by Thailand and the UNHCR in June which led to the repatriation of some 8,000 Kampucheans from camps in Thailand (most of them Khmer Rouge loyalists) prompted Vietnamese troops to launch a military strike into Thailand and seal key areas of the frontier, bringing the repatriation programme to a halt. Simultaneously, Vietnamese-led forces lauched fresh attacks against Khmer Rouge strongholds in western Kampuchea not far from Thailand. In neighbouring Laos at about the same time, a clash on the Mekong River between a Thai naval patrol boat and Pathet Lao troops resulted in the Bangkok Govern- ment closing the whole of its frontier with Laos, sharply reducing imports to the landlocked country and causing considerable economic hardship there. In August, UN Secretary-General Waldheim flew to Hanoi and then to

Bangkok in an attempt to use his good offices to stabilise the situation along the border between Indo-China and Thailand.

By mid-July Thailand was playing reluctant host to nearly 300,000 people displaced from Indo-China, according to the Thai Military Supreme Command. The total included 158,327 persons who had arrived from Laos, Kampuchea and Vietnam since 1975 and been given refugee status by Thai authorities. This group comprised 115,355 Laotians, 9,503 Vietnamese, and 7,632 Kampucheans who had left their country before the fall of Phnom Penh in January 1979. The remaining people in holding centres in Thailand were 158,327 Kampucheans who had arrived since the overthrow of the Khmer Rouge regime. They were classed as 'illegal immigrants'.

The Soviet invasion of Afghanistan in December 1979 and the creation of another massive flow of refugees, this time from Afghanistan into Pakistan, moved international attention away from the Indo-China conflict and its refuges. Thailand and its ASEAN partners were alarmed at this trend which occurred at a time of growing economic recession in the Western industrial democracies. It was felt that rising unemployment would only contribute to reductions in the number of resettlement places made available for Indo-Chinese refugees in ASEAN countries. In addition, ASEAN-sponsored efforts to negotiate with Vietnam to bring about a withdrawal of Vietnamese forces from Kampuchea and a political settlement had made little or no progress. Attempts to expand an orderly departure scheme for would-be refugees wishing to leave Vietnam had produced only meagre results. Vietnam on the one hand and the US and other Western countries on the other could not agree on who should be able to emigrate or how they should be screened.

In this uncertain and ominous atmosphere, ASEAN's strategy was to keep as much international pressure as possible on Vietnam and its principal ally, the Soviet Union, over both political and refugee issues in Indo-China. The two related questions were prominent in statements issued after a meeting between ASEAN and European Economic Community Foreign Ministers in March 1980 and between ASEAN Foreign Ministers and their counterparts from the US,

Japan, Canada, Australia and New Zealand in June. To sustain the flow of international relief supplies to Kampuchea and prevent even more refugees turning to Thailand for food and shelter, ASEAN members helped to sponsor a UN meeting on humanitarian assistance to Kampuchea in May.

But these moves were no more than palliatives in the absence of progress towards settlement of the underlying political causes of the Indo-Chinese refugee turmoil. The situation has the potential to erupt again at any time. A massive surge of Kampuchean refugees into Thailand would create severe strains within that country and probably lead to demands from the Government in Bangkok that the West guarantee to resettle the newcomers if they could not be sent home. Tension between Thailand and Vietnam, and between Indo-China and ASEAN, would rise dangerously. If another armada of boat people were unleashed by the Vietnamese authorities, the consequences for ASEAN could be grave: rifts would open within the Association and its five member States would push unwanted boats away from their shores in the direction of neighbouring countries; tension would erupt between ASEAN and Western Governments over ASEAN's practice of refusing entry to boat people and the West's failure to resettle them fast enough; and irreconcilable suspicion and hostility would develop between the non-communist and communist halves of Southeast Asia in which China and the West would side with ASEAN and the Soviet bloc with Indo-China.

Vietnam holds the key to this Pandora's box and thus, in a sense, has the capacity to dictate future events in Southeast Asia. Whether or not international opinion has restrained Vietnam, it held back the outflow of refugees throughout 1980. But there is no certainty that if other things do not go Vietnam's way, this restraint will continue.

Indo-Chinese Refugees

1. From the first outflows in 1975 up to 31 August 1980, refugees from
   Indo-Chin were accepted for *permanent resettlement* by the following major recipient countries (figures to nearest '000):

USA	283,000 (+ 300,000 direct from Vietnam in 1975)
France	67,000
Canada	63,000
Australia	41,000
Germany (FRG)	15,000
UK	11,000
Hong Kong	3,000
Japan	600 (with a commitment to a total of 1,000)

2. *Official financial contributions* to UNHCR Special and General
   Programmes, including refugee processing camps in ASEAN countries
   made by the following major donors (figures to nearest US $ million):

	1978	1979	1980 (to June)
USA	47.4	90.8	92.5
UK	12.8	16.1	15.3
Japan	11.6	68.1	64.1
Sweden	10.8	16.1	15.4
Netherlands	8.5	14.3	9.4
Denmark	8.0	8.6	6.4
Norway	7.8	6.4	9.6
Germany (FRG)	7.1	27.4	8.9
Australia	5.9	5.5	8.8
Canada	2.4	4.1	5.6
Switzerland	–	4.0	2.0

Source: UNHCR, *Report on the Status of Contributions to
Voluntary Funds*, 18 August 1980.

6

Looking Outwards: ASEAN's External Relations

Allan Gyngell

As earlier chapters have shown, the most immediate task for ASEAN's founders was the development of a basis of under-standing and trust between the five member governments. For as long as this remained the main focus of ASEAN's activities, the question of developing formal relations with external powers was low in the Association's list of priorities. Although its formation was prompted by the impact of external events on the region, ASEAN in the Bangkok Declaration did not see itself as a mechanism for formal dealings with the outside world. There were no readily apparent advantages for members in such collective approaches, the Association was not mature enough organisationally to cope with external relationships, and members still jealously guarded their national interests.

In the early to mid-1970s, however, as the Association matured, as members became more confident in their dealings with each other, and as they began to experience rapid economic growth,[1] a number of significant international developments focused ASEAN attention urgently on the external environment, and caused an important shift in the expectations which its members had of ASEAN. These developments included the OPEC oil price rises in 1973, the 1975 communist victories in Indo–China and the final with-drawal of US military power from mainland Southeast Asia in 1976, the beginnings of Sino–American and Sino–Japanese rapprochement and internal changes in China from 1976 leading to its commitment to economic modernisation.

Faced with these developments, and the uncertain regional

and global environment to which they gave rise, the Association's members felt a need to demonstrate greater public solidarity and cohesion. 'As never before', Lee Kuan Yew told the 1976 Bali Summit meeting, 'the future of non-communist South East Asia rests in the hands of the leaders and peoples of non-communist South East Asia.' The concept of 'ASEAN unity' became, therefore, the primary way of demonstrating their resilience in the face of external uncertainty and threat.

But they also began to identify positive pressures for more active co-operation. The OPEC members and the Group of 77 were beginning to demonstrate ways in which the 'South' could bring pressure to bear on the 'North' through collective effort.

Partly as a result of their dealings as a bloc with Japan and Australia (considered in more detail in Chapters 7 and 8) and with the EC, the ASEAN countries were becoming increasingly aware of the efficacy of joint action as a means of pursuing common economic and political goals and the need to restructure the Association to do so more efficiently. This need was met by the organisational reforms adopted by the Bali Summit.

This chapter examines first the development of ASEAN's formal 'dialogue' relationships with its main external trading partners, and then the common approach ASEAN had developed towards its communist neighbours and to the major extra-regional powers. The underlying question it addresses is the extent to which developments in Southeast Asia are leading to the emergence of a common ASEAN foreign policy.

The Dialogue Relationships

ASEAN's third-country dialogues grew out of its early dealings about trade matters with Japan and the EC. Since March 1976 each dialogue relationship has been co-ordinated by a particular member country. Indonesia is the contact country for Japan and for the EC (which nevertheless maintains a regional liaison office in Bangkok), Malaysia is the contact country for Australia, Singapore for New Zealand, the Philippines for the USA and Canada, and Thailand for the UNDP and ESCAP. The central ASEAN Secretariat in Jakarta was made the initial contact point for the embryonic dialogue with India.

ASEAN has made similar demands of each of its dialogue partners – improved investment flows, higher levels of development assistance, greater access to markets for ASEAN exports, support for an export earnings stabilisation fund. But as the separate dialogue relationships have progressed and ASEAN has gained closer knowledge of the situation in the individual countries, differences have emerged in areas of concentration and ASEAN's requests have become more specific.

In many ways the development of ASEAN's dialogue relations has mirrored the pattern of its internal growth. An initial emphasis on the non-controversial economic, development assistance and social matters prescribed in the Bangkok Declaration has more recently shifted to more overtly political issues as ASEAN's confidence in its political influence and international acceptance has built up.

THE EUROPEAN COMMUNITIES (EC)

ASEAN's basic interest in a dialogue with the EC stems from the Community's economic importance. This importance reflects in part the continuing strength of economic links formed during the colonial period. Trade with the EC in 1979 accounted for 16 per cent of ASEAN's total trade, ranking third behind the United States (17 per cent) and Japan (26 per cent). It is also the third largest foreign investor in the ASEAN region, with 14 per cent of the total. From the Community's viewpoint the relationship is less central. Trade with ASEAN is only 2.3 per cent of the EC's total external trade. But it is growing: both exports and imports doubled in the five years to 1978. Both blocs – roughly equivalent in population size – identify strong prospects for further growth in the economic relationship.

It became necessary for ASEAN to take specific account

of the EC after Britain's accession to membership led to the loss of Commonwealth trade preferences for Malaysia and Singapore. The Joint Declaration of Intent annexed to the accession treaty had made particular reference to the Community's willingness to examine any problems which might emerge for the developing Commonwealth countries of Asia after the termination of the Commonwealth pre-ference scheme in 1972, 'taking into account. . .the situation of the other developing countries in the same geographical area'. The EC accepted that this declaration applied to the other ASEAN partners as well.

ASEAN set up a Special Co-ordinating Committee of ASEAN Nations (SCCAN) in 1972 to co-ordinate its links with the EC. Formal relations between the two groups were institutionalised with the establishment in 1974 of a Joint ASEAN—EC Study Group as an alternative to the commercial co-operation agreements which had been negotiated bilaterally between the EC and the other Asian Commonwealth countries. The Joint Study Group met annually from July 1975 but its results were limited. It led to EC financing of a number of technical studies of regional integration projects, such as the development of ASEAN port facilities; to assistance with ASEAN trade promotion in Europe; and to investment seminars in Brussels in April 1977 and Jakarta in February 1979.

It became clear to ASEAN officials, however, that as long as the relationship continued to be the responsibility of the Commission itself, rather than of the Council of Ministers, it would lack the political backing necessary to achieve real progress. ASEAN pressed, therefore, for meetings between the diplomatic representatives of the five ASEAN countries in Brussels (the ASEAN Brussels Committee) and the Committee of Permanent Representatives of the member states of the EC. The first such meeting was held in November 1977, and led in turn to the first ASEAN—EC Ministerial Meeting in Brussels on 20 and 21 November 1979.

There were no major breakthroughs at this meeting. A Joint Declaration issued afterwards covered the main areas of discussion. The Community made clear its opposition to a separate Stabex arrangement with ASEAN of the sort which it had established at Lomé with the former European colonies in Africa, the Caribbean and the Pacific. Nevertheless the Commission expressed 'its willingness to examine, within a global context, what possibilities there were for guaranteeing the stabilisation of the export earnings of the developing countries, including ASEAN, as a complement to other measures'. On trade matters, ASEAN expressed concern about Community measures which might restrict exports. There were some minor gains for ASEAN. The participants agreed to promote the establishment of an ASEAN–EC trade and investment forum; the EC undertook to pay more attention to ASEAN regional projects in its future development assistance programmes; an EC regional office was to be set up in Bangkok in 1979; and the two groups agreed that it would be desirable to place their relationship on a more formal footing by discussing a co-operation agreement. This last was particularly welcome to ASEAN.

The ASEAN–EC Co-operation Agreement was negotiated during 1979. Although it contains little more than an expression of principles and intentions – the two groups commit themselves to closer co-operation in the areas of trade, industrial co-operation, investment and the transfer of technology – it does provide a formal framework within which consultation can take place. A Joint Co-operation Committee was set up 'to promote and keep under review the various co-operation activities envisaged between the parties'. The committee was to meet at least annually.

The Agreement, which was for an initial period of five years, was signed at the Second ASEAN–EC Ministerial Meeting held in Kuala Lumpur on 7 and 8 March 1980. The Ministers described the Agreement as having 'ushered in a new area of relations between ASEAN and the Community'. The meeting also discussed the usual agenda for ASEAN dialogues: commodities, commercial co-operation, trade promotions and private sector co-operation.

The most dramatic aspect of the Kuala Lumpur Meeting was the decision by Ministers to issue a strongly worded Joint Statement on Political Issues in order to condemn the Soviet and Vietnamese invasions of Afghanistan and Kampuchea. Although the earlier Brussels meeting had expressed concern about the Indo-Chinese refugee problem, the Kuala Lumpur statement was the first time the two groups had taken a joint position on major political issues.

Significant though the EC's political support of ASEAN was, however, when the Joint Co-operation Committee met again in November 1980, ASEAN hopes of EC concessional funding for the long-delayed industrial projects, and of a Stabex scheme, were no further advanced.

THE UNITED STATES

No formal relationship existed between the United States and ASEAN as a group until 1977. ASEAN, uncertain of America's political commitment to the region after 1975, also had enough significant economic reasons for wanting a formal dialogue with the United States to outweigh the doubts of those who argued that ASEAN should avoid formal links with any of the great powers. The United States in 1979 was ASEAN's second largest trading partner, and second largest foreign investor. Total trade in 1979 was more than US $16 billion, and was expected to reach US $21 billion in 1980. The United States market for ASEAN's exports of manufactured goods was expanding rapidly.

The first conference between ASEAN and United States officials was held in Manila on 8–10 September 1977. The US delegation was led by Under-Secretary of State for Economic Affairs, Richard Cooper. The meeting was a breakthrough for both sides. United States views of ASEAN had been ambivalent. Some officials argued privately that ASEAN was too fragile an entity to allow the United States to put too much weight on it.[2] Others suggested that although ASEAN was a positive force in Southeast Asia, formal US endorsement of the Association could prove to be the 'kiss of death', justifying Soviet and Vietnamese claims that ASEAN was a Western stooge.

The Manila conference dealt mainly with economic issues, partly at least because of the political constraints on dealing with broader political subjects. ASEAN sought US support for ASEAN industrial projects, greater access to the US market, US agreement to drop revised tax deferral arrangements for US companies operating abroad, and a request that US law be amended to allow Indonesia — a member of OPEC — access to the United States' GSP (Generalised System of Preferences).

The results of the meeting did not live up to ASEAN expectations. There was disappointment at the relatively low level of US participation, and few specific commitments emerged. The US rejected ASEAN's Stabex scheme for stabilising regional export earnings (as the EC and Japan did) on the grounds that globally-based efforts as part of a broader north—south dialogue were preferable. On development assistance, ASEAN projects were said not to conform with the 'basic needs' approach of the US aid programme. The tax deferral issue and requests for greater access to the US market were referred to Washington.

Little progress was subsequently made with these deferred issues. Indonesia remained excluded from the US GSP and the Administration reportedly rejected ASEAN's requests for changes to the GSP. The tax deferral amendment went ahead.

Between the Manila meeting in September 1977 and the second ASEAN–US meeting in August 1978, however, the United States gave further signs that it had begun to pay greater attention to ASEAN. Erland H. Heginbotham, a senior State Department official, told the *Asian Wall Street Journal* in March 1978 that although the first year of the Carter Administration might have given 'the appearance of a lessened interest in Asia', the second year would see increasing signs that the US had been 'building for expanded relationships in Asia'. Heginbotham said that, while economic consultations would be important in the dialogue, the United States would not follow Japan in providing ASEAN with large aid projects.[3]

In May 1978 Vice-President Mondale visited three of the ASEAN states during which he announced several major arms sales and aid commitments, and emphasised the continuing US role in Southeast Asia and its support for ASEAN. Speaking in Hawaii on his return, he praised the emergence of

ASEAN as 'one of the most encouraging developments in South East Asia'.[4]

It was in this environment of positive US statements of reassurance that the second dialogue meeting, this time at Ministerial level, was held in Washington on 3–4 August 1978. The US delegation was led by Secretary of State Vance and other Cabinet-level officers, and the ASEAN delegation was received by President Carter, Vice-President Mondale and Congressional leaders. But although the tone of the meeting was encouraging for ASEAN leaders (President Carter reaffirmed 'strong US support for the goals and aspirations of ASEAN'), there were again few substantive results beyond an important Administration pledge of support for the Common Fund in the negotiations for a New International Economic Order, an announcement upgrading the lending activities of the United States' Export–Import Bank in Southeast Asia, and agreement to encourage the formation of an ASEAN–United States business council. It was agreed that a permanent working group of US and ASEAN representatives in Washington should be established to co-ordinate the relationship.

Following the Washington meeting, an EXIM Bank mission visited the ASEAN countries, and in July 1979 the ASEAN–US Business Council, linking US private business with the ASEAN Chambers of Commerce and Industry had its inaugural meeting.

By the time of Secretary of State Vance's meeting with ASEAN Foreign Ministers after their meeting in Bali in June 1979 the Indo-China refugee crisis and the Vietnamese occupation of Kampuchea had given the ASEAN–United States relationship renewed political and strategic importance. At Bali the United States was for the first time present at an overtly political meeting with ASEAN. Mr Vance told the meeting that the United States was a Pacific power which saw co-operation with ASEAN as vital to the peace, prosperity and stability of Southeast Asia. The Secretary of State reaffirmed in specific terms the United States' commitment to Thailand. 'We are,' he said, 'committed morally and by treaty to support the ASEAN states. We have made this clear to all concerned – and directly to the Soviet Union and

Vietnam.' Mr Vance also announced doubling of the US Indo-China refugee intake, and identified five areas of high priority for future US–ASEAN co-operation: energy, trade, commodities, food production and improved nutrition, and the strengthening of technical co-operation, especially on food and energy.

The presence of Mr Vance's successor, Senator Edward Muskie, at the June 1980 meeting of ASEAN Foreign Ministers in Kuala Lumpur underlined the extent to which the United States' earlier scepticism about ASEAN had been set aside. It also underlined how far concern about Vietnam and the Soviet Union had led ASEAN to overcome its reluctance to be identified politically with the United States.

The third ASEAN–United States dialogue meeting was held in Manila on 10–12 September 1980. In a message to the meeting the Philippines' Foreign Minister Romulo described the ASEAN–United States dialogue as a 'microcosm of the North–South dialogue'. The meeting discussed commodity problems, trade access and other economic issues. It agreed to establish an Economic Co-ordination Committee, associated with the ASEAN Washington Committee, comprising the ASEAN Ambassadors in Washington, as a forum for discussing economic issues in Washington. The United States indicated that the EXIM Bank would finance at least $2 billion in transactions with ASEAN over the following five years. The United States also reiterated its 'strong commitment to regional development projects with ASEAN'. for which $30 million had been allocated. These included a plant quarantine project, a watershed conservation and management programme, and a programme to combat drug abuse. ASEAN agreed to consider a United States' proposal for the establishment of an ASEAN–US Consultative Group on Energy.

Elements of the political aspects of the relationship also emerged. In their joint Press statement delegates described the dialogue as 'the forum for their consultation in support of peace and stability and economic development in South East Asia'.

NEW ZEALAND

The ASEAN–New Zealand dialogue began in February 1975 and has progressed steadily. Emphasis has been placed on development assistance projects, including forestry, animal husbandry, and measures to assist ASEAN exporters.

Formal meetings of the dialogue partners were held in 1975 (twice), 1977 and 1979. The New Zealand Foreign Minister also attended meetings with ASEAN Foreign Ministers in 1979 and 1980. Although the small size of the New Zealand market gives it only a limited potential for ASEAN exporters, a Joint Trade Study Group was formed after the third dialogue meeting in May 1977 to study problem areas in trade between the two sides. The second meeting of the Study Group was held in September 1979. New Zealand Foreign Minister Talboys said of the New Zealand–ASEAN relationship in 1979: 'We have. . .set out to underpin the political links with a growing economic relationship. This has been the most important fact behind the sequence of dialogue and other meetings.' The ASEAN region is a major focus of New Zealand attempts to develop new markets. In the six years from 1974 to 1979 New Zealand exports to the five ASEAN countries increased by 233 per cent to NZ $169.6 million, and imports by 306 per cent to NZ $147.9 million. The balance of trade was generally in New Zealand's favour.

CANADA

Although the ASEAN–Canada dialogue was initiated in 1975, it took a long time to develop. The purpose of the dialogue, said the then Canadian Secretary of State for External Affairs, Mr Allan MacEachern, in August 1975, was to 'enhance our lines of communications and to facilitate cooperation in development assistance'. The trade and economic aspects of the relationship received little initial attention from Canada (in 1977 only 0.5 per cent of Canada's external trade was with the five ASEAN countries). The first dialogue meeting was not held until 3–4 February 1977 in the Philippines. The ASEAN side identified a large number of other potential areas for co-operation. ASEAN also raised the question of access to the Canadian market and the encouragement of greater Canadian investment in the region. The Canadian response was hesitant.[5] A second dialogue meeting was held in Ottawa in October 1977. Again, there was little positive movement. A satellite communications project was dropped and other potential aid projects reviewed. ASEAN again called for trade and economic concessions from Canada. Canada responded that further consideration of the ASEAN position would be given within the context of the Multilateral Trade Negotiations.

No further movement was evident in the ASEAN–Canada dialogue until June 1980, when Dr MacGuigan, the Secretary of State for External Affairs, met ASEAN Foreign Ministers after their meeting in Kuala Lumpur. A memorandum of understanding on the first ASEAN–Canada joint project – a forestry programme in Thailand – was signed, and negotiations were continuing about a second project, in the fisheries sector. Dr MacGuigan also held discussions about an agreement with ASEAN on technical and economic co-operation. Canada's 'period of caution' regarding contacts with regional groups was, he said, over. He told the Press that Canadian interest in ASEAN would remain a fundamental element of its policy.

UNDP

A formal programme of co-operation between ASEAN and the UNDP and ESCAP has been in existence since October 1976. Under this dialogue UNDP organises specialist assistance to ASEAN's regional programmes in a variety of areas. Areas of technical assistance have included the supply of and demand for food, environmental protection of marine areas, and technical support for the ASEAN secretariat.

INDIA

India is the first developing country with which ASEAN

has attempted to establish a relationship. Indian interest in a formal dialogue was first raised with the Malaysian Foreign Minister, Tengku Rithauddeen, during a visit he made to India early in 1978. In March 1979 a formal approach was made to the ASEAN Central Secretariat in Jakarta, and the ASEAN Secretary-General, Datuk Ali bin Abdullah, visited India to explore the idea further. At that stage, however, political factors intruded and ASEAN annoyance with what was seen as Indian bias towards Vietnam on the Kampuchea question delayed an ASEAN response until March 1980, when the Indians were advised that the way was open for a dialogue.

Factors influencing ASEAN's positive response seem to have included its recognition of the economic potential of ASEAN–India trade, its belief that a dialogue with India, a leading member of the non-aligned movement and the Group of 77, would offset the Western bias which ASEAN's other dialogue relationships suggested, and a hope that political discussions with India might moderate the degree of New Delhi's political support for Hanoi.

India's Secretary-General of External Affairs, Mr Eric Gonsalves, toured the ASEAN countries in May 1980 and attended the first dialogue meeting of senior officials in Kuala Lumpur. The meeting went smoothly. Proposals were discussed for trade promotion, for technology transfers, scientific exchange, and co-operation on energy matters. India offered to host a workshop in early 1981 at which officials could identify areas of future co-operation, and proposed exchanges of consultancy services in the engineering and industrial sectors as well as pooling of technical and managerial resources and skills.

Despite the positive elements in the meeting, however, political difficulties again affected the relationship when, in July 1980, India recognised the Heng Samrin regime in Kampuchea. ASEAN Foreign Ministers issued a statement strongly critical of the decision and it seemed that, for the time at least, neither side would want to press ahead with the projects identified at the first dialogue meeting.

THE SOUTH PACIFIC

A desultory relationship between ASEAN and the countries of the South Pacific has developed slowly over a decade. The main focus of the relationship has been Papua New Guinea, the largest of the South Pacific states. PNG shares a border with Indonesia and has sometimes seen itself as a bridge between Asia and the Pacific. PNG was represented as an observer at the ASEAN Foreign Ministers' meetings in Manila in 1976, Bangkok in 1978, Bali in 1979, and Kuala Lumpur in 1980. After a visit to Indonesia in December 1980 the PNG Prime Minister, Sir Julius Chan, was reported to be seeking to strengthen his country's links with ASEAN.

PNG has pressed for the development of formal relations between ASEAN and the regional body representing the South Pacific countries, the South Pacific Forum. In August 1977 the Forum agreed that the South Pacific Bureau for Economic Co-operation (SPEC) should institute a dialogue with ASEAN.

Although both associations seem to see merit in closer co-operation, they have not easily been able to identify specific areas in which they might move. The former Director of SPEC visited the ASEAN countries in November 1979 and discussed possibilities for co-operation with the central ASEAN Secretariat. Trade, transport, tourism and industrial co-operation were identified. It was also felt that represent-atives of each organisation might attend meetings of the other. No formal decisions about these matters had been made by either ASEAN or the Forum at the time of writing.[6]

Links between ASEAN and the Forum are unlikely to develop rapidly. ASEAN's interests continue to lie pre-dominantly in the development of relationships with its major trading partners, and the Forum has little experience of 'dialogue relationships' in ASEAN's sense. It is possible, however, that during the 1980s the political attractions of forging closer links between the small Pacific states and the ASEAN countries will increase for both sides, and that this will lend a new logic to the relationship.

REPUBLIC OF KOREA

The possible establishment of a dialogue relationship between ASEAN and the Republic of Korea, a growing trading partner for the ASEAN countries, has been suggested from time to time. Although a private sector link – the ASEAN–Korea Business Club – has been formed, no progress has been made towards an official relationship. ASEAN's wish to avoid becoming embroiled in the Korean question appears to have been an important factor in this.

Despite the slow and sometimes confused way in which the dialogue relationships have developed, they have brought ASEAN significant benefits. First, they have helped ASEAN to obtain a number of important practical concessions from its trading partners which would not have been possible for the ASEAN countries acting alone. These concessions have included agreement with Japan on limiting artificial rubber production, the EC's agreement to apply cumulative rules of origin to ASEAN products, and the upgrading of US lending and investment activities in the region. Large sums in loans and grants have also been pledged to regional development assistance schemes, including Japan's support for the ASEAN Finance Corporation and for the industrial projects.

Secondly, the dialogues have been important in consolidating a feeling of unity within ASEAN. They have forced the five countries to think about their common economic needs and to formulate joint approaches to their external partners.

Thirdly, they have contributed to the development of an ASEAN consciousness among people within the five countries well outside the traditional foreign affairs areas. Joint development assistance projects in a wide variety of fields, many of them based on the pattern established by Australia from 1974, have brought together a wide range of ASEAN scientists, technicians and other professional people who represent a new constituency for ASEAN.

Finally, the dialogues have been good public relations exercises for the Association. Awareness among political leaders, government officials and businessmen in the dialogue countries of ASEAN's existence, and of the need to take its interests into account, as well as to take advantage of the opportunities it presents, have increased markedly.

ASEAN and the Region

The establishment of the dialogue relationships was only one way in which ASEAN's existence influenced the individual foreign policies of the five member governments. It also provided a forum for co-operating policies towards regional issues such as the refugee exodus from Vietnam and the invasion of Kampuchea. But is there, in a wider sense, a common view among the ASEAN countries about the sort of regional environment which they want to create?

The 1967 Bangkok Declaration sees Southeast Asia (not simply the five ASEAN countries) as a region which has 'mutual interests and common problems' which can be protected or resolved by common action. The Association is 'open for participation by all states in the South East Asian region subscribing to the aforementioned aims, principles and purposes'.

Secondly, the Declaration embodies the idea — later seen in the ZOPFAN proposal — that 'external interference in any form or manifestation' is harmful to the stability of the region, and that 'all foreign bases are temporary' and are 'not intended to be used directly or indirectly to subvert the national independence and freedom of states in the area'.

Although these ideas have sometimes been criticised as mere rhetoric, and have been relegated more than once by ASEAN spokesmen to the status of long-term aims, they have had a discernible effect on the chequered development of ASEAN's relationships with its Indo-Chinese neighbours.

Relations between ASEAN and the Indo-China countries were from the beginning marked by deep mutual suspicion. Vietnam saw ASEAN — a number of the members of which had actively supported the United States during the Vietnam war — as no more than a front for Washington's interests, a 'new SEATO'. For their part, the ASEAN countries feared what they saw as Hanoi's expansionist aims, and the potential it had for supporting communist insurgent groups in the region.

In May 1975, however, the ASEAN Foreign Ministers showed a conciliatory approach to Hanoi, following its victory. They expressed their willingness to establish cooperative relations with the countries of Indo-China.

Vietnam remained hostile, alleging after the Bali Summit in February 1976 that the ASEAN countries were 'colluding with one another to repress the revolutionary movements in their countries'.[7]

From about mid-1976, however, following the US military withdrawal from Thailand, signs of change became apparent in Vietnam's position. It began to give greater emphasis to its regional diplomacy. In March, Foreign Minister Nguyen Duy Trinh announced a four-point programme to guide Vietnam's foreign policy, which gave new emphasis to the region. As one commentator has pointed out, the word 'region' appears in three of the four points.[8] The final point was particularly significant. It called for 'the development of cooperation among the countries of the region for the building of prosperity in keeping with each country's specific conditions, and for the cause of independence, peace and genuine neutrality in South East Asia'. The similarities with ASEAN's ZOPFAN proposal were clear.

In July 1976, Vietnam's Deputy Foreign Minister Phan Hien visited the Philippines, Malaysia, Singapore, Indonesia and Burma. His tone was positive and conciliatory. Although he emphasised that Vietnam was interested in developing its relations with its neighbours only in a bilateral framework, he was reported as saying that Hanoi was not interested in joining ASEAN or subscribing to the Zone of Peace proposal 'for the moment'. The implication was that this might change.

Relations deteriorated sharply again in August 1976 when Vietnam joined Laos in rebuffing Malaysia's attempts to have the non-aligned meeting in Colombo renew an earlier endorsement of ZOPFAN. There were angry exchanges on both sides.

At the bilateral level, relations between the ASEAN countries — apart from Thailand — and Vietnam gradually improved during 1977, and Vietnam's criticism of ASEAN declined in strength and frequency. Although the ASEAN countries remained concerned about Vietnam's long-term aims, and were worried about the prospect of Hanoi securing large-scale economic support from Japan and other Western countries, they maintained their public position of readiness to develop co-operative relations. At their second summit meeting, in Kuala Lumpur in July 1977, ASEAN leaders again expressed the Association's willingness to develop peaceful relations with all the countries of the region. Vietnam now began to talk about ASEAN as being unwittingly misled by the United States.

Foreign Minister Trinh again visited the region in December 1977 and January 1978, and though he stated that ASEAN was still 'inappropriate', he raised the concept of a new and wider organisation, to embrace all the countries of Southeast Asia, based on the principles of 'peace, independence and neutrality'.

In July 1978, as Vietnam's relations with Kampuchea and China deteriorated, Phan Hien paid ASEAN another visit. Vietnam now accepted, he said, that ASEAN was a regional organisation concerned primarily with economic development. He also followed up a proposal, first made by Vietnam in New York in May 1978, for discussion with ASEAN about the concept of a 'Zone of Peace, Independence and Genuine Neutrality'. The idea was not explained in detail, and ASEAN leaders expressed suspicion about what 'genuine neutrality' meant.

In September and October the Vietnamese Premier Pham Van Dong visited ASEAN capitals with offers to sign treaties of friendship and non-aggression with Hanoi's neighbours. He also reiterated that Vietnam would not support communist insurgent movements in the region. The ASEAN countries reacted cautiously, co-ordinating their responses and refusing to accept the proposals for individual treaties. Then, in November, as tension grew on the Vietnam–Kampuchea border, Hanoi signed a Treaty of Friendship and Co-operation with the Soviet Union, with provision for joint consultation about security issues. Article 6 of the Treaty read: 'In case one of the parties becomes the object of attack or of threat of attack, the High Contracting parties will immediately begin mutual consultations for the purpose of removing that threat and taking appropriate effective measures to secure the peace and security of their countries.' Finally, on 25 December, Vietnam invaded Kampuchea. Phnom Penh fell on 7 January and Vietnamese forces moved on to within a few kilometres of the Thai border.

The invasion of Kampuchea profoundly altered the strategic situation in the region. By destroying the buffer state between Thailand and Vietnam, it threatened Thai security interests so directly that the search for a *modus vivendi* between regional states which had preoccupied Southeast Asia's diplomats for the preceding four years came to an abrupt halt. At the same time the invasion led directly to a new escalation of great power rivalry in Southeast Asia. Vietnam's actions had only been possible because of the extensive economic and military support it was receiving from its Soviet ally. In return, the Soviet Union was making greater use of Vietnamese military facilities, particularly for its navy. China continued support of the defeated Khmer Rouge forces, many of whom sought sanctuary in Thailand, and moved to establish closer relations with the ASEAN countries, particularly Thailand. Chinese officials declared that they would support Thailand in the event of any Vietnamese attack on Thailand. The United States also made statements renewing its pledges of support for Thailand.

The focus of ASEAN diplomacy shifted. International forums such as the United Nations became the centre of ASEAN's efforts to prevent international recognition of the Heng Samrin Government, installed by the Vietnamese in Kampuchea. The Association's members began to pay greater attention to co-ordinating their approach to debates in such bodies. Meetings with dialogue partners, like that with the EC in March 1980, also became occasions for rallying support for ASEAN policies.

Within the Association there was general agreement about the ends of those policies: bringing about Vietnam's withdrawal from Kampuchea in a way which would ensure Thailand's security. There was no unanimity, though, about the means which should be adopted to secure them.[9] Debate took place within and between the ASEAN countries about whether Vietnam's motivation in invading Kampuchea had been territorial expansionism or a genuine, if misplaced, fear for its own security, and about whether the best means of pressing for Hanoi's withdrawal was the maintenance of all available pressures from any source, or the provision of inducements for change, or a mixture of both tactics.

The policy finally adopted was designed to deny international recognition and legitimacy to the Heng Samrin regime, and to dissuade Western and Third World governments from moving to derecognise the ousted government of Democratic Kampuchea, despite the domestic pressure which many of them faced to do so because of the emerging evidence of the barbarity of Pol Pot's rule. ASEAN's tactics were based on an assumption that a combination of political, economic and military pressure could force Hanoi to reconsider its position. The political pressure would come through the force of international criticism of Vietnam; economic pressure through the denial of Western, particularly Japanese, assistance to Vietnam's shaky economy; and military pressure from the Khmer Rouge resistance forces, supported by China and based in Thai border areas and mountainous areas of Kampuchea. This combination of elements would, it was argued, eventually make the costs of the occupation too high for Hanoi to bear.

Some within ASEAN, however, believed that Vietnam actions were motivated in part at least by its mistrust of China. It was for this reason that President Suharto of Indonesia and Prime Minister Hussein Onn of Malaysia put forward at a meeting in March 1980 a proposal which came to be described as the Kuantan doctrine, after the town in which the two leaders met. The proposal itself was unexceptionable in ASEAN terms: a call for Vietnam to move to a position of neutrality between China and the Soviet Union. But it was assumed by observers at the time[10] that it represented an attempt by Malaysia and Indonesia to find a way out of the diplomatic impasse which had arisen over Kampuchea.

The position of those within ASEAN, particularly Thailand and Singapore, who were privately arguing for ASEAN to maintain the pressure on Vietnam, was considerably strengthened by Hanoi's limited military incursion against Khmer resistance forces inside Thai territory on

23 June 1980. The incursion took place on the eve of the ASEAN Foreign Ministers' Meeting, and while Vietnamese Foreign Minister Nguyen Co Thach was still in Indonesia as part of a tour of ASEAN capitals.

The communiqué issued after the Kuala Lumpur Foreign Ministers' Meeting three days later was, therefore, a firm restatement of the ASEAN position on Kampuchea. It reiterated the belief of the ASEAN members that their security interests were directly threatened by the conflict in Kampuchea, their concern at the presence of Vietnamese troops inside the country, their regret at Vietnam's failure to respond to calls for a durable political solution, and their commitment to the United Nations resolution 34/22 on the Kampuchea question and the ASEAN–EC Joint Statement on political issues of 7 March 1980. The Foreign Ministers also requested the UN Secretary-General to convene an international conference on Kampuchea.

The communiqué emphasised ASEAN's continuing solidarity. The Foreign Ministers

> strongly reaffirmed the solidarity of ASEAN member countries in, and their continued total commitment to, their position on the Kampuchea conflict, particularly on the fundamental issues of total withdrawal of Vietnamese forces from Kampuchea, the exercise of the right of self-determination of the Kampuchean people, free from outside interference, subversion and coercion and non-interference in the internal affairs of the states of Southeast Asia.

The Kampuchean question has become the central element in the relationship between the ASEAN countries and their Indo-China neighbours. Hopes for the development of more co-operative relations between the two groups must await some resolution of the apparently irreconcilable interests which each side asserts for itself in Kampuchea.

Even when relations have been at their most bitter, the ASEAN countries and their communist neighbours have continued to regard each other as different sorts of adversaries from their external backers. Both sides continue to assert, in a way which would not have made sense before ASEAN's formation, that regionalism, in the sense of a system of co-operation between states in Southeast Asia, even with different social, cultural and political backgrounds, is a goal which should continue to be sought, regardless of the formidable obstacles which exist.

ASEAN and the Great Powers

The second major theme of the Bangkok Declaration was the need to free the region from the threat of great power rivalry. This idea has re-emerged frequently in ASEAN statements and communiqués. In the Kuala Lumpur Declaration of November 1971, the ASEAN countries agreed that 'the neutralisation of Southeast Asia is a desirable objective', and called for 'joint action to secure the recognition of the region as a Zone of Peace, Freedom and Neutrality free from any form or manner of interference by outside powers'.

The Kuala Lumpur Declaration was based on, but was less precise in its terms than, earlier Malaysian suggestions that Southeast Asia should be declared a neutral zone, with its neutrality guaranteed by the United States, the Soviet Union and China (see Chapters 2 and 3).

The ZOPFAN proposals have not been further defined with any precision, and the mechanism by which they would limit great power rivalry remains vague. Attitudes to the proposals vary within the ASEAN group. Malaysia, the originator of the idea, generally puts most emphasis on it, despite its continued participation in the Five-Power Defence Arrangements. Indonesia prefers to emphasise its own concept of regional resilience. Singapore is sceptical about ZOPFAN's practicability. Thailand and the Philippines remain in formal security alliances with the United States which they would be reluctant to abrogate in the present circumstances of regional instability.

Nevertheless, ZOPFAN is an important long-term aim for the ASEAN countries, in part because it represents a potentially significant area of shared interest with Vietnam. Much of the discussion which has taken place between Hanoi and

ASEAN since 1977 has revolved around the concept of a Zone of Peace, and the search for a political settlement of the Kampuchean dispute may eventually involve – as President Suharto and Prime Minister Hussein Onn seemed to suggest in their March 1980 Kuantan proposals – a move towards the exclusion of some forms of involvement in the region by outside powers.

In the continuing absence of a framework like ZOPFAN, however, pressing problems arise for the ASEAN countries in dealing with the present manifestations of great power competition in the region.

THE UNITED STATES

Although the Association's members assert from time to time their equidistance from all the great powers, and although three of them are members of the non-aligned movement, formal and informal security ties and vital economic links with the West lead them to regard the United States as the most benign of the major external powers.

They have, however, found their relationship with the United States difficult to manage. On the one hand they have sought a continuing flow of arms from the United States, they have obtained US reaffirmation of its treaty links with the Philippines and Thailand, and have welcomed a continued 'off-shore' US military presence based on Subic Bay naval base and Clark Field air base in the Philippines as a necessary balance to the growing Soviet military involvement in Vietnam.

But the ASEAN members also resent accusations that they are stooges of the United States. They recognise that Washington's global interests do not always coincide with their own regional ones, and they have no expectation of, nor desire for, a return of American troops. Following a tour of the region in May 1978, Vice-President Mondale found that 'the non-communist nations continue to look to the United States for help. They do not seek our direct military involvement. . .But they do want us to sustain a military presence to serve as a deterrent and a source of psychological reassurance.'

The ASEAN countries also have doubts about the constancy

of US support and the extent of its commitment to the region. These doubts grew during the period from the enunciation in February 1971 of the Nixon Doctrine, which asserted that 'it is no longer possible in this age to argue that security or development around the globe is primarily America's concern. The defence and progress of other countries must be first their responsibility, and second a regional responsibility', to the final withdrawal of US troops from mainland Southeast Asia in May 1976.

It was widely hoped by ASEAN leaders that the 1976 US Presidential elections would resolve the perceived uncertainties in Washington's policy towards Southeast Asia. The first signals from the new Administration of President Carter, however, seemed even more disturbing to ASEAN governments.

After Deputy Assistant Secretary of State Richard Holbrooke's talks in Paris with Vietnamese officials in May 1977 it seemed that the Administration might move towards early normalisation of its relations with Hanoi; questions were being asked in Washington about whether the US bases in the Philippines should be retained; statements about the Administration's human rights policies appeared selectively critical of America's allies, singling out the Philippines in particular; and many ASEAN leaders saw serious danger in proposals for US troop withdrawals from the Republic of Korea.

The nervousness of ASEAN leaders about the drift of US policy led them to seek assurances from the Carter Administration through Japanese Prime Minister Fukuda when he visited Washington in March 1977. As a result, the communiqué issued after Mr Fukuda's talks with President Carter contained a reference to Japan and the United States making joint efforts to aid ASEAN. (Other questions were raised by President Carter's references to an expanded Japanese role in Southeast Asia. Some saw this as an American move towards greater reliance on Japan as a protector of 'Western' interests in the region.)

In the two years following the Carter–Fukuda communiqué the United States was able to provide greater reassurance to the ASEAN countries through a series of high-level visits and statements of support. (See details of the ASEAN–US dialogue above.)

The exodus of refugees from Indo-China and the subsequent Vietnamese invasion of Kampuchea heightened the importance of the United States to the ASEAN countries. The United States was the major country of resettlement for the tens of thousands of Vietnamese refugees seeking asylum in the ASEAN countries, and after the invasion, its security ties with Thailand, through the Manila Pact, its arms supplies and its diplomatic support for the ASEAN position developed a new significance. Richard Holbrooke described 1979 as 'a year which was marked by the tremendous increase in US involvement in Asia, after some years of decline and drift'.[11]

Kampuchea and related developments during 1979 (particularly the growing Soviet use of Vietnam's naval bases) shifted the focus of ASEAN–US relations from bilateral and multilateral economic issues back to concerns about security and defence. President Reagan's election at the end of 1980 seemed unlikely to lead to any reversal of that approach.

CHINA

From the early 1970s, China's belief that its security was threatened less by the United States, which was withdrawing its military power from Southeast Asia, than by the Soviet Union, led it to reverse its hostility towards ASEAN. By 1975 it was making favourable references to the Association which it had earlier condemned as a US-sponsored 'military alliance specifically directed against China'.[12] In 1974 and 1975 Malaysia, the Philippines and Thailand all established diplomatic relations with China, and Lee Kuan Yew visited Peking in 1976. (Because of Singapore's concern about being seen as a "Third China" in Southeast Asia, it has consistently said that it will not establish diplomatic relations with Peking until after Indonesia does so.

But despite the shift towards better relations between the ASEAN countries and China, and the more moderate policies adopted by the post-Mao leadership in Peking, deep suspicion of China's long-term aims remains an enduring factor in

Sino—ASEAN relations. This suspicion has its roots in long-standing historical, cultural and racial fears. China's support for the communist insurgencies in the region (and for its perceived support for the attempted *coup* in Indonesia in 1965, the failure of which led to the establishment of President Suharto's New Order Government) remains a serious stumbling block to better relations, despite Peking's claimed separation of state-to-state and party-to-party relations, and its assertion that it now gives no more than moral support to the insurgent groups. The fear that it might use the extensive overseas Chinese communities in Southeast Asia for its own political ends also remains potent. There is suspicion, too, that its modernisation programme will lead it to compete with the ASEAN countries for markets in the West, and will give it, over time, the ability which it now lacks, to project concentrated military power into the region.

However, the defeat by Vietnamese forces of the China-backed government of Pol Pot in Kampuchea led to a closer alignment of interests between Peking and ASEAN than had been seen in the past. This was particularly true of Sino—Thai relations, which had never been marked by the same degree of suspicion as China's relations with Malaysia and Indonesia. In the light of China's February 1979 invasion of Vietnam, its promises that it would 'not stand idly by'[13] in the event of a Vietnamese attack on Thailand were probably a more potent threat to Hanoi than was Thailand's formal alliance with the United States.

Both Thailand and China saw their interests served by maximising military pressure on Vietnam in Kampuchea, and this reportedly involved the secret channelling of Chinese assistance to the Khmer Rouge forces through Thai territory.

But in spite of these parallel interests, some of Thailand's ASEAN partners, particularly elements in the Indonesian military leadership, continued to believe that there were dangers in the development of too close a relationship with Peking. In June 1979, the Malaysian Deputy Prime Minister, Dr Mahathir, told a conference that Southeast Asian nations faced the threat of an 'emergent and militarily capable China' which had unequivocally demonstrated by its military incursion into Vietnam its willingness to 'act regardless of the usual norms of world opinion'. ASEAN had to accept, Dr Mahathir said, 'the implication of such a candid display by China in terms of big power potential for disruption in the region'.

The changing direction of China's foreign and economic policies, the prospect of a developing strategic relationship with the United States, and the potential for expanded trade links, will undoubtedly lead to a further reappraisal of ASEAN–Chinese relations. The potential exists for a much more productive relationship than in the past. But such a reappraisal can only succeed if it takes place over time and without pressure. The Kampuchean conflict provided a temporary convergence of interests between the ASEAN countries and China, but it also raised wider questions of regional order in Southeast Asia which will need to be resolved before the necessary reassessment of ASEAN–Chinese relations can take place.

SOVIET UNION

Soviet attitudes towards ASEAN have changed gradually from outright hostility to tentative and conditional approval of the grouping. From about mid-1978, a more positive tone began to appear in Soviet commentaries about ASEAN. In July 1978, for example, a news bulletin from the Soviet Embassy in Bangkok reported that 'ASEAN has been set up by the five ASEAN states in their own interests. Herein lies its strength'. This marked a substantial shift away from earlier accusations that ASEAN was a tool of the United States. References also appeared during 1978 to possible co-operation between ASEAN and COMECON. The change in the Soviet position was recognition that ASEAN had become an established feature of regional affairs. Moscow may have felt that continued hostility to the Association would have played into Peking's hands. There was clearly a close correlation between the new Soviet attitude to ASEAN and the more positive approach to regional diplomacy which Hanoi adopted during 1978. Moscow's official attitude now seems to be that ASEAN is an acceptable economic and social organisation which is in constant danger of being lured by imperialist forces from its proper goal of co-operation with the socialist states of the region.

The establishment of the Soviet–Vietnamese alliance and Moscow's military and material support for Hanoi's invasion of Kampuchea altered very significantly ASEAN's perceptions of the Soviet Union. It was no longer the most remote of the great powers, but one whose influence was growing through its support for Hanoi (estimated to cost it US $2 million per day) and its access to former United States naval facilities at Cam Ranh Bay in Vietnam. The ASEAN countries faced the question of whether the Soviet–Vietnamese alliance – the central framework for the projection of Moscow's military and political power in Southeast Asia – was a temporary phenomenon, resulting from Hanoi's fear of China and from its isolation from the West, or whether it would be a continuing factor in the regional power structure.

JAPAN

Japan's relations with ASEAN are considered in greater detail in Chapter 8. In general terms, the period after Prime Minister Fukuda's successful visit to the region in 1977, during which he met ASEAN leaders at the Kuala Lumpur summit meeting, saw the development of a better balance between Japan's massive economic interests in the region and its willingness and ability to play a commensurate political role.

Tokyo's more sensitive appreciation of ASEAN's political sensitivities (on questions such as relations with Vietnam), and the increasing contacts between Japanese and ASEAN leaders, has been welcomed, although suspicions that Japan is motivated essentially by economic ambitions remain strong.[14]

Japan cannot yet play a major part in the military balance in Southeast Asia, and there are still some in the region who would not want it to do so. Nevertheless, there is a general expectation that, over time, this position will change and that, in Lee Kuan Yew's words,[15] Japan 'can be a positive contributor to a quadrilateral great power balance in East Asia and the Pacific'.

Conclusions: An ASEAN Foreign Policy?

As we have seen, elements of a common ASEAN foreign policy are already evident. In their dealings with the communist states of Indo-China, for example, the ASEAN countries have preserved a significant degree of unity of purpose. The group has not always been unanimous on the responses which should be adopted: Thai and Singaporean leaders, for example, have been more critical in public of Vietnamese actions than have the Indonesians or Malaysians. But when these differences of view have been portrayed by those outside ASEAN as evidence of the Association's weakness, members have been quick to close ranks. ASEAN has thus provided a framework within which differences of approach have been successfully resolved or moderated.

There are, though, limits which all members recognise to the scope of ASEAN political co-operation. ASEAN has, for example, had little influence on members' policies towards the Arab–Israeli dispute. On questions such as the Middle East, ASEAN members instead tend to seek common identity with broader Third World groups such as the non-aligned movement or the Islamic Conference. They find it unnecessary, and possibly counterproductive, to develop identifiable ASEAN positions on such questions except where, as in the case of the Soviet invasion of Afghanistan, the issue is perceived (because of the parallels with Hanoi's policies in Kampuchea) as impinging directly or indirectly on the Southeast Asian region.

This may begin to change during the 1980s in response to growing international interest in Southeast Asia as a centre of potential economic growth, as a source of raw materials, and as an area of growing strategic and political importance. Japan, India, the members of the EC, and the countries of the Middle East are all likely to have a more substantial economic and political presence in the ASEAN region at the end of the 1980s than they did at the beginning. One effect of this growing international involvement will be to increase the number of international issues which will impinge directly on Southeast Asia, and on which its views will be sought.

The real test of ASEAN's impact as a moderating and co-ordinating influence on the individual foreign policies of its five members has, perhaps, not yet come. Common policies emerge without great difficulty in the face of a collectively identified threat. The more difficult tasks now confronting the ASEAN members are to arrive at a new analysis of the nature of any threat to their security in the more complex regional environment of the 1980s, to identify more precisely the sort of regional order which they want to help to create, and to work out ways in which these challenges can be met.

China, long identified as the major long-term threat to the ASEAN countries, continues to be the principal concern of many military leaders in Indonesia. Thailand, on the other hand, has encouraged closer links with Peking as a means of balancing the threat it feels from Vietnam. If the strategic relationship between the United States and China grows, the ASEAN countries will need to make far-reaching decisions about the sort of great power involvement which they want to see in Southeast Asia.

The potential for disagreement between the ASEAN members is considerable. But political leaders and officials in the five countries now have more than a decade of experience in identifying common goals and formulating common strategies. That evidence suggests that the challenges will be met.

7

ASEAN and Australia

Frank Frost

Australia's relationship with ASEAN was one of the most significant aspects of the Association's development in the latter half of the 1970s. While Australia in terms of economic strength was not a trading partner for ASEAN of the order of the US, Japan or the EC, it was a Western country located close to the Southeast Asian region which had long expressed a major interest in regional developments and which was willing to develop close working relations with the new body. The Australian relationship provided ASEAN with an opportunity to put into action several of its key policies in external relations after 1975, with a country which was unusually willing to consider and to give publicity to ASEAN demands, even if those demands could not all be easily met.

For Australia, the ASEAN relationship came to be of considerable importance and received extensive official and public attention. While Australia was in most respects very much a member of the 'First World' of 'developed' states, it had a traditionally strong interest in pursuing relations with its northern neighbours in Southeast Asia. In the 1970s, successive Australian governments were actively attempting to promote an image of a non-racist, pluralist nation with effective links with traditional First World allies but also with a sympathetic concern for Third World issues. Australia was thus both keen to develop relations with ASEAN and willing to consider seriously any ASEAN criticism of Australia's regional role. ASEAN probably had more impact and influence in Australia than in any other of its extra-regional associations.

Australia was the first extra-regional state to formally recognise and establish relations with ASEAN on a multi-lateral basis (in April 1974), and the course of the relation-ship reflected the changing concerns and emphasis of the ASEAN members after 1975. Emphasis was initially placed heavily on trade and economic relations questions in 1975 and 1976, but these issues were joined both by a major dis-pute over civil aviation policy in 1978 and 1979, and by a renewed stress on regional security issues from late 1978, in the wake of the refugee crisis and the Kampuchea conflict. In the period up to 1980, ASEAN—Australia relations were a focus for some significant conflicts of interest, but they also served as an avenue for extensive communication and discuss-ion of a wide range of issues and for close co-operation in some important policy areas.

To explore the issues raised by the ASEAN—Australia relationship this chapter will first outline the origin and development of Australian perceptions of ASEAN in the period up to 1975. It will then discuss the three major areas of significance and controversy in relations from 1975 — trade and economic relations, civil aviation and the impact of the Indo-China crises. The chapter will conclude with an overall assessment of the relationship to 1980.

Australia and ASEAN 1967—75

Australia had extensive political and diplomatic associations with some of the ASEAN members in the period after the Second World War, but these associations were not neces-sarily an ideal preparation for the challenges of ASEAN—Australia relations in the late 1970s. Australia in the 1950s and 1960s developed strong bilateral links with several South-east Asian states (notably Indonesia, Malaysia and Singapore) and multilateral co-operation was pursued through a variety of avenues including the Colombo Plan, SEATO, ASPAC and the Five-Power Defence Arrangements. In this period, how-ever, issues of economic relations were relatively insignificant: Australian policy concerns were dominated by considerations of regional security, including the problem of Indonesia's 'Confrontation' of Malaysia, and the Vietnam war. In its early years, Australia tended to look at ASEAN as a possible focus for regional security arrangements — an approach which had little immediate utility, given ASEAN's essentially non-military character.

When ASEAN was formed in 1967, Australian official concern about the threat to regional security thought to be posed by the Vietnam war was at its zenith. Australia at that time had military forces in Malaysia and Singapore and a force of 8,300 in South Vietnam, and it placed great emphasis on the contribution to regional security made by the Five-Power Defence Arrangements (linking Australia with Malaysia and Singapore) and SEATO (which associated Australia with Thailand and the Philippines). The Australian Government accordingly welcomed the formation of ASEAN as an association created by some of the states of the region themselves which could promote security and stability through regional economic and political co-operation. In keeping with this emphasis, some Australian observers seemed to view ASEAN as a potential military alliance with which Australia might be usefully associated. The Minister for External Affairs (Mr Freeth), for example, stated in April 1969 that Australia would regard a defence role for ASEAN as 'a healthy development' although he acknowledged that such a role was unlikely in the immediate future.[1]

With ASEAN in its early years maintaining a very low-key existence there was of course little scope for any Australian link with the association. The Liberal—Country Party governments of the period confined themselves to general expressions of support for ASEAN and reacted cautiously to its first major political proposal — the adoption of the 'Zone of Peace, Freedom and Neutrality' concept for Southeast Asia in 1971. The Australian Government did not regard the proposal as immediately practicable.[2] Until 1972, then, ASEAN did not loom large in Australian perceptions of Southeast Asia.

ASEAN became of somewhat more interest to Australia with the election of the Labour Government in December 1972. As an avowedly non-military organisation devoted primarily to economic and social co-operation, it fitted in well with the general wish of the Labour Government to de-emphasise ideological and military alliances in its relations with Southeast Asia. Labour policy strongly promoted non-military regional co-operation as a way of reducing ideological tensions and promoting economic development. In a speech during his visit to the region in January and February 1974, Prime Minister Whitlam emphasised that in his view, of all the regional associations and arrangements in Southeast Asia, '. . . ASEAN is unquestionably the most important, the most relevant, the most natural'.[3] In contrast to its predecessors, the Labour Government endorsed the ASEAN concept of a 'zone of peace' for the region. Despite this generally favourable orientation, ASEAN–Australia relations were not entirely without problems during the Labour Government period. The announcement by Prime Minister Whitlam of a proposal for the establishment of a new Asian and Pacific forum led to some feelings among ASEAN leaders that their Association could be overshadowed by such a new grouping. In the event, however, the forum proposal remained in the theoretical stage.

In keeping with the Labour Government's favourable orientation towards the Association, Australia moved to establish its first formal links with ASEAN in 1973 and 1974. Preliminary meetings were held between Australian and ASEAN representatives in Canberra in May 1973 and Bangkok in January 1974, at which the ASEAN members indicated their interest in economic co-operation with Australia on a joint basis. At a meeting in Canberra in April 1974 between the Australian Foreign Minister (Senator Willesee) and the Secretaries-General of the ASEAN National Secretariat it was duly agreed that Australia would contribute A $5 million for joint ASEAN projects and that it would also offer training assistance for ASEAN experts engaged on ASEAN projects. Most of these funds were subsequently spent on two projects: one aimed at developing, distributing and utilising new forms of low-cost, protein-rich foods, and the other aimed at an overall improvement in methods of handling, transporting and storing fruit, vegetables, grain, fish and livestock products. This multilateral aid commitment was the genesis of a wider programme, the Australia–ASEAN Economic Co-operation Programme, which became an important element in Australia–ASEAN relations from 1977 (see below).

A Foreign Affairs Department statement of April 1974 commented optimistically that this initiative was '. . . a positive contribution to the development of a special relationship between ASEAN and Australia. The desire of the ASEAN states to associate with Australia reflects a growing appreciation of Australia's regional policies.' The development of a direct ASEAN–Australia link undoubtedly was a useful step, but the significance of ASEAN as a regional grouping was still very limited. The nature of ASEAN, however, changed dramatically after 1975, as did its importance for Australia.

In 1975, Australian concerns in the Southeast Asia region were focused heavily on the implications of the fall of the non-communist regimes in Indo-China and with the problem of East Timor which became a major issue in Australia–Indonesia bilateral relations. ASEAN was not yet a major orientation. The incoming Liberal Party Prime Minister Mr Fraser, however, announced that ASEAN would be an important focus for Australian regional policies. During a visit to Kuala Lumpur to attend the funeral of the Malaysian Prime Minister, Tun Razak, Mr Fraser said on 18 January 1976 that '. . . I think it is possible for ways to be found for Australia to identify and develop the common interests we have with the ASEAN countries, and then work together with them to help achieve [them]'.[4] He specified trade as an area where co-operation was desirable and would be sought.

ASEAN–Australia Trade Relations and Problems

ASEAN did indeed become of much greater significance for Australia from 1976. The first major issue to arise was trade and economic relations which became the subject of a concerted ASEAN 'joint approach' in late 1976. On the face of it, the fact that ASEAN–Australia trade relations became a major regional political issue in the late 1970s was a rather paradoxical development. Australia has never been a primary focus for the ASEAN countries' trade and the reverse has also been true. However, for reasons which will be specified, a combination of factors brought some Australian policies into sharp conflict with the interests of several ASEAN members after 1974.

To help provide a context for consideration of the origins and evolution of ASEAN–Australia trade problems it is useful to examine first the development and structure of the trade itself. Both Australia and ASEAN are heavily oriented in trade towards the major industrialised economies of the US, Japan and the EC. ASEAN–Australia trade is significant but is for each party overshadowed by other international links. Australian exports to ASEAN in 1978/79 represented 7.7 per cent of total exports while Japan took 28.8 per cent, the EC 14.1 per cent and the US 12.6 per cent. ASEAN in the same period supplied 4.7 per cent of Australia's imports while the EC supplied 25.6 per cent, the US 23.5 per cent and Japan 17.6 per cent. From ASEAN, Australia in 1978 took 2 per cent of exports, compared with Japan (25 per cent), the US (21.3 per cent) and the EC (14.3 per cent); Australia supplied 4 per cent of ASEAN's imports compared to Japan (24.9 per cent), the EC (14.4 per cent) and the US (14.2 per cent).[5]

ASEAN–Australia trade, while comparatively small, has been significant enough to merit serious political attention for one major reason: Australia has had a consistent trading surplus as Table 7.1 indicates. By 1978/79 Australia exported goods valued at A $1,091 million to ASEAN, including wheat, sugar, dairy products, iron ore, iron and steel and zinc. The annual growth rate of these exports since 1972/73 was 18.7 per cent, compared with average for total exports of 14.8 per cent. ASEAN continued to be a useful market for Australian manufactures, and received 15.9 per cent of total exports of these products in 1978/79. Australian imports from ASEAN in 1978/79, by contrast, amounted to A $641.9 million, including petroleum products, coffee, tea, cocoa, spices, wood and rubber. Australia has also imported increasing amounts of manufactured goods from ASEAN; a 1979 report by the Department of Trade and Resources put the annual rate of increase of imports of these goods at 46.3 per cent since 1972/73, although it was of course only at that time that ASEAN began to direct many manufactured goods to Australia.[6]

The balance of trade situation with Australia differs among the ASEAN states. As the figures given in Table 7.2 indicate, Thailand and Indonesia have both run balance-of-trade deficits with Australia, but Thailand has been traditionally less oriented towards trade with Australia than other ASEAN members, while Indonesia has the prospect of increasing exports of petroleum products as Australian resources are run down. Singapore has recently had trade surpluses with Australia although a high proportion of Singaporean exports in recent years has consisted of transhipped Middle East petroleum. The Philippines and Malaysia have continued to experience trade imbalances with Australia and the Malaysian deficit had risen rapidly by 1978/79. A detailed official report on ASEAN–Australia trade prepared by the Department of Trade and Resources in 1979 noted that:

> In the past the Philippines and Malaysia have been the most vocal [ASEAN members] about the unfavourable trade balances with Australia because in their cases the imbalance is relatively large in relation to most of their other trading partners with which their trade is unfavourable. In the case of Malaysia, which overall runs a trade surplus, Australia is the country with which they have the largest deficit. For the Philippines, with the exception of oil suppliers and Japan, of the developed countries Australia runs the largest surplus with them.[7]

As this report also pointed out, the ASEAN–Australia trade deficit has been consistently offset by a net capital inflow from Australia through aid, investment and tourism. In 1980, Australian bilateral aid commitments to ASEAN amounted to A $314 million out of a total of A $512 million (excluding Papua New Guinea), investment was estimated to total about A $500 million and over 117,000 Australian tourists visited the ASEAN countries in 1978. The ASEAN members, however, have continued to give a high priority to exports as an avenue towards economic development and have tended to closely associate trade imbalances with problems of developed country restrictions and protectionist policies. These concerns were very much in the minds of members when trading relations with Australia began to become a focus for critical scrutiny in 1975 and 1976.

A conjunction of three factors brought the issue of trade relations to the centre of attention in ASEAN—Australia relations from 1976. The first factor was a developing pattern of increased exports, particularly of manufactured goods, from some of the ASEAN countries (notably Singapore, Malaysia and the Philippines) to Australia from the late 1960s onwards. As a number of Australian observers (including the Industries Assistance Commission, the Bureau of Industry Economics, and Australian economist Dr Clive Edwards) have pointed out, this development needs to be seen as part of a wider pattern of economic change in Southeast and East Asia generally.[8] When states in these regions began to industrialise in the early post-war period their emphasis was on import-substitution and this led to inefficient industries with excessive cost-levels and inadequate domestic markets. In the 1960s, however, there was a trend in a number of Asian states faced with rapidly growing populations and workforces to develop highly competitive labour-intensive export industries. Taiwan and South Korea began this trend in the late 1950s and early 1960s and once they had adopted policies of encouraging export industries their industrial expansion was rapid. Among the ASEAN states, Singapore adopted broadly similar policies in 1965 and Malaysia and the Philippines placed heavy emphasis on export industries from the late 1960s onwards. The success of these industrialisation policies clearly depended on continued access by the ASEAN states to their major outlets in Japan, the USA, the EC and Australia. For Australia, the process led to increased competitive pressure on a number of industries, particularly textiles, clothing, footwear and wood-products, with the prospects of wider sections of industry coming under similar pressure as the East and Southeast Asian states' industries developed and diversified.

The second factor which became significant after 1975 was the difficulties experienced by the Australian economy after 1974 and consequent alterations in external economic policy. In the early 1970s ASEAN exports to Australia became increasingly competitive *vis-à-vis* Australian-produced goods because of a number of developments in the Australian economy, including a high rate of wage increases, the introduction of equal pay for women, the 25 per cent tariff cut in July 1973 and large currency revaluations in 1972 and 1973. In 1974, however, the deteriorating economic climate led to significant alterations in Australian policy including the imposition from March of a series of quotas on imports and a currency devaluation in September. In a number of cases, for example textiles, clothing and footwear, these quotas had a serious effect on imports from some ASEAN countries.

In a process which has been described in detail by Clive Edwards, these Australian restrictions had a major impact on a number of ASEAN exporters, especially in Malaysia and the Philippines, at a time when these states faced serious balance-of-payments problems in the wake of the 1973 oil price rises, and thus needed to maintain and expand all possible export markets. The ASEAN states concerned undoubtedly found the Australian import restrictions frustrating, particularly since Australia was simultaneously maintaining a large overall surplus in its balance of trade with the ASEAN states ($342 million in 1975-6).

Edwards has argued that the Australian restrictions also had an unfavourable psychological and political impact on states whose economic expectations in foreign trade were rapidly changing.

> History had cast them in the role of raw material suppliers. The experience of the fifties and sixties seemed to indicate that, in the field of manufacturing, they could not be internationally competitive. The exhilarating experience of 1973-74 *permanently* changed this depressing scenario. The ASEAN countries realised that there were manufactures that they could export at highly competitive prices. Unfortunately, it was at this moment of euphoria that Australia struck.[9]

It was against this background that a third crucial factor came into play — ASEAN's rapid development of a new sense of purpose from 1975 onwards. Before 1975, the trade problems of the ASEAN members would no doubt have been taken up on a bilateral, uncoordinated basis. In 1975 and 1976, however, as earlier chapters have indicated, one of the major areas of co-operation which ASEAN was now seeking to undertake was the expansion of its 'joint approaches' to extra-regional countries on patterns of trade and economic relations. Australia, which had professed a particular interest in the Southeast Asian region and had established an institutional link with ASEAN, and which had now impinged on some members' economic interests, was an obvious target for such an approach. From 1976, the ASEAN members made a series of approaches to Australia on economic issues. The approaches were made with considerable diplomatic and public relations skill and had a major impact on Australian thinking if not always on Australian policy on the central issues of ASEAN concern.

Reports about the unfavourable impact of Australian trade policy changes among ASEAN members (especially Malaysia and the Philippines) began appearing in the Australian Press in late 1975 and early 1976. The first major ASEAN salvo, however, took the form of a memorandum, formally transmitted to Australia in November 1976, but 'leaked' in July to the Southeast Asia correspondent of Australia's most influential business journal, the *Australian Financial Review.* The ASEAN memorandum made the front page of that journal on 27 July 1976. It stated that:

> For a developed country Australia has one of the highest tariff rates, especially on labour-intensive light industrial goods exported by developing countries. An increasing number of such items as furniture, footwear, yarns, textile and garment products etc., are constantly placed under tariff review for protection purposes.

The document included detailed criticisms of Australian import restrictions and suggestions for liberalisation, including the removal of import quotas on twenty-six categories of products, liberalising rules on labelling and packaging, relaxing health and sanitary regulations on five products and the initiation of consultations between Australia and ASEAN before unilateral action was taken by the former on trade matters.

This approach was followed up by ASEAN both jointly and on an individual basis (essentially from Malaysia, the Philippines and Singapore). On an individual basis, both Malaysia and the Philippines engaged in informal restrictions on Australian imports. Singapore also played a leading role in promoting the ASEAN cause. Its Government was highly sensitive to the international economic issues of trade and protection, and its Prime Minister, Lee Kuan Yew, was not averse to attempting to correct what he saw as retrograde policies pursued by Australia. In a notable comment in June 1977, for example, he argued that trade liberalisation by Australia would

> remove a source of considerable frustration and bitterness on the part of countries like the Philippines, Indonesia and Malaysia, which feel this is a one-sided business — of a very wealthy continent, sparsely populated, with enormous natural resources, not yet fully developed with an industrial capacity commensurate with those resources, yet wanting to make all the little things. It wants labour-intensive products like shirts and garments, knitwear, shoes and socks, all for itself, behind high tariff walls. Buying little and selling more. Of course, let me add that successive Australian governments have been conscious of this and have made up with dollops of aid — it's like giving toffees and chocolates away. That's not the kind of relationship which generates mutual esteem, respect and an adult mutual continuing inter-dependence which in the long term is the only sound relationship we can develop. . . And if that's the way the world is going to be — if the relationship between the countries of ASEAN and Australia is the relationship between the developed and underdeveloped world — then I see strife.[10]

ASEAN also continued its approach on a joint basis. A further detailed critique of Australian policies was presented in an ASEAN paper in November 1978, which was reported to have stated in part that, 'Australia seems to regard developing countries only as a source of supply of certain materials for her industrial outputs'.[11] The document called on Australia to liberalise tariffs, assist ASEAN export promotion efforts in the Australian market and promote ASEAN–Australia co-operation in industrial development in the region.

AUSTRALIA'S RESPONSE

The ASEAN challenge to Australian trade and economic relations policies had a major impact in Australian government, business and academic circles. There had been a long-standing debate in Australia about the structure of its economy and the question of protection for secondary industry. While the challenge from ASEAN on this issue after 1976 was unexpected, it came from a region in which Australia had been consistently closely interested, and the ASEAN criticism was thus given a credence which similar criticism from Europe or even East Asia would probably not have received. Many Australian observers, including some businessmen, academics and journalists, readily accepted the ASEAN claims and argued for Australian trade liberalisation.

The Australian Government adopted a more reserved approach. It emphasised Australia's continuing interest in maximising political and economic relations with the ASEAN region and it initiated a series of joint projects and regular consultations. However, it simultaneously continued to maintain policies of protection for endangered Australian labour-intensive industries, and it attempted to put the best possible face on the existing ASEAN–Australia economic relationship.

Australian Government responses to the ASEAN criticism began in earnest in 1977. A Standing Interdepartmental Committee on Relations with ASEAN was established in January to bring together the many departments involved in ASEAN relations, and several Australian missions visited the region in the months leading up to the Kuala Lumpur Heads of Government Meeting in August, which was to be attended by Prime Minister Fraser. At the Kuala Lumpur summit, Mr Fraser held discussions with his ASEAN counterparts on a variety of issues including global economic problems such as the need for stability in commodity prices and improved marketing facilities, Australian aid and consultative projects and trade problems. Australia did not offer immediate concessions on trade issues, but did agree to increase its overall foreign aid commitment to the ASEAN countries, and it offered to provide assistance to the ASEAN joint industrial projects. The discussions also resulted in an agreement on a series of meetings (including a trade fair and an industrial co-operation conference), a joint research project into the ASEAN–Australia economic relationship and an arrangement for regular consultation on trade matters.

Considerable progress was subsequently made in establishing the pattern of relations agreed upon at Kuala Lumpur. Building on the original multilateral aid projects initiated in 1974, the ASEAN–Australian Economic Co-operation Programme by 1980 involved a series of projects at a cost of A $34.5 million in areas including the development of low-cost protein-rich foods from locally available sources, studies on post-harvest handling, transportation and storing of grain, meat and cereals and assistance to education, population programmes and regional animal quarantine. The joint research project into economic relations was initiated in 1980. An Industrial Co-operation Conference was held in Melbourne in June 1978 and ASEAN Trade Fairs were mounted in Sydney (October 1978) and Melbourne (August 1980). Private business links were also developed on a multilateral basis; an ASEAN–Australia Business Conference was inaugurated in Kuala Lumpur in June 1980. In November 1978 agreement was reached on the ASEAN–Australia Consultative Meetings (AACM) between the ASEAN Canberra Committee (comprising the head of ASEAN diplomatic missions in Canberra) and the Australia Interdepartmental Committee on Relations with ASEAN. Under the AACM a working group on trade matters was set up to provide ASEAN members with 'early warning' of Australian policy changes.

The consultation and discussions provided by these forums were undoubtedly of some value to ASEAN. Since sudden and seemingly arbitrary changes in Australian tariff policy had been a major problem for some ASEAN producers in 1974 and 1975, the AACM was potentially useful. But while

Australia was prepared to consult extensively, the Government made it clear in a number of statements and actions that in the domestic economic environment of the late 1970s in Australia, major liberalisation in areas of trade relevant to ASEAN would not occur. On the same day as Prime Minister Fraser's report to the Australian parliament on his successful talks with ASEAN leaders (17 August 1977), the Ministers of Industry and Commerce and Business and Consumer Affairs announced that the Government would attempt to maintain existing levels of employment in the textiles, clothing and footwear industries for the following three years. Further guarantees were given during the 1977 election campaign and in August 1978, an additional tariff surcharge of 12½ per cent was imposed for revenue purposes on a number of products of concern to ASEAN members. A further commitment to attempt to maximise employment in the textiles, clothing and footwear industries was announced in August 1980.

Although the substance of Australian external economic policy conceded little to ASEAN claims, Australian spokesmen asserted consistently that ASEAN's market access in Australia was expanding rapidly, that Australia in fact imported considerably larger amounts of sensitive goods (such as textiles and footwear) *per capita* than ASEAN's other major markets, that ASEAN countries should look at their problem of adverse balances of trade with Australia in a global context and that as the Australian economy recovered and expanded, ASEAN exporters' opportunities would also further expand.[12] Government leaders, while maintaining support for endangered Australian industries, also rather audaciously launched extensive attacks on the protectionist policies of the European Community — an irony that was not lost on ASEAN officials.

By 1980, the prospects for ASEAN—Australia trade as an economic factor and as a political issue were still a matter of some doubt. In a regional climate dominated by concern over Sino—Vietnam relations and the ongoing problem of Kampuchea, ASEAN's criticism of Australian trade policies was no longer being pushed with the stridency of 1976 and 1977. ASEAN concern continued, however, and it was illus-

trated in a speech delivered by Malaysia's Finance Minister
Tengku Razaleigh Hamzah, to the first ASEAN—Australia
Business Conference in June 1980. Tengku Razaleigh
reminded his audience of the link which ASEAN leaders saw
between economic growth and political stability and
commented pointedly that:

> Unfortunately there are many countries in the north which
> ironically are concerned with global security but which at
> the same time, adopt international economic and trade
> policies and practices, that in the longer-term erode the
> very foundation of security that they try to promote.

He praised the steps which had been taken to develop and
institutionalise ASEAN—Australia co-operation but noted
that protectionism was still a problem. He added that:

> While ASEAN and other developing countries have
> strongly supported Australia's efforts in combating pro-
> tectionist policies emanating from the United States, the
> EEC and OECD countries, it is understandably difficult for
> us simultaneously to experience the adverse effects of
> Australia's own protectionist policies.[13]

Reports of the tenth ASEAN Economic Ministers' meeting in
Bangkok in October 1980 indicated that the ministers continued to be concerned at Australia's protectionist policies
and that Australian-sponsored consultations and research
were not regarded as an acceptable substitute for action on
trade liberalisation.[14]

Whether the ASEAN members would see a significant reduction in Australian trade barriers was uncertain. Structural
change was occurring in Australian industry — employment
in the textiles, clothing and footwear industries, for example,
declined from 171,500 in 1971 to 120,000 in 1979 — but
this was more by default than by any concerted Government
or industry planning. The Australian policy of encouraging
the institutionalisation of relations with ASEAN while forestalling action on trade barriers appeared to have been reas-
onably successful in containing the ASEAN criticism on the

issue by 1980, but whether Australia would be willing and able to make greater concessions during the next decade was highly uncertain.

Trade was not the only issue of contention to gain prominence in ASEAN—Australia relations in the late 1970s. The framework for discussion and negotiations set up by 1978 provided a ready avenue for consideration of additional ASEAN claims. Australia's civil aviation policies provided another source of ASEAN concern from 1978.

The Civil Aviation Dispute

The dispute over the Australian International Civil Aviation Policy (ICAP) is a particularly interesting example of the dynamics and potential of ASEAN—Australia relations. At the outset, it was not an issue which necessarily fitted easily into the context and framework of this relationship. The issue impinged directly on the interests of only one ASEAN member in a major way (Singapore) and it was not automatically to be expected that Singapore would receive backing from its ASEAN partners on the issue. In terms of the norms of international civil aviation regulation and negotiation, Australia probably had a stronger case to back up its policy aims than it did in the area of trade relations. For a variety of interacting economic and political reasons the ICAP issue nonetheless became a *cause célèbre* in the relationship.[15]

The genesis of the problem lay in an emerging conflict of interests between Australia and Singapore in the 1970s. Australia's national airline Qantas had steadily come under increasing competition on its most important air-routes (Australia to Europe) from a number of airlines, including Singapore Airlines (SIA). The financial position of Qantas came under pressure at a time when there was also a rising demand for cheaper fares from sections of the Australian public and travel industry. In order to secure cheaper fares and to ensure that a new arrangement to achieve these fares would safeguard Qantas' position, the Australian Government and Qantas devised a policy which would limit foreign airlines' capacity on the Australia—Europe route, and guarantee high 'load factors' for the entire flights between Australian and European ports by discouraging (through a high-cost sur-charge) 'stopovers' by passengers *en route*. This policy could be justified on the grounds that it was in accord with the norms of international airline negotiating procedures, and that it was an assertion of legitimate Australian economic interests. Singapore, however, was able to place the issue squarely in the ASEAN—Australia context.

Singapore had a great deal to lose through the Australian policy. Its national airline had been operating under the SIA name only since 1972 (when Malaysia—Singapore Airlines was dissolved) but it had achieved by 1977 the highest passenger and freight load factors of any international airline. Singapore was understandably proud of its airline, which itself by 1978 accounted for over 3 per cent of the country's GNP. Part of its successful growth had been based on the Australia—Europe route in which the airline had gained as much as 30 per cent of the traffic by 1978. ICAP threatened to significantly reduce SIA's participation in this traffic and the discouragement of stopovers threatened to damage Singapore's tourist industry which was heavily dependent on this type of short-stay tourism. No other airline from an ASEAN member was dependent on Australia to Europe traffic to anything like the same degree as SIA. Singapore's ASEAN partners were not automatically sympathetic towards its economic problems, and it had been involved in an acrimonious dispute with Malaysia over civil aviation. Australian officials seem to have assumed that SIA could be isolated effectively through the initiation of favourable bi-lateral negotiations with other ASEAN countries. Singapore, however, was able to successfully mobilise ASEAN support to challenge the Australian policy.

The ICAP issue fitted easily into the framework of both Australia—ASEAN relations and the wider issue of North—South economic relations. It was relatively easy for Singapore to depict the Australian policy as an act of discrimination against a successful airline from a rapidly developing Third World state, which was being penalised for its success in competing in the Western-dominated, technically sophisti-cated airline business. The apparent attempts by Australian negotiators to play on the differing interests of ASEAN members in aviation issues also struck sensitive nerves, because in a context of a deteriorating situation in Indo-China it seemed most important for the ASEAN members to maintain solidarity and cohesiveness.

After preliminary complaints in early and mid-1978, ASEAN jointly criticised the ICAP policy at the end of October, and in December the ASEAN Economic Ministers agreed that negotiations with Australia on ICAP would be on a group basis. Joint negotiations were held with Australia in January 1979, but the results were inconclusive. In February the Economic Ministers met again: their joint communiqué included the statement that, 'ICAP could not be confined to ASEAN and Australia alone. . . ICAP is a manifestation of the tendency of developed countries to change the rules as soon as the developing countries have mastered their own rules and overcome the obstructions posed by them. . .'.[16] ASEAN's major demands were that its airlines should be able to participate in the Australia—Europe low fare scheme with or without stopovers, that stopovers should not be prohibitively costly for low fare passengers, and that for ASEAN—Australia cheap fares, the cost per kilometre should be roughly equivalent to that charged between Australia and Europe.

The ASEAN case was pursued actively in early 1979, partly through negotiations with Australia and partly through a variety of comments and statements by Singaporean and other ASEAN spokesmen which gained extensive coverage in the Australian media. In May 1979 a preliminary agreement on the issue was reached, just before the UNCTAD V meeting in Manila which was to be attended by Prime Minister Fraser. It was agreed that ASEAN airlines could obtain limited access to the Australia—Europe cheap fare market on a temporary basis subject to review; ASEAN airlines were to be allowed to carry 18,200 passengers on this basis in each direction. Australia also agreed to a stopover payment of A $150 — less than the original Australian proposals, though higher than the ASEAN request. Australia also made proposals on the question of ASEAN airlines, capacities and traffic rights in flights to Australia and 'general agreement' was reached on cheap fare advance payment flights between Australia and ASEAN. This agreement was subsequently accepted by the ASEAN Economic Ministers in September. The agreement did not meet all ASEAN demands, and it fell far short of what SIA was originally aiming for. It did, however, seem to effectively defuse the issue as an ASEAN problem and much of the controversy on the question had subsided by the end of 1979.

The ICAP dispute was significant in a variety of ways. The ASEAN states showed an impressive ability to coalesce on an issue which for them was potentially far more a divisive than a cohesive influence. They linked the dispute with Australia to the wider context of North–South relations – an effective ploy given Australian sensitivities on this issue. The dispute also illustrated that the framework for public and governmental discussions of ASEAN–Australia issues which had been developed initially to discuss trade relations could be most effectively used to consider other issues as they arose and used to exert pressure on Australia for concessions. While the ASEAN approach did not achieve all its aims, it did force significant Australian policy changes, and the ICAP challenge probably constituted ASEAN's single most influential joint approach in economic relations up to 1979.

For Australia, the ICAP issue demonstrated the tensions inherent in the predominantly European orientation of much of its population and the need to attempt to consider carefully the interests of its neighbours in ASEAN. Despite the Government's professions of interest in and concern for ASEAN, it was still clearly a difficult task to attempt to get elements in the Government (such as the Department of Transport) to develop an awareness that ASEAN had significance as a cohesive grouping. The dispute also showed that the ASEAN members had a considerable capacity both to advance their cause through the Australian domestic media and to cause Australia considerable embarrassment by placing ASEAN–Australia issues in the context of the North–South dialogue.

Immigration and Refugees Policy

The preceding consideration of trade relations and civil aviation policy has illustrated that the ASEAN–Australia relationship in the late 1970s served as a focus for consideration of some significant conflicts of interest. Australia and ASEAN, however, continued to have important interests in common particularly in relation to stability in the Southeast Asian region and the problem of great power interference. Towards the end of the decade, areas of long-term common interest for Australia and ASEAN became readily apparent as the refugee crisis and the Kampuchea conflict posed significant threats to security and stability. These common concerns were a stimulus towards greater harmony in the relationship.

One issue which became increasingly important in the ASEAN–Australia context was that of Australian immigration and refugees policy. In the 1970s immigration policy was a low-key but nonetheless important focus for closer Australian contacts with ASEAN countries because extensive networks of person-to-person links were being built up through the increasing number of settlers in Australia from ASEAN countries. Australia's restrictive immigration policy had been a formidable obstacle in its relations with Southeast Asia for twenty years after the Second World War. In 1966, however, Australia began to liberalise its policy and this process was furthered by successive Australian governments in the 1970s. Increased immigration rates were clearly a beneficial long-term factor for ASEAN–Australia relations, but in 1977–8 the immigration issue was complicated by the worsening refugee situation in the region.

As Chapter 5 points out, the refugee exodus from Vietnam and the other Indo-China states had a profound impact on the ASEAN members, especially Thailand, Malaysia and Indonesia. The refugees were an economic and administrative burden and a source of social and political tension. The refugee exodus, particularly the boat refugees from Vietnam, were also of very real concern to Australia. In 1976, some refugee boats began arriving in northern Australia, having travelled onwards from Malaysia and Indonesia, and in November 1977 a number of boats arrived in Darwin. The boat arrivals provoked a hostile public reaction in Australia since they raised the spectre of a possible uncontrolled influx of Asian immigrants. The prospect of continued boat arrivals threatened to undermine support for the Government's policy of accepting Indo-China refugees through organised channels and it also threatened to reawaken controversy about the general question of Asian immigration. These problems provided a strong impetus for ASEAN–Australia co-operation on the issue.[17]

The Government adopted an active policy of gaining the co-operation of the ASEAN states (especially Malaysia and Indonesia) on the refugee issue. Australia announced a major increase in its intake in May 1978 (to 9,000 per year) and it then sought the assistance of Malaysia and Indonesia in preventing the onward passage of boats from their points of first asylum to Australia. The Government sought actively to assist the ASEAN members' efforts to 'internationalise' the refugee problem by gaining increased financial assistance and particularly increased resettlement commitments from Western states. Australia initiated the proposal which led to the first Geneva conference on Indo-China refugees (in December 1978) and it played a major role in supporting the diplomacy of the ASEAN states in 1979, leading up to the Bali Foreign Ministers' Meeting in June (which Australia's Foreign Minister attended) and the crucial second Geneva conference in July. By 1980, Australia was accepting 14,000 Indo-China refugees per year and by 31 October 1980 a total of 41,937 had been accepted since April 1975. Australia had now accepted more refugees *per capita* than any other country of asylum except Hong Kong and the policy had maintained a high degree of public acceptance.

Refugee policy was an area of considerable success in ASEAN–Australia relations. Australia had lent valuable support on an issue of major concern to all of the ASEAN members and it had demonstrated a capacity itself to make a contribution towards participating in the resolution of a serious regional problem.

Australia, ASEAN and the Indo-China Conflicts

The tensions raised by the Indo-China conflicts from 1978 provided a further focus for ASEAN–Australia co-operation. The Australian Government shared the ASEAN members' concern at developments in Vietnam's policies, especially its move towards closer relations with the Soviet Union and its Government's role in the refugee outflows. Like ASEAN, Australia was quick to denounce the Vietnamese invasion of Kampuchea and also like ASEAN, while it condemned the subsequent Chinese incursion into northern Vietnam this criticism was not pursued with anything like the same conviction. Between 1976 and 1978 the Fraser Government had pursued a conciliatory policy towards Vietnam, which included a small aid programme, support for Vietnam's entry into the UN in 1977 and emphasis on the need to encourage Vietnam to broaden its international contacts and sources of financial assistance. In January 1979, however, the aid programme was cancelled and Australia adopted a strongly condemnatory position on Vietnam's regional policies.

Australia offered its full diplomatic support to the ASEAN joint stand on Kampuchea – the most assertive political move by the Association up to 1980. Australia argued for the ASEAN position on recognition for the ousted Democratic Kampuchean regime and for its continued membership of the UN. Australia also co-sponsored the important ASEAN resolutions on Kampuchea, calling for an immediate Vietnamese withdrawal and self-determination for the Khmer people, which were adopted by large majorities in the UN General Assembly in November 1979 and October 1980. Australian policy on Kampuchea was a positive contribution towards harmony in relations with ASEAN in 1979 and 1980. The Australian Government's policy, however, was not universally supported domestically. There was widespread public antipathy towards the policy of continued recognition for the DK regime, irrespective of whether the policy was in accord with ASEAN's wishes. By late 1980, the force of public opinion on the issue was reflected by a Government announcement on 14 October that Australia would move to 'de-recognise' the DK regime on a bilateral basis although it was also indicated that this move would be accompanied by continued strong Australian support for the ASEAN position on Kampuchea in the UN and elsewhere. There was also concern on the wider question of Australian policy towards ASEAN in the context of Southeast Asia as a whole – a number of Australians (including academics and some Labour Party Members of Parliament) felt that the Australian Government was devoting insufficient attention to the need for the creation of a climate of *détente* between Vietnam and ASEAN – a process which Australia might be able to encourage.[18] At the end of 1980 it seemed likely that if the political impasse between Vietnam and ASEAN over Kampuchea persisted, support in Australia for the ASEAN position would continue to be a source of some controversy.

ASEAN and Australia: Present and Future

ASEAN relations with Australia had by 1980 come to involve a series of interactions on a wide range of economic and political issues. The relationship was not easy to sum up or characterise, because areas of close co-operation (such as refugee policy) coexisted with areas of continuing discord (such as trade relations). There was, however, little doubt that the relationship had proved to be of relevance and value to both parties. ASEAN had derived benefit from its joint approaches to Australia – its major substantive trade demands had not yet been accepted, but its challenge to Australia's ICAP had been one of its most influential efforts at collective negotiation. The institutional framework of the relationship gave ASEAN the opportunity to introduce new issues for discussion and negotiation when necessary and it had received useful political support for its joint policies on the refugees issue and on Kampuchea. For Australia, the ASEAN relationship had also had a very considerable impact.

It had highlighted the continuing significance of Southeast Asia to Australia and had stimulated much useful discussion and revaluation of Australia's regional political and economic role. Australia had not made any substantial concessions to ASEAN's trade demands, but the fact that the Australian Government had not adopted more liberal protection policies during a period when the country was experiencing its most difficult economic problems since the Second World War did not mean that the ASEAN criticism had been ignored by the Australian community or that it would not have a substantial long-term influence.

However, while much had been gained, the ASEAN–Australia association continued to be marked by uncertainties. In Australia there was a widespread realisation that the country's commitment to ASEAN had been marked by inconsistencies and that Australia's regional image had suffered as a result. This concern was expressed clearly in a major Government–sponsored report on 'Australia and the Third World', issued in 1979, which commented that:

> ... insofar as there is some evidence of a generalised disillusionment and impatience with Australia in the region – and there is such evidence – we need to consider the extent to which inappropriate and dated attitudes, a failure to match aims with actions and an inability to coordinate procedures in terms of clear priorities may be contributing to them.[19]

The report went on to state that it was vital that Australia should clearly establish what its domestic and foreign policy interests are in relations with Southeast Asia, and especially with ASEAN, and develop a capacity to balance these interests. It continued:

> ... if we recognise clearly that the stability, prosperity, self-confidence and unity of the ASEAN countries are themselves major Australian interests, we will be less inclined to justify contradictions in our policy by saying that while of course we want better relations with ASEAN countries and we do not want to divide them, we also have our own interests to look after.[20]

The trade and civil aviation issues suggested that translation of these principles into practice by Australia would be far from easy.

ASEAN leaders also seemed to see the course of the Australian relationship as a factor of some uncertainty, for reasons which accorded closely with the Australian self-perception reflected in the report just quoted. Australia often seemed to appear as a rich, relaxed society professing an interest in the region but basically oriented towards Europe and the Americas, which lacked sufficient knowledge about ASEAN and which could not see that a commitment to rationalise its economy would not only be in the interests of its neighbours but would serve its own interests as well.

At the beginning of the 1980s, the ASEAN–Australian relationship had come to serve as an important means for the discussion of both common and differing interests. In early 1981, it appeared that after several years of at times heated discord, the relationship was in a period of consolidation. Consultation between ASEAN Foreign Ministers and their Australian counterparts had become an annual event and together with the regular Forum of senior officials these meetings seemed to be making progress in reducing the degree of contention in the relationship. By April 1981, the Director-General of ASEAN–Malaysia, Encik Yusof Hitam, returned from a Forum in Canberra to describe the ASEAN–Australia relationship as 'comfortable' and as one in which the sides were not making large demands on each other.[21] While these comments reflected a move towards consolidation and a reduction in tensions, long term questions about the scope and potential of the relationship remained. A major question seemed to be whether the relationship would produce significant moves towards closer economic co-ordination and co-operation (necessarily involving concerted Australian action on trade), or whether after six years of development it would remain essentially on a plateau, with continued close diplomatic and securtiy co-operation, but with a tacit agreement to disagree on some of the crucial economic issues which had inspired much of the ASEAN criticism of Australian policy from 1976.

8

ASEAN and Japan: More than Economics

Alan Rix

Japan has actively fostered its relations with ASEAN only in the last few years. The five individual members of ASEAN, however, have had close and fruitful relationships with Japan for a considerably longer period. This chapter views ASEAN–Japan relations as the outgrowth of this longer period of Japanese interest and involvement in Southeast Asia, and the pursuance of its considerable interests there. It traces the important early steps in Japan's return to the region after the Allied Occupation of Japan, Japanese political initiatives in the 1960s and, after the first tentative brush with ASEAN, the see-saw of summit diplomacy and the final move towards a 'new' or at least fresh dialogue relationship.

Perception of the continuities in Japan's post-war Southeast Asian policy is fundamental to an understanding of the sudden spurt in ASEAN–Japan contacts after the Bali Heads of Government summit of February 1976. What Japan is attempting in its ASEAN policy is essentially no different from its concurrent bilateral policies in so far as they constitute a regional approach, although it is today more focused, more outspoken and more overtly political.

The ASEAN–Japan dialogue has a strong economic base. In 1978 ASEAN accounted for 10 per cent of Japan's total trade. Only the United States took a larger percentage (22 per cent) and even the EC traded marginally less with Japan. It was not, however, total trade with ASEAN that was most important to Japan, but the goods themselves. From ASEAN came most of Japan's imports of bananas (mainly from the

Philippines), palm oil (Malaysia), aviation kerosene (from refineries in Singapore), natural rubber (Malaysia and Thailand), tropical timber (Indonesia and Malaysia) and tin (Indonesia, Malaysia and Thailand). Fifteen per cent of Japan's oil came from ASEAN, and 20 per cent of her sugar imports. On the export side, ASEAN was a major market for Japanese trucks and truck assemblies, motor cycles, motor cars, cement and iron and steel. Apart from trade, ASEAN was an important investment target, accounting for 20.3 per cent of total accumulated Japanese investment in the period 1951 to 1976 and 20.0 per cent in 1978 alone. About one-third was invested in manufacturing industry (one-third of this in textiles) and about half in the mining sector. Japan also made significant investments in off-shore processing industries — petrochemicals, aluminium refining. ASEAN was, in addition, the major recipient of Japanese official aid, taking just over 40 per cent of that given in 1960–77 and, in 1978, 29 per cent.

For ASEAN, Japan looms large too. Japan is ASEAN's largest single trading partner and the largest for Thailand, Indonesia and the Philippines. Japan takes upwards of a quarter of ASEAN's exports and provides about a quarter of the region's imports. In 1977, trade with Indonesia was even more significant than this (it was around the 40 per cent mark in both exports and imports, in which the purchase of Indonesian oil was important) but with Singapore it was much lower (10 per cent of exports and 18 per cent of imports).

Return to the Region

After the Second World War, the Japanese were virtually excluded from the Asian region for six years during the Allied Occupation of Japan until the signing of the San Francisco Peace Agreement in September 1951. This agreement opened the way for renewed Japanese contact with the countries which its own military occupation had helped towards Independence. In a sense, the Allied Occupation was merely a hiatus in long-standing Japanese interest in, even need for, Southeast Asia. Japan's relations with ASEAN reflect an overwhelming geopolitical concern of the Japanese with this populous, strategically-placed group of countries and its abundance of natural resources and labour.[1]

At a policy level, the government of Yoshida Shigeru was assessing with some uncertainty the future foreign policy of Japan; Yoshida himself saw the United States, Great Britain and Southeast Asia as the cornerstones of a post-Occupation Japanese foreign policy.[2] The relationship with the US was, of course, paramount, but for both economic and security reasons, the US authorities actively encouraged the development of Japanese interest in economic co-operation with Southeast Asia.

The economic basis to Japan's relations with Southeast Asia — and the ASEAN five in particular — had a strong political and security rationale. Prime Minister Yoshida's abortive suggestion for an 'Asian Marshall Plan' (an assistance programme for Asia to be funded mainly by the United States) was indicative of a desire to cement US–Japan co-operation in Asian development, Japanese security interests and Japanese economic well-being.[3] These three aims — Asian development, Japanese economic security and the stability and security of Southeast Asia — have remained, along with Japan's natural desire to build a favourable image in the region, the basis of Japan's Southeast Asian policy since the 1950s right through to the present.

TRADE AND ECONOMIC SECURITY

Until the mid-1960s Japan's relations with Southeast Asia developed rapidly on the commercial side. Reparations brought increased Japanese exports to the region in the form of plant and equipment, financed largely through government credit facilities, such as the Export–Import Bank of Japan. The incentive to export meant that Japanese private enterprise showed a great interest in Asia. The Federation of Economic Organisations (*Keidanren,* one of Japan's major business groups) was active in its own economic diplomacy in the 1950s and 'was to emerge as a major spokesman for Japanese aid efforts'.[4] Keidanren leaders perceived clearly the market potential of the region, and were instrumental in developing business awareness of Southeast Asia.

According to Olson, however, Government attempts to educate Japanese public opinion about the region were poor.[5] Indeed, after Yoshida stepped down as Prime Minister, the pursuance of a Southeast Asian policy proceeded more cautiously. Prime Minister Hatoyama Ichiro's concerns were mainly with the Soviet Union (with which diplomatic relations were successfully opened in 1956) but his successor, Kishi Nobusuke, oversaw several initiatives in Southeast Asian policy. The most public were his two trips to the region in May and November 1957, the first by a Japanese Prime Minister after the War.

By the time Ikeda Hayato became Prime Minister in 1960 there was no doubt about Southeast Asia's importance to Japanese foreign policy or her economy. While there may have been an element of condescension in Japanese attitudes (as witnessed by Ikeda's reported remark that 'Asia thinks of Japan as an advanced elder brother'),[6] the groundwork was laid for a massive growth in Japanese economic relations with the region in the 1960s. Ikeda and his successor in the 1960s, Sato Eisaku, reiterated the common themes of interdependent economic and political futures for Japan and the region.[7] During that decade Japan was the fastest-growing economy in the world, and became one of the world's leading economic powers. As Asia's only advanced nation she became a leading, if reluctant, Asian power. There were steady moves to assert Japan's influence through multilateral and regional forums, but bilateral ties still preoccupied Japan's policy-makers in their dealings with the region.

The total value of Japan's trade with the ASEAN countries as a whole about tripled between 1962 and 1971 but, because of Japan's rapid economic growth and a trend to heavy industry, the ASEAN countries' share of Japan's exports and imports fell over the 1960s from taking 15.8 per cent of its imports in 1962, to buying only 8.8 per cent of exports in 1971 and supplying only 11.1 per cent of imports. In the years up to the formation of ASEAN in 1967, there was no across-the-board spurt in Japanese trade with Southeast Asia. Japan's total exports were concentrated in industrial manufactures and ASEAN declined as a market for these goods. But the position of the ASEAN countries in Japan's trade in foodstuffs, raw materials and energy goods improved, reflecting the importance of several Southeast Asian commodities to Japan's economy, and the development of the Southeast Asian countries themselves. Historically, Indonesian oil and timber and Malayan tin and rubber have been well known to the Japanese. It was in the 1960s that Japanese involvement in the development of trade in these and other raw materials and food began again.

REGIONAL STABILITY – JAPAN'S INITIATIVES

In a conscious attempt to go beyond the bilateral economic preoccupations of Japan's relations with the region, and to affirm her political presence in regional minds, Japan was party to several multilateral initiatives after the mid-1960s. These were Japan's convening the Ministerial Conference on the Economic Development of Southeast Asia (MEDSEA), the founding role of Japan in the Asian Development Bank (ADB) and Japan's participation in the Inter-Governmental Group on Indonesia (IGGI). While not without their own economic rationale, they served to signal Japan's earnest commitment to fulfilling the international obligations which it had begun to appreciate went with its economic status. (Japan had been admitted to the OECD in 1964 and, in acceding to IMF Article VII status in the same year, had opened the way for freer exchange and trade transactions.) They also interlocked neatly with Japanese trade, aid and investment policies towards the region.

MEDSEA was first convened at Japan's suggestion in April 1966 in Tokyo. Ten nations attended: Japan, the five countries later to form ASEAN, Laos, South Vietnam, Cambodia and Burma. Seen in many ways as an adjunct to ECAFE, which was financially weak and geographically more broadly spread, MEDSEA stemmed largely from Japan's desire to participate more actively in, and to encourage, regional cooperation, which Japan saw as one example of a trend towards regional stability, through regional self-help. One of the primary concerns of MEDSEA's developing members, however, was Japan's aid activity in the region. Japan, while using the Conference as a convenient public forum for its aid policies, was careful to underscore the 'co-operative' nature of the meeting — a theme in Japanese thinking which is still strong in 1980.

Some of MEDSEA's achievements relate to the ADB. It was MEDSEA, for example, which suggested the idea of a special fund for soft loans to agriculture within the ADB. The Bank itself was set up in 1966 for the purpose of regional development financing, a concept which Japanese officials had strongly supported. Japan lobbied strongly for Tokyo as the location for the Bank's headquarters, but had to settle instead for Manila, with the Presidency going to a succession of Japanese officials, a practice which has contributed greatly to Japan's leadership role in the Bank. The Bank had, indeed, been instrumental in multilateralising a strong Japanese institutional presence in Asian regional — and now ASEAN— development.

Japan's other important initiative was to participate in international assistance to one of the ASEAN group, Indonesia. Following the political crisis in that country in 1965–6, and the ensuing economic collapse, Indonesia sought a moratorium on its foreign debt as one element of a package of economic stabilisation policies. Japan hosted a meeting of creditors in September 1966 and later joined the group which was formed to co-ordinate future aid programmes to Indonesia. The IGGI, which was crucial to Indonesia's economic reconstruction, has been essential to the development of Japan–Indonesian aid relations. Structuring the donor–recipient relationship in this way meant that Indonesia became the largest single beneficiary of Japan's aid in later years. Likewise, the arrangement served Japan well, isolating the aid component of an extremely sensitive bilateral relationship from constant political and bureaucratic pressures and legitimising what was in many ways the crux of Japan's Southeast Asian policy–aid to Indonesia.

AID AND INVESTMENT: SECURITY, STABILITY AND DEVELOPMENT

Appreciating the extent of Japan's early foreign aid effort in Southeast Asia is indispensable to an understanding of Japan's relations with the ASEAN states from the late 1950s onwards.

The Kishi years were notable for the tentative steps into Asian diplomacy as reparations were actively implemented – even though this occasioned some accusations of corrupt practices over reparations contracts with Indonesia. Nevertheless, the Government was cautious about moving too quickly and it was in the period of Ikeda's prime ministership that domestic attitudes to foreign aid to Japan's Southeast Asian policy began to change. Japan became more confident of its Asian profile and Ikeda's trips to the region in 1961 and 1963 (when, in Japan's most independent diplomatic initiative in the region, Ikeda offered to mediate in the Malaysian–Indonesia confrontation) preceded the rapid expansion of economic ties from the mid-1960s.

The pattern of geographical distribution of Japanese aid was established in the 1960s. While investments in the 1950s showed a marked emphasis on Latin America and the Middle East – indeed by 1964 Asia accounted for only 19 per cent of Japanese direct foreign investment since 1951 – by 1969 Asia took 30 per cent of Japan's direct investment, and the five ASEAN countries themselves took 13 per cent of the total. In the same way, official development assistance became heavily concentrated in Asia after the middle of the 1960s. In 1963, 56 per cent of total economic co-operation flows – ODA (Overseas Development Aid), investment, other Government loans and investments – was directed to Asia, but 99 per cent of ODA. In 1969, 74 per cent of total flows went to Asia and 100 per cent of ODA. Half of ODA flowed into Southeast Asian countries. Japan's Asian policy was underpinned by flows such as these (mainly concessional loans for economic infrastructure projects), and it was not until the mid-1970s that regions other than Asia began to encroach on Asia's share. Until the end of 1975, 85 per cent of all OECF loans went to Asia, 78 per cent to six countries alone – Indonesia, South Korea, the Philippines, Thailand, Burma and Malaysia. There was indeed remarkably little change in the pattern of recipient nations and regions between 1965 and 1975. The accumulated value of yen loans was concentrated in South Asia up to 1960, but by 1965 the Southeast Asian tally matched this. After 1965, Southeast Asia drew well ahead as the leading recipient region. The top recipient nations have seldom varied and, along with India, South Korea, Taiwan and Burma, four ASEAN nations – Indonesia, Malaysia, the Philippines and Thailand – have always been among the top ten. The important recipients were all Asian and Indonesia's rise to first rank was the most remarkable.

These concentrated aid flows from Japan tied economic co-operation closely to foreign policy, for Japan viewed the economic development of Southeast Asia very seriously. For reasons of 'security and stability' the Japanese Government argued that the region and its economic development were of paramount importance to Japan. Expansion in Japanese aid and direct investment was also encouraged by economic policy development in both Japan and the recipient countries. Japan's balance of payments began to move into surplus after 1965, allowing the Government to ease controls on overseas investment, although this liberalisation was gradual and it was not until July 1971 that overseas investment became completely open in Southeast Asia, as export manufacturing plans were begun and foreign investment policies (first relaxed in the 1960s) allowed in more foreign capital and technology. Indonesia enacted its Foreign Investment Law in 1967, while Singapore and Thailand had encouraged foreign investment since the early 1960s. The purpose of the investment, however, has not been uniform across the five ASEAN nations. Differences in the level of economic development and the endowment of natural resources in each of the five countries mainly accounted for the nature of this investment.[8] Although Japanese investment in Indonesia, Thailand and the Philippines is still mainly of an import-substitution type in contrast to investment in Singapore, which is directed to higher technology export-oriented manufactures, there is a greater trend to export directed manufactured investment in all the ASEAN countries, alongside natural resources investment in all but Singapore.

Japan and the Early Years of ASEAN

By 1967, then, Japan enjoyed established relations with all five nations about to join together as ASEAN. Japan had signed friendship, commerce and navigation treaties with them. These relationships were, however, quite distinct and were not seen as in any sense a whole by Japanese policy-makers, except in so far as each was a recognisable independent state in a region of declared strategic and economic importance to Japan. This was not just a one-way reliance, however − Japan was a major trading partner of each of the five nations by 1967, accounting for 27 per cent of Indonesia's trade, 17 per cent of Malaysia's, 20 per cent of the Philippines' and Thailand's trade and 8 per cent of Singapore's. This made Japan the largest trading partner of the Philippines (after the United States), Malaysia (after the United Kingdom) and Singapore (after the United Kingdom). Furthermore, it was the chief natural resources exports of these countries in which Japan was most interested − the oil, rubber, timber, sugar, coconut oil and palm oil.

The Bangkok Declaration of August 1967 brought ASEAN into being; in Japan, comment on the event was limited and may have been less had not the Prime Minister, Mr Sato, been scheduled to visit Southeast Asia in September−October 1967. Japan's recognition of ASEAN was primarily as one advance in regional co-operation, a policy which Japan itself had been actively promoting through multilateral forums.

Non-official comment in Japan recognised the widespread implications of the formation of ASEAN. The number of its members and their geographical location made it significant, according to the *Asahi Shimbun,* but it was Indonesia's participation which gave the group its political and military character. Indonesia's Foreign Minister, Adam Malik, was quoted as saying than an even wider membership was possible, maybe including even Japan (he was later reported as saying that this was not possible) and it was implied that he, at least, appreciated the anti-communist character of ASEAN.[9] In the context of the escalating Vietnam war, the Association's potential political nature could hardly be denied. Other comments made similar points. ASEAN was strongly political, even though its avowed intentions were expressed more in economic than political terms. It was even said that changing international circumstances *required* a grouping such as ASEAN. Newspapers such as the *Nihon Keizai Shimbun* sought out the economic relevance of ASEAN – and saw a potential 'pressure group of primary producers' knocking on Japan's door[10] but the regional security implications were uppermost in Japanese minds, not resources controls. Indeed, only one year later, on the occasion of the ASEAN Foreign Ministers' Meeting, one Japanese newspaper was asking whether the economic priorities of the new Association would be retained, and dubbed ASEAN a 'wolf in sheep's clothing' in reference to its apparent political overtones.[11]

At the time of its formation in 1967 official Japanese comment on ASEAN was circumspect and remained so for several years afterwards. In fact it was not until the 1972 edition of the Foreign Ministry's *Diplomatic Blue Book (Waga gaiko no kinkyo)* that ASEAN was actually discussed as one of the main Asian regional organisations. Until that time the Foreign Ministry had regularly cited increased regional co-operation as a welcome development, but made no special mention of ASEAN. Prime Minister Sato did not even refer to ASEAN by name in his speech to the Japanese Diet on 5 December 1967, when he reported on his Southeast Asian trip. There was no mention of ASEAN in Diet policy speeches until Foreign Minister Ohira spoke on 22 January 1973 of the group's contribution to regional co-operation, which Japan 'highly appreciated'. The ASEAN 'Foreign Ministers' declaration of Southeast Asian neutrality at their gathering in November 1971 was duly noted in Japan as a sign of independent initiative, but it merely reinforced the Japanese perception of the political (and, to Japan, the strategic) role of ASEAN. The term 'regional co-operation' was not given a specific economic meaning; indeed, ASEAN was likened to ASPAC in its regional implications.

Prime Minister Sato's two-leg Southeast Asian–Pacific tour

in September–October 1967 only confirmed the as yet cautious Japanese approach to the future of regional economic co-operation. The joint statements included *pro forma* reference to the fact that Japan welcomed regional co-operation such as was demonstrated by ASEAN and other groupings, but the real substance of the talks was bilateral.

Sato's reported remarks about his tour make it clear that he saw problems in the ASEAN concept. He said that there were too many regional organisations and that Asia was too varied a region to be called cohesive.[12] Nor was ASEAN the focus of Japan's Asian policy at the time – Sato's preoccupations were with Korea, the China question, US policy in Asia and Japan's immediate economic interests in the region. These included trade and economic co-operation with ASEAN member countries particularly Indonesia – but were pursued through forums such as MEDSEA or the ADB in which Japan had a dominant voice, rather than dialogue with a regional association like ASEAN. That rather different form of 'bilateral' dialogue was a new experience for the Japanese, who felt more comfortable in accustomed country-to-country relationships.

JAPAN, ASEAN AND RUBBER

At the Sixth ASEAN Foreign Ministers' Meeting held in Pattaya in April 1973, Japan came under strong criticism for the effects of its synthetic rubber exports on ASEAN natural rubber producers. This was the first such action on an economic front by ASEAN, as a regional grouping, towards a non-member country and what followed involved the first contact at a policy level between Japan and the ASEAN countries as a group. In spite of some Japanese response, the problem was not immediately solved – in fact, in October 1973 it was raised in a wider forum at MEDSEA and in 1976 a further protest was made by ASEAN over Japan's rubber exports.

Malaysia appears to have been the instigator of this action. Malaysia's dissatisfaction with rubber prices had been expressed in talks with Prime Minister Sato when he visited in September 1967.[13] Sato agreed that some form of international price stabilisation mechanism should be studied. Certainly, the Malaysians had a point. Natural rubber was Malaysia's most important export commodity and its main provider of income and employment. But the world price of natural rubber halved between 1960 and 1971. The effect on the Malaysian economy was 'unfortunate but not catastrophic',[14] although the variability in the price decline caused serious problems for the main suppliers, smallholders whose supply tends to be price-inelastic. Lower synthetic rubber prices and improved quality were important factors in natural rubber's price decline.[15]

The ASEAN criticism of Japan was an effective common approach. One Southeast Asian critic saw this form of ASEAN action as 'a storm signal for Japan'.[16] Rubber provided an opportunity for useful and extended Japan–ASEAN dialogue. Why this had not occurred before was obvious enough: Japan was satisfied with its bilateral relationships and was not convinced of the economic effectiveness of ASEAN as a grouping. Nor, until rubber, had there been an immediate and distinctive issue. Even though the criticism of Japan was largely promoted by Malaysia, it led to the setting up of the Japan–ASEAN Forum on Rubber following the second officials' meeting in March 1974. This offered the first scope for formal dialogue between ASEAN and Japan.

The rubber problem was dealt with in practical terms. At the second officials' meeting Japan agreed to ensure that her synthetic rubber production would not adversely affect the natural rubber market. The Forum convened again in July 1975 and discussed Japanese assistance for rubber production. Technical assistance by the Japan International Co-operation Agency for Thai rubber production was later agreed upon and, although recorded in the aid statistics as bilateral technical aid, was in fact intended as Japan's contribution to improving ASEAN rubber production. The next meeting of the Forum, in November 1976, confirmed Japanese assistance for tyre research and a grant of ¥600 million for this purpose was made to Malaysia in March 1977.

While the Rubber Forum was a first step in closer Japanese relations with ASEAN, and showed Japanese willingness to accommodate pressure, two particular events were far more effective in making the Japanese aware of the ASEAN nations, of feeling in those countries about Japan's presence in Southeast Asia, and of the need to pay more attention to Southeast Asian – and ASEAN – demands. One event was the visit of Prime Minister Tanaka to the region in January 1974, a visit which provoked violent, and ostensibly anti-Japanese, demonstrations; the other was the Bali meeting of ASEAN Heads of Government in February 1976 at which ASEAN leaders reaffirmed the purposes of ASEAN, especially in economic co-operation, and, importantly in terms of relations of the group as such with other governments, established a permanent ASEAN Secretariat.

THE TANAKA VISIT

The violence which accompanied Prime Minister Tanaka's visit to Singapore, Thailand, Indonesia, Malaysia and the Philippines seriously shocked many Japanese. Even beforehand, Thai students had criticised Japan for its trade imbalance with Thailand and for restrictive Japanese import barriers, but Tanaka was, ironically enough, intending that the trip be fairly routine. Anti-Japanese sentiment, such as criticism of the practice of Japanese businessmen to 'take away the meat and leave only the bones of the host economy',[17] was thought to be manageable – and visits to only Thailand and Indonesia were thought necessary at one stage in planning for the visit.

It was a trip with several immediate policy purposes. Tanaka wished to mollify criticism in Southeast Asia and assure countries there of Japan's good intentions. He also felt it important to show Japan's goodwill in assisting the economic development of the nations of Southeast Asia and its aspirations for regional stability and security. Thus, decisions had been hastily taken in December 1978 to form a Japan International Co-operation Agency for technical aid and development financing and to create a new ministerial portfolio for economic co-operation.

It was also considered necessary to renew Prime Ministerial acquaintance with the region. Tanaka's slightly higher profile in foreign policy had been dubbed 'autonomous' diplomacy, perhaps a polite term for a stable, non-involved and 'all directional' diplomacy carried off in Tanaka's gruff, direct style. Tanaka's Southeast Asian trip (it was *not* termed an ASEAN trip) came on top of the oil crisis and its strong reinforcement in Japanese minds of their vulnerability in resource supplies.

Some commentators held high hopes for the tour – it was referred to as the 'finishing touch' to Tanaka's series of summit diplomatic moves.[18] Japanese views of Southeast Asia were still cast, however, in the aid framework, where Japanese responsibilities lay in providing economic and technical aid on the assumption that developing countries welcomed such largesse and that stability, security and peace would thereby result. It was a mechanistic, even condescending, policy.

The result of this policy was growing dissatisfaction in Southeast Asian countries. As foreign investment increased in Thailand in the 1960s, Thai policy became more restrictive. Anti-Japanese sentiment was expressed in a boycott organised by students against Japanese goods in November 1972. This encouraged the Foreign Ministry to attempt to switch the focus of aid policy from export promotion and the mutual benefits of aid flows, towards assistance designed to help recipients. This was partly a domestic argument – the Foreign Minister trying to persuade MITI and the Finance Ministry of the benefits of a more liberal approach to foreign aid.

Criticism of the Japanese economic presence in Southeast Asia was not a matter simply for governments to deal with. Indeed, the keenest criticism by Southeast Asians was of Japanese attitudes and behaviour (which often reflected ignorance of local sensitivities) and Japanese business practices which, according to many, exported Japanese pollution, exploited lowly paid Southeast Asian workers and discouraged local participation in management.

The five major Japanese economic organisations recognised the possible effects of unrestrained Japanese business activity in developing countries and in June 1973 issued guidelines on investment practices for Japanese investors in those nations. These guidelines encouraged investors to respect the develop-

ment aims and policies of the host nations, employ and promote locals, properly select and train Japanese staff and give
them more authority in the field, promote technology transfer, and more general aims of harmonising with the local
society. This statement came just six months before Tanaka's
visit to Southeast Asia, in too little time to have any significant effect on investors' behaviour. In fact, as we shall see,
the economic organisations were spurred to make a more
searching assessment of Japanese investment after the Tanaka
trip.

Tanaka's stop in the Philippines was largely uneventful. It
was in Thailand that student riots began; they continued in
Malaysia and were at their worst in Indonesia, where several
students died. The riots were not only in protest against the
Japanese presence — there were domestic problems and
policies which students opposed — but the Tanaka visit was a
handy opportunity for the students to make their views
known to their own governments and to the outside world.

The visit could not be called a success. Tanaka had little in
the way of initiatives to offer the nations he visited, and no
decisions of significance were made. ASEAN received
perfunctory mention in the five joint communiqués issued,
Japan merely recognising ASEAN's contribution to regional
co-operation, security and stability. The only hint that
Tanaka was thinking of ASEAN as something more than a
regional collective useful to Japan in strengthening her
security interests in Southeast Asia was his statment in Kuala
Lumpur that, in seeking assurances on the stable long-term
supply of resources, he hoped that ASEAN as a whole would
be able to set up some form of common co-operative mechanism.

A New Form of Dialogue: The Bali Summit and After

The meeting of ASEAN Heads of Government in Bali in
February 1976 gave ASEAN new energy in both intra-
regional co-operation and in forming approaches to external
economic relations. There were initial doubts in Japan about
the viability of the programme, an ambitious one ostensibly

based on strategic concerns which followed the end of the war in Vietnam in 1975. One report claimed that 'there have been no new concrete results in economic co-operation from this summit meeting'.[19] But in three important areas out of the four which emerged from the meeting (trade preferences, industrial co-operation, commodity stabilisation and a common front in external economic relations), Japan was to become closely involved. As a result, Japan's policy towards Southeast Asia has become primarily a policy of economic co-operation. The Japanese need for assurances of stability in the region has been answered firmly by ASEAN, but almost too successfully. Japan is, in a sense, no longer the most active, or even the most visible, economic presence of the region. That role has been taken up by ASEAN itself.

Official Japanese statements on the Bali Summit were effusive by comparison with previous government reactions to ASEAN. Against a background of the fall of the non-communist governments in South Vietnam and Cambodia in May 1975, Prime Minister Miki had in August 1975 praised ASEAN's role in helping stabilise Southeast Asia and offered Japanese co-operation.[20] Foreign Minister Miyazawa had repeated this offer in September. In February 1976 Miki, although his request to attend had been refused, sent a message to the ASEAN Heads of Government in the same terms, noting that the meeting was 'an historic step towards achieving the common goals of growth and stability in Southeast Asia'. Again, Miki was backed up by Miyazawa who forecast greater contact between Japan and ASEAN through the new Secretariat, and said that Japan wanted to consider how it could co-operate with ASEAN's new economic programme. While the preoccupation was still with the trilogy of peace, prosperity and stability, Miki went further than previous Japanese leaders in setting Japan and ASEAN on a closer economic and political path. The approach in his speeches was direct: it was ASEAN as a grouping which he was addressing, not its several individual members.

In spite of this encouragement, economic co-operation was slow to get off the ground, although, as Arndt and Garnaut point out, ASEAN'S joint efforts *vis-à-vis* the developed world have 'probably made more headlines since Bali' than the other decisions taken.[21] These efforts have been directed against Japan, principally in relation to improved market access and Japanese support for ASEAN industrial co-operation. It was over a year, however, before any sign of initiatives in Japan's relations with ASEAN became obvious. This was due partly to Japanese uncertainties about the new ASEAN approach (itself characterised by a hesitant 'honeymoon period') and its likely success. But it was due also to a continued Japanese preference for bilateral emphasis in trade and aid policies and to the thinking that lay behind Japanese policy. Japan's aid programme, for example, was based on project aid requested and designated for specific projects. In 1976 foreign aid had not yet acquired the more prominent political support which came in 1977 on the heels of a stronger Japanese commitment to aid and co-operation with ASEAN.

The process of getting to know each other was gradual and not always without its problems. Only a few months after the Bali Summit, the Ninth ASEAN Foreign Ministers' Meeting criticised Japan again, expressing dissatisfaction with Japanese action on synthetic rubber and canned pineapples. While ASEAN was happy with its relations with Australia, New Zealand, the EC and Canada, talks with Japan on these two items had produced 'only limited results'. Criticism of Japan's trade with the region highlighted trade imbalances, Japan's interest in the region's resources to the exclusion of the region's manufactured goods, and at the same time (because of Japan's domestic economic downturn) her steady demand for key commodities such as tin, natural rubber, timber and copper.[22] The question of rubber continued to trouble the relationship and in September 1976 a stronger set of demands was presented to Japan by the ASEAN Secretariat requesting cuts in synthetic rubber production and support for technical assistance and rubber research.

The Bali Meeting was a further assertion of the will of the ASEAN countries to manage their affairs independent of Japan. The Tenth MEDSEA Meeting, scheduled for late 1975, was postponed because of preparations for Bali. It was never reconvened and was not greatly missed, for by that time it had fulfilled its purpose of giving form to Japanese support for regional co-operation. While the decline of MEDSEA may have solved a management problem for Japanese officials, however, it did leave them without a focus for a Southeast Asian policy. Japan's influence in the Asian Development Bank was strong, but it was not associated with the development of Southeast Asia alone. ASEAN provided a substitute, albeit one to be approached initially with care. It was a framework, moreover, which had been constructed not by Japan but by its own members.

Miki's support for ASEAN as part of a new Japanese call for Asian–Pacific co-operation to underscore a new security alignment in the region, harked back to his Asian–Pacific concept of the late 1960s. It was spelled out in a speech in Washington in August 1975 and the aid component was expanded into an 'Asian New Deal' proposal floated in January 1976. ASEAN interest, however, was in more specific areas of co-operation and Miki's idea advanced no further.

These very tentative Japanese advances towards a relationship with ASEAN became more purposeful by 1977, but the management of bilateral relations was still a strong element of Japan's Southeast Asian policy. Sunobe Ryōzō, a former Japanese Ambassador to Indonesia, expressed one reason for continued ambivalence. 'The projects which the group is promoting', he said, 'will take time to mature. Look how long it took the EC. These are considerable hurdles to be overcome in promoting an economic association such as this. Japan should respond to the extent that the group advances.'[23]

This sort of caution gradually eased and as the Japanese became more willing to build constructive channels to ASEAN, ASEAN became more receptive to Japanese advances. In September 1976 Japan proposed the creation of a Japan–ASEAN Forum, to which ASEAN agreed in November. The first meeting was held in March 1977 in Jakarta, and it was decided that successive forums would discuss problems of industrial development, trade, food and agriculture. In commenting on the Forum, the Japanese Foreign Ministry was careful to point out that whether or not Japan could respond to the several demands of ASEAN on aid and trade matters depended a great deal on the ability of ASEAN to successfully co-ordinate its own position and to have the details of complex problems such as export stabilis-ation (Stabex) and the industrial projects properly worked out. Japan was later able to use the lack of ASEAN prepared-ness to postpone its own decisions on these questions.

Economic co-operation was to the fore in both Japanese and ASEAN thinking, although it is not easy to separate gen-uine initiatives from policies with a Japanese 'domestic' pur-pose. In January 1977 the Japanese Foreign Ministry announced a 'new' aid policy aimed at 'stabilising' the South-east Asian region. The policy was even-handed, providing for increased aid to both ASEAN and Indo-China, but it had one immediate purpose – that of convincing the Ministry of Finance to support the Foreign Ministry's budget request for the following fiscal year. It was also noteworthy for its announcement that Japan would look favourably on ASEAN requests for assistance with the ASEAN industrial projects.[24] At the same time, Japan maintained active and expanding bi-lateral relations with member countries (in aid, trade and investment), and with ASEAN's neighbours (Vietnam, for example).

The same ambivalence was evident on the ASEAN side. Each nation naturally maintained close ties with Japan – thus Indonesia was careful to preserve Japan's long-standing commitment to the Indonesian aid consortium, IGGI. Indonesia's Foreign Minister was quoted as saying that 'ASEAN has to be nice to Japan – because Japan is wealthy'. At the same time, dissatisfaction was expressed with Japan's 'lukewarm' attitude (attributed to President Marcos of the Philippines) and 'promises only' approach (Prime Minister Lee of Singapore). ASEAN countries demanded more aid from Japan, but still threatened resources cartel tactics. Prime Minister Lee indicated that only if Japan could promise to expand its aid would Japanese attendance at the following ASEAN summit be considered.[25]

THE FUKUDA DOCTRINE

The visit by Prime Minister Fukuda to ASEAN in August 1977 appeared to mark a radical change not only in Japan's attitude to ASEAN, but also in the substance of relations themselves. The 'Fukuda Doctrine', enunciated as a set of principles governing Japan's Southeast Asian policy, was one of the main foreign policy statements of the Fukuda premiership. But the Doctrine marked no new directions in Japanese policy: while it restated Japanese Southeast Asian diplomacy, it encapsulated twenty years of Japanese experience in the region. In the wake of Tanaka's failure, it was a bold step, and one which demonstrated Japan's perpetual need to sort out its relations with Southeast Asia in a way that would secure its interests there. There were sound economic and political reasons for the Fukuda trip. The dual approaches of both sides to growing dialogue needed discussing and ASEAN demands for economic concessions had to be assessed. In the few months between the Japan–ASEAN Forum in March and Fukuda's visit which coincided with the Second Heads of Government Meeting, the Japanese Government rushed to prepare some sort of policy – and slogan – for Fukuda's ASEAN summitry. Assessment initially centred on the three key ASEAN proposals (which had been put to Japan at, among other meetings, the March Japan–ASEAN Forum) for Japanese assistance with an 'Asian Lomé Agreement' for regional preferential trade, an export income stabilisation scheme (Stabex) and support for the ASEAN industrial projects. Early indications were that the trade preferences question would be difficult to agree to because of the continuing Tokyo Round of Multilateral Trade Negotiations. There were also doubts about Stabex in view of the possible demands of other developing countries, and reservations were expressed about the effects of commitment to the ASEAN projects on the traditional bilateral loan framework.[26]

The visit of Mr Fukuda to Southeast Asia – he pointedly included Burma in his itinerary, not just the ASEAN nations – was notable in three ways:

(a) Mr Fukuda had relatively easy meetings with ASEAN leaders and made a rather limited set of commitments to the Association;
(b) he engaged in active bilateral diplomacy and produced a long list of commitments to each of the ASEAN countries;

(c) he made a forthright statement of Japan's Southeast Asian policy, which included an important reference to Japanese co-operation with Indo-China.

Fukuda's position *vis-á-vis* ASEAN was delicate. One newspaper dubbed him a 'Hamlet' on ASEAN policy, [27] while ASEAN nations' attitudes to Japan were as ambiguous as ever. Foreign Minister Romulo of the Philippines called Japan a 'shrewd merchant', while Rajaratnam of Malaysia stressed that 'we don't believe in Santa Claus from Japan or anywhere else'. There had been criticism of a vague statement made in July by Japan's Ambassador to the Philippines, Mikanagi Kiyohisa, that 'Japan's aid to ASEAN must also build Japan's friendship with Indochina'. Many took this to mean that Japan saw Indo-China as important as ASEAN and, given the reference to Indo-China in the Fukuda Doctrine announced later, they may have been right. At a news conference after the Kuala Lumpur summit Fukuda spoke of the need for peaceful coexistence between Indo-China and ASEAN, and added that Japan could act as a 'bridge' in this respect. He did not elaborate on exactly what this required of Japan.

Fukuda's most notable pledge to ASEAN was his promise of US $1 billion to ASEAN industrial projects, provided that feasibility was satisfactorily proven. No commitments were made to Stabex other than a general agreement for a joint study of the possibilities. Fukuda also agreed to consider Japan's tariff structure as it affected ASEAN. Promises of assistance to cultural exchanges were also made. As Fukuda outlined in a Press conference on 4 August, before his departure, it was not his style to 'buy the goodwill of Asian countries' by throwing money around. He was after 'true friends' as a basis for an economic relationship – this principle he certainly applied in his discussions with ASEAN leaders. He moved no further than careful responses to ASEAN requests.

In Manila, Fukuda outlined his 'three pillars' of Japan's Southeast Asian Policy, best known as the 'Fukuda Doctrine':

(a) Japan rejects the role of a military power, and seeks the peace and prosperity of Southeast Asia;

(b) Japan wants a 'relationship of mutual confidence and trust based on "heart-to-heart" understanding';
(c) Japan is an equal partner of the ASEAN countries and will co-operate positively in their own efforts, while aiming at a relationship of mutual understanding with Indo-China.[28]

Fukuda's speech was the most positive Japanese assessment of ASEAN Japan had then made. Most notable was the full credit Fukuda gave to ASEAN successes, but his reluctance to acknowledge ASEAN's existing solidarity; he preferred to view regional solidarity as something yet to be achieved, and only slowly. Its path was made more difficult by regional diversity. Fukuda simultaneously sounded a cautionary note about the dangers of regional economic blocs and the preference for global approaches. In explaining Japan's pledges to ASEAN as the fruits of this new Japanese stance, Fukuda gave little credit to ASEAN for the pressure it had steadily applied to Japan since the Bali Summit, even if the demands themselves were ill-formed.

THE NEW ASEAN—JAPAN DIALOGUE

It has been remarkable how, in the years since 1977, Japan—ASEAN contacts have burgeoned at government, business and private levels, while progress on the central questions of aid, trade access and other economic issues has been difficult and slow.

Although the high diplomacy of Mr Fukuda was not repeated by his immediate successor, Mr Ohira, Japan has adopted a deliberate policy of high-level discussions. Ministers and officials from both sides have been in constant contact since mid-1977. The Second Japan—ASEAN Forum, which met in November 1977, followed up the several proposals raised during Mr Fukuda's August visit to Southeast Asia, but there was no progress on any item. The Minister for International Trade and Industry, Mr Komoto, was positive towards assistance for the ASEAN projects during talks in ASEAN capitals in May 1978, but the most noteworthy ministerial visit was that by Foreign Minister Sonoda to coincide with the ASEAN Foreign Ministers' Meeting in June 1978. This occasion produced a great deal of goodwill on both sides, but still no specific commitments. Prime Minister Ohira travelled to Manila in May 1979 to deliver a speech at UNCTAD V and, in a separate statement, pledged a $10 million scholarship scheme for ASEAN students, in keeping with his UNCTAD policy of 'people-building', as a new plank in Japan's technical assistance programme. Mr Sonoda attended meetings with the ASEAN Foreign Ministers in July 1979 (as did his successor, Dr Okita, in July 1980), and the ASEAN Economic Ministers met their Japanese counterparts in Tokyo in November 1979. After Ohira's broader foreign policy approach, embracing the United States, China, Australia and the Pacific as a whole, Mr Suzuki, who became Prime Minister in July 1980, gave early signs of wishing to strengthen ties with ASEAN, as part of a more concentrated regional commitment.

Private enterprise has followed government in establishing regular contacts. The Japan—ASEAN Economic Council first met in November 1978, and a Japan—ASEAN Chambers of Commerce and Industry meeting was also instituted. They tended to be, in their initial stages, an alternative and direct channel for ASEAN pressure on the Japanese Government, but have begun to consider more appropriate areas such as investment, technology transfer, industrial co-operation and banking. Joint action has developed to the point where an ASEAN—Japan Development Corporation was established in July 1980 to assist in financing ASEAN private sector industrial ventures.

The fate of Mr Fukuda's promises of August 1977 is indicative of the difficulties for Japan in dealing with an economic grouping of which it is not a member but about which it has lingering doubts and with whose individual members it has strong economic ties. The reference in Mr Fukuda's August 1977 Manila speech to ASEAN's potential solidarity expressed an important reservation in Japanese official minds about how well prepared ASEAN was to co-ordinate its industrial projects or its approach on trade concessions, or to handle loan finance. It was not until April 1979 that agreement was reached on assistance to the first of the ASEAN projects, Indonesia's urea fertiliser plant. Japanese assistance was to be 70 per cent of the total original cost through OECF and Export–Import Bank Loans to the Indonesian Government did, however, provide grant funds through the Japan International Co-operation Agency to conduct a feasibility study in the Indonesian project. A loan of ¥33,000 million was signed in October 1979 between Japan and Indonesia for construction of the plant. As with Japanese assistance to the ASEAN rubber industry, aid had to be offered on a bilateral basis rather than through ASEAN financing machinery. JICA also completed a study of the Malaysian urea project, but agreement on a loan was delayed: Malaysia sought similar concessional terms to those given to Indonesia, and Japan took the view that Malaysia's level of development precludes it from such a loan. ASEAN mutterings have been heard about the slowness of Japanese procedures, and about contracts being tied to Japanese suppliers.

Progress on trade questions has been even slower. ASEAN demands on trade preferences and improved access to the Japanese market were initially stalled until negotiations (in the context of the Tokyo Round of Multilateral Trade Negotiations) between Japan and ASEAN – and, more significantly, Japan and the individual ASEAN members – were concluded in mid-1978. Japan reduced tariffs on a number of items, including bananas (an important trading item between Japan and the Philippines), palm oil, coconut oil, shrimps and canned pineapple, but ASEAN requested larger tariff cuts and action on non-tariff barriers. The Economic Ministers' Meeting of November 1979 revealed that these requests were still being pursued and that Japan had made little response on trade access or trade preferences.

Negotiations on Stabex have not advanced very far. An experts' meeting due in May 1978 was cancelled by ASEAN two days beforehand, and the meeting was carried over until September. The Japanese were unable to agree amongst themselves prior to the meeting and a decision was held over to await the outcome of discussions within UNCTAD on the proposed common fund. UNCTAD failed to move very far on this question at its Fifth Conference in May 1979, and

ASEAN Economic Ministers were still pressing Japan to establish Stabex when they consulted with the Japanese in November 1979.

No progress on this or other trade questions was made at the Fourth ASEAN–Japan Forum in May 1980.

One result of the limited progress on the central aspects of ASEAN economic policy towards Japan has been repeated criticism from within ASEAN of Japan's alleged failure to make good its promises. The establishment of an ASEAN Cultural Fund with the Japanese Government support of ¥5 billion has prompted some appreciation, but cynicism has also been expressed about the motives of Japan's 'cultural diplomacy'.[29] The ASEAN centre established in Tokyo in 1979 has not yet lived up to the expectations either of ASEAN or of Japan for trade, investment and tourist promotion. Much of the ASEAN complaint derives from a failure on the part of Japan to keep the commitments made by Mr Fukuda, but more relates to fundamental Japanese attitudes towards developing countries of which ASEAN is, to the Japanese, a representative example. Some of this criticism is exaggerated – after all, Japan has to consider its ASEAN policy in the context of its more general economic co-operation policies and its stance towards the North–South problem.

It is undeniable that since mid-1977, ASEAN has become integral to Japan's Asian policy. As a stabilising force in Southeast Asia, ASEAN has been assiduously nurtured by Japanese diplomacy (even if fed a limited diet). The joint approach to foreign economic policy adopted by ASEAN was not altogether welcomed by Japanese officials, but such an approach can help achieve the Japanese objective of 'peace and security in the region'. That theme is still, after twenty-five years, a key to Japan's Southeast Asian policy. The traditional distinction between assistance to the group, and to its individual members, is in practice still maintained, but the distinction is sometimes difficult to discern. A large loan to Thailand, for example, in January 1979, was said 'to underscore Japan's moral support for ASEAN' in the face of the Vietnamese invasion of Kampuchea.[30]

It has not only been Japan's follow-up on promises to

ASEAN that has symbolised the lack of a special relationship. Just as important have been Japan's continued desire to assist Vietnam, and its recent eagerness to have China designated a 'developing country' and Japan's economic co-operation therefore classified as 'aid'. In December 1979 Prime Minister Ohira visited China and pledged a loan of ¥50 billion for 1979 for six infrastructure projects, and a grant of ¥1 billion for technical assistance. Japan assured ASEAN at the November 1979 Economic Ministers' Meeting that aid to China would not disadvantage the ASEAN countries. It is not likely that Japan's posture towards ASEAN will change as a result of aid to China, as long as the projected doubling of Japan's official development assistance in the three years 1977—80 is achieved, and that further expansion of the aid budget is agreed to by the Finance Ministry. Aid policy is not based on a pie of fixed size, but the potential impact of China on an aid programme limited more by bureaucratic processes than political will could, over the longer term, affect the relative, rather than the absolute, level of the share of Japan's aid programme going to ASEAN. Conversely, Japan is likely to ensure that ASEAN is kept happy — after all, Japan is not about to abandon ASEAN for China, for political sense dictates that Japan will need ASEAN just as much in the years ahead as now. Japan's stern, if even-handed, policy towards Vietnam (not cutting off aid, but postponing its disbursement, while at the same time increasing aid for refugees in Thailand and supporting the transit camps in Indonesia and the Philippines) is an example of how Japan is not going to let slip what influence it has in the region.

The visit of Prime Minister Suzuki Zenkō to the five ASEAN countries in January 1981 only confirmed the Japanese approach: improvement in some areas of political and economic relations (such as agreement on financing Malaysia's industrial project and a promise to meet cost overruns on Indonesia's), but reluctance to make firm commitments on the longer-term issues of market access, aid, investment and technology transfer.

Conclusion

A relationship which began cautiously and diffidently in the early 1970s is now one of the most active for Japan and for ASEAN, and presents each side with some demanding policy issues. There are two contrasting aspects to Japan's approach to ASEAN since 1977. On the economic front, the response to key ASEAN demands, and to ASEAN complaints, continues to be *ad hoc*. The tendency for Japanese promises to be made faster than they can be implemented, Japan's delayed response to the vexed question of market access, and her continuing tendency to distinguish bilateral and ASEAN channels, are of nagging concern.

On the political side, however, successive Japanese Prime Ministers since Fukuda have fostered the growth of the Japan–ASEAN relationship and, with it, Japan's closer involvement in regional affairs. Japan's growing practice of taking ASEAN into its counsels over matters of regional concern — aid to Vietnam, assistance for refugees, recognition of the government in Phnom Penh, the proposal for safe havens inside Kampuchea, the Pacific Community concept — has done much to demonstrate to ASEAN governments Japan's consistent view about the importance of regional balance and stability. Japan's desire to act as a 'bridge' or interpreter of Asia to the West, however ill-defined, still appears strong, although Japan has not opted to use ASEAN as its exclusive channel to the region.

Japan is nevertheless committed to a policy of co-operation with and constructive assistance to ASEAN. The short history of ASEAN–Japan relations suggests that their full potential has yet to be realised. Yet it will be worked out alongside a changing and more broadly-based Japanese interpretation of economic security and regional stability, and of its own political role. The future of ASEAN–Japan relations lies as much in attitudes to the major powers, energy and resources, as it does in Japan's willingness to keep its promises and put flesh on the bones of the relationship.

9

ASEAN: The Five Countries

Ho Kwon Ping

Ten years ago, or even five, the ASEAN countries were hardly spoken of collectively. Their individuality was underscored by the memory of the conflicts between several of them since independence, and by the separation that had grown upon them as colonies of distant powers. That the differences between the countries are now so often ignored is a mark of what ASEAN has achieved. Yet their differences still influence what happens within ASEAN and outside it.

The Peoples of ASEAN

The countries of ASEAN located between the two great culture worlds of India and China have historically seen a swirl of converging migrant communities. All but Thailand are island chains separated by shallow seas, easily traversed by traders and migrants. The result is great racial diversity, described with technical precision by Buchanan:[1]

> Many physical types are represented here: the negritoes of the island interiors, the slender brown-skinned Nesiots (akin to the Mediterranean race of Europe) whose distribution is from South China to the Indonesian Islands, the broad-headed straight-haired mongoloid peoples who spread southwards from China mingling with or displacing earlier peoples. Upon this racial diversity is superimposed a great diversity of linguistic groups. In the earliest period the mainland was dominated by peoples speaking

languages of the Mon-Khmer group; the islands by peoples speaking Malayo–Polynesian languages. The linguistic homogeneity of the mainland was subsequently shattered by the irruption into the area of peoples speaking languages of the Sino–Tibetan group — Burmese, Thai, Vietnamese. These peoples pushed the earlier Mon-Khmer peoples into the forested uplands so that today, with the exception of Cambodia, all the major lowlands of mainland South-East Asia are dominated by people speaking languages of the Sino–Tibetan group; the peoples of the islands and Peninsular Malaya remained, by contrast, solidly Malay in their speech, though many dialectal variations emerged... to these groups must be added the later immigrants, especially Indian and Chinese, drawn into South-East Asia by the European economic development of the late nineteenth century.

The blinkers of colonialism ensured that for centuries the Indo-China countries looked to France, Indonesia to Holland, Malaya and Singapore to Britain, the Philippines to Spain and later to America. The cutting off of Southeast Asia from itself was complete and its effects are still strongly felt.

A political legacy of the colonial period was the injection of indentured workers and merchants, who stayed to form political sub-cultures. The overseas Chinese community in ASEAN countries has become a wealthy, culturally distinct enclave (though class and income differentiation within the Chinese community certainly exists) often in friction with its adopted society. It is sometimes said that the overseas Chinese control the economy and the 'native' races control the military and government. In Thailand and to some extent in the Philippines a symbiotic relationship has developed, and racial frictions have declined accordingly. In Indonesia discriminatory measures against Chinese education and business have been applied with little resistance because of the relative smallness of this community. But it is in Malaysia, where the Chinese population is a substantial minority, that the legacies of colonial migration have caused the most friction. Even today, the scars of the 13 May 1969 racial riots remain indelibly imprinted in the national psyche, and every policy —

social, political, economic, educational — reflects both the racial tensions and the urgent need to strike compromises.

Religion has not been a unifying force between the ASEAN countries as it has in Western societies. Thailand is overwhelmingly Buddhist, except its southern provinces which are predominantly Muslim and for that reason — plus economic grievances — have spawned a secessionist movement. In the Philippines the dichotomy between the Christian north and the Muslim sector in the south again gives rise to a religiously and economically inspired secessionist movement led by the Moro National Liberation Front (MNLF). Except for the tiny Hindu outpost of Bali, Indonesia's several thousand islands were converted to Islam during the wave of Islamic religious expansion into Southeast Asia several centuries ago. The spread of Islam also reached Malaysia, where today religion has exacerbated the racial tensions, with the Malays practising Islam and the Chinese retaining Confucian–Taoist beliefs. Islam has played a unifying role for the Malay peoples of Malaysia and Indonesia, but for the other peoples of ASEAN, it has accentuated the historical differences.

Besides religious and racial diversity, there are regional differences between the people of individual ASEAN countries. The upland hill tribes of all ASEAN countries, of course, have long been ethnically distinct from the majority lowland settlers. But there are also subtle tensions and differences between the peoples of the same racial heritages. The northeasterners of Thailand have Laotian and Vietnamese ancestries, which have been noted with suspicion by the mainstream Thai people of the Central Plains. The non-Javanese peoples of Indonesia — for example from Sumatra or Sulawesi — are acutely aware of the dominance of the Javanese in national life. Because of the lack of communication regional linguistic differences have emerged within the same country.

Across countries, the linguistic gulf is even wider. Except for Malaysians and Indonesians (and the southern secessionists of Thailand and the Philippines), Malay is not used elsewhere in ASEAN. But then the Thais and Filipinos also speak totally different languages, while in Singapore Chinese dialects

and English are the *lingua franca* – though Malay is nominally the national language. Because of this babble of different
tongues, English, a colonial language, has become the working medium for intra-ASEAN communication.

One of the most striking features of the demographic pat-
tern of ASEAN is the patchiness of its distribution. Java
alone accounts for one-third of the region's population,
crowded on to less than one-thirtieth of the area's land
surface. The bulk of the Thai population is clustered in the
Central Plains and the megalopolis that Bangkok has become.
Malaysia's population is concentrated on the west coast of
Peninsular Malaysia: East Malaysia is sparsely inhabited. The
Philippine people are centred in the northern islands of
Luzon and the Visayas, with Mindanao remaining, like
Kalimantan, a rich but sparsely populated or exploited land.
This unevenness of distribution has been a feature from early
times and is a reflection of dominant dietary staples – rice
and fish; the unevenness has nevertheless been increased by
modern economic development, as improved agricultural
services and new and better varieties of crops as in Java, or
improved irrigation techniques as in Thailand, made possible
an increasing accumulation of population in the already
closely-settled areas. Elsewhere, as in the west Malaysian peninsula, plantation or mining development led to an increasing
concentration of population in areas formerly only thinly
peopled. Singapore, the city-state, is the most densely populated of all, with only a tiny fraction of its land area left over
for agriculture.

In all the ASEAN countries except Singapore, the population is growing much faster than did the population of
Europe during its period of rapid growth. Moreover, in contrast to Europe, demographic changes have not been accompanied by an economic revolution of equal dimensions to
provide for the growing population of Indonesia, Thailand
and the Philippines. These countries face the problem of
accommodating physically and economically an increase of
111 million people in the next twenty years. And since the
majority of those who will enter the labour market in the
next two decades are already born, population planning is of
only marginal relevance in confronting the immediate prob-

lem. In addition, the number of potential parents already born is so large that, even if family size should fall, the absolute population increase each year will continue to be very great.

Furthermore, the ASEAN demographic structure is heavily weighted with young, working-age people, and therefore the provision of adequate schooling and technical training is a basic prerequisite of growth. But except in Singapore and to a certain degree Malaysia, the countries of the area are caught in a vicious circle in which poverty leads to inadequate schooling and poor technical training facilities, and this in turn back to low productivity and poverty. These pressures are of fundamental importance to economic planning in ASEAN.

Despite a long tradition of urban life, dating back to pre-colonial trading centres, the ASEAN countries — again excepting Singapore — have been essentially rural societies. But this has begun to change as a result of the increasing flow of migrants to the cities. One of the most striking features of the post-independence period has been the mushrooming growth of some of the great cities. The degree of urbanisation varies: in Malaysia about two-fifths of the population is urban, in the Philippines somewhat less than one-third, while in Thailand the proportion is much smaller. The pace of urbanisation has accelerated greatly in recent years, faster than population growth. The population of Kuala Lumpur increased at the rate of 7 per cent per annum between 1947 and 1970, as against the national average of 3 per cent; that of Bangkok at a rate twice the average for Thailand as a whole between 1947 and 1960.[2]

Exacerbating this is the tendency for urbanisation to concentrate on a single 'primate city' — Bangkok, for example, is more than six times larger than Thailand's next largest city. Such growth rates give rise to complex urban problems: housing and transportation difficulties, shortages of essential services such as water and sewerage, spiralling land prices and many social dislocations. And the relative wealth of the cities attracts consumer-oriented industries and a disproportionate share of the country's professionally trained personnel (in Bangkok the ratio of doctors to patients is ten times higher than the Thai average, and much the same is true of Manila), leading to a widening gap between a stagnating or slowly developing countryside and the ostentatious and precariously based wealth of a handful of cities. This growing divergence between the rural and urban sectors of society is an important factor in the political stability of ASEAN nations.

Political Change

Liberal democracy on the Western model is not a characteristic of today's ASEAN societies. Though the formal institutions of government resemble Western structures, largely because they were inherited colonial legacies, the actual style of government, reflecting deeper social traditions, is authoritarian, ranging from paternalism to outright military rule. Indonesia and Thailand are run by generals, and the Philippines in January 1981 ended eight years and four months of martial law, without significantly diluting the powers of the president. Singapore is effectively a one-party state with the interface between the bureaucracy and the ruling party barely distinguishable. And Malaysia is run by a coalition of political parties each exercising paternalistic control over its own communal constituency and resolving problems at the top.

Political articulation by the masses – which in every case except Singapore are rural-based – is rudimentary and closely controlled by government. The historically agricultural and colonial structures of the member nations resulted in a bifurcated class structure immediately after independence: the mass of the traditional peasantry on one hand, and the landed, semi-feudal élites and small corps of urban professionals and bureaucrats on the other. But with the growth of cities, political power revolves around the relatively small urban middle class of entrepreneurs and bureaucrat–capitalists, which had barely existed fifty years ago. Nowhere is this clearer than in Thailand where, as seen above, the dichotomy between town and country has become so deep that governments can fall due to urban unrest over issues which do not touch the bulk of the peasantry.

If this phenomenon of class differentiation is indeed occurring, and if the 'capitalisation of ASEAN' is rapidly proceeding, it may mean that the ideology of traditional national liberation movements, operating largely in the jungles and attempting to overthrow supposedly feudal structures, is no longer as relevant as it was before or immediately after independence. The Maoist strategy of encircling the towns and establishing liberated sectors in the remote rural areas applies only to certain parts of ASEAN countries which have historically been isolated from the general economic growth, and experienced political, cultural and economic discrimination from the centre. Thus the Communist Party of Thailand (CPT) still maintains its hold over the most depressed parts of northeast Thailand, and the Muslim separatist movements in southern Thailand and southern Philippines are religious—cultural wars as much as political. But the CPT is now considering the need to intensify its urban organising and agitation, while in the Philippines – the ASEAN country with the earliest industrial experience – urban guerrilla activity has now begun in Manila, apparently led not by the New People's Army (NPA) which has operated in depressed provinces, but by amalgams of groups opposed to the regime.

There is no doubt that the massive demographic shift in post-war years from the farms to the cities has considerably changed the *loci* of political power. True, there has been class transformation in the rural sector also, with the rapid commercialisation of agriculture into export agribusiness and the displacement of farmers from their lands. But the pace of social change has been greatest in the cities. For example, the rural Thailand, Indonesia and Philippines of fifty years ago are still recognisable today, but Bangkok, Manila or Jakarta are no longer even a shadow of what they were, transformed beyond belief by the forces of migration and export-oriented growth.

Because of a greater proportion of urban and rural poor in universities and high schools than ever before, due to improving educational opportunities, students now provide potentially important linkages between town and country, peasant and worker, traditionalism and modernism, though they are constrained from expressing their views in direct action. With many coming from poor backgrounds, their sense of social consciousness has been growing: witness the role of Thai students in the 1973 ouster of the Thanom–Praphat regime and subsequently in the 1973–6 democratic interregnum; Malaysian students in the 1973 Baling riots in northern Malaysia; students in all the countries visited by Japanese Prime Minister Tanaka in 1974; Indonesian and Philippine students today in criticising the New Order and New Society, and calling for their end.

Among many of the youth – who comprise over half of the total population in ASEAN – the Chinese and Vietnamese paths to development may contain lessons, but are no longer paragons of development. Non-Marxist challenges to the established order are emerging within ASEAN, sometimes led by the activist Christian groups, other times by fundamentalist Muslim groups inspired by the Islamic resurgence. They still rage against foreign investment and multinational corporations, against dictatorship and the absence of human rights, but their leadership is not coming from the communist parties, nor are they simply communist fronts. By labelling them as such, ASEAN governments may be hastening the process of polarisation.

Political Legitimacy

The recent turmoil in South Korea sent tremors down a political fault-line running along the Asian rim of the Pacific Basin. Even if the repercussions are not about to be felt today or tomorrow, the same pent-up forces which produced the Kwangju insurrection of 1980 could emerge in other authoritarian, rapidly developing countries. More than Japan, South Korea was the model for the newly industrialising countries of ASEAN to emulate. Many of these countries watched with envy as the Korean economy took off on export-oriented industrialisation propped up by massive international borrowings and investment, American military support and no-nonsense, stony-faced Korean generals. These same countries must now anxiously watch Korea's internal turmoil, question the rationale of 'development authoritarianism' and wonder if much the same fate awaits them.

ASEAN countries share some common development patterns with Korea and, even more importantly, they suffer the same effects of a trade-off between rapid capital accumulation and political liberalisation. The forced-march pace towards economic growth in South Korea (and to some extent Hong Kong and Taiwan) produced Asia's economic 'miracles' — but also widened income gaps and produced social dislocations to which the political leadership responded by suppressing dissent. Governments extolling the material benefits of economic growth have not been able to gloss over the lack of civil liberties and popular participation in national life — even though authoritarian leaders insist that the 'masses' are not concerned with abstract concepts of democracy and that Western models are not relevant to their societies.

In the Philippines, Thailand, and Indonesia the panacea of material improvements is not substantial enough to compensate for authoritarianism. Unbalanced growth has created a conspicuously widening gap between élites and masses. What are seen by their critics as flagrant corruption, militaristic forms of social control, excessive reliance on and cosiness towards foreign investment and multi-national corporations, have not endeared these regimes to the national bourgeoisie, students or intellectuals. The peasant population, though largely quiescent, has seen real living standards decline.

Some ASEAN leaderships have a degree of popular support: others retain their hold on legitimacy by suppressing dissent under wide definitions of subversion. The case of Indonesia provides an example.

Fourteen years after President Suharto brought in Indonesia's New Order, economic development has been at best patchy; at worst, regressive and inequitable. The military's continuing involvement in politics and the fundamental assumption that development will lead to stability and shared prosperity is being challenged from various quarters. Increasingly vocal criticisms of Suharto and his regime have come not only from the students or extremist religious groups, but also from within the élite.

A recent demonstration of this opposition was the statement of concern delivered to Parliament by former government and military leaders in mid-1980. The 'Petition of 50' was highly critical of Suharto's two controversial speeches in March and April 1980 dealing with the duty of the armed forces to choose sides in supporting the state ideology, *Pancasila.* It was Suharto's assertion that the government and himself better personified Pancasila than any other political party or group, and that the army could legitimately manipulate the constitutional process to protect Suharto's definition of Pancasila, which triggered the outbursts of protest.

When it came to power, the Suharto regime was a coalition of five major forces: the military élite; the devout Islamic community, both urban and rural; the Protestant and Catholic minorities; the small indigenous entrepreneurial, professional and bureaucratic middle class; and a Westernised intelligentsia. The government's political base has shrunk since then, and the regime's legitimacy is being openly challenged by some of its erstwhile supporters. But there is no agreement about a successor — a situation which Suharto has fostered.

The failure of the opposition to forge a working alliance — as in the Philippines — has been an important factor in Suharto's and Marco's continuing rule. In the case of Indonesia, the Muslims have one vision of the sort of state Indonesia should become, but they are split between modernists and traditionalists. The secular nationalists have their own, quite different views. The Western-oriented liberals, though they join with Muslims and nationalists in their condemnation of the New Order's excesses, tend to be suspicious not only of Islam but of the inward-looking attitudes of old-style nationalists.

Under the New Order, 'guided democracy' gave way to 'developmental authoritarianism'. As Suharto pushed ahead destroying all vestiges of Sukarno's legacy, Parliament became a rubber stamp. Today, there are signs that elements in the ruling circle are beginning to feel unease over the direction of the government, and the danger of keeping the lid closed on accumulating pressures. The same people who emasculated political parties in the late 1960s are toying with the idea of relaxing the political system. This re-think is motivated mainly by a desire to ensure the continued stability of the regime and control over the political processes.

It is, after all, in the sitting-rooms of the middle class and the *nouveaux riches* that Suharto and his family are disparaged. It is a dilemma which also afflicts the Thai and Philippine leadership. These governments depend for immediate support on their armies, but their claims to legitimacy rest on support from the wealthy and middle classes. Loss of support from these élites could lead to a general erosion of legitimacy and serve as a catalyst for a snowballing movement of discontent which, if it reached the urban and rural poor, would be difficult to halt.

There is no Indonesian, Thai or Philippine version of Ayatollah Khomeini, capable of forging a united front between unlikely political allies. As for the Philippines, Benigno Aquino remains a populist figure, perhaps as symbolic of the resistance movement as Kim Dae Jung was to South Korea, but definitely without the messianic aura and unquestioning loyalty which Khomeini mustered around himself. In none of the three countries do the likely contenders for power seem capable of putting forward credible programmes for reform. Their concentration is more on how to take over power than on what to do when they have it.

The Military Élites

The role of the military is an important element in the political life of the ASEAN countries. Generals have often intervened in the political arena and stayed there for good. This is certainly the case in Thailand and Indonesia — and potentially in the Philippines, where the military found a political role as the pillar of President Marcos's martial law regime, and even with martial law formally ended, could move in quickly to fill the vacuum should anything untoward happen to Marcos.

Power does come from the barrel of a gun in Indonesia and Thailand, where ex-generals with military backing rule as heads of government. In Singapore and Malaysia, the socio-political roles of the military have been strictly circumscribed; but soldiers in the other ASEAN countries do not simply command ships and planes, pursue insurgents and play war games. They are supposed to be important agents of modernisation, bringing new values of discipline, organisation, efficiency and technical knowledge to tradition-bound societies.

Yet growth and democratisation and, with them, the essence of modernity, could remain blocked by a conservative, defensive and entrenched military élite. It is not generally remembered now that even Malaysia neared the brink of military intervention during the 13 May 1969 racial riots, and that it was averted only because the civilian government managed to establish order.

Indonesia's fourteen-year-old New Order is a military order. Ever since the 1965 attempted *coup* which triggered a massive military retaliation against, and purge of, the PKI, and opened the way for an eventual military takeover, the sprawling archipelago of 140 million people has been run like an army encampment.

The Indonesian armed forces, with 300,000 men in the army, 70,000 in the navy and 40,000 in the air force,[3] have since emerged as a distinct ruling élite, controlling all the essential governmental organs and state-owned enterprises. Military involvement in almost every facet of public life has been explicitly legitimised by the *dwi fungsi* (dual function) concept, which states that the military's role is not simply to protect the nation in wartime, but also to undertake a nation-building task.

The president is a retired four-star general, and so too is the Speaker of the national Parliament. The president-director of Pertamina (the state oil company), the chief of Bulog (the national logistics board) and the head of Golkar (the government-sponsored mass political movement) are all two-star generals. Even where civilians serve as ministers — and there are fourteen civilians in the 24-man inner cabinet — there are numerous generals, admirals and air marshalls to fill the key watchdog positions in the administration. Overall, about a third of the Indonesian army is reported to be engaged in civil and administrative duties.

The Indonesian military has not been able to pull off an 'economic miracle', partly because the military's self-defined role has been indiscriminately broad, leading to insufficient use of the technocratic élite and often producing less than ideal economic results, such as Pertamina's multi-million-dollar débâcle in 1975.

In the face of corruption, inefficiency and red tape, the military government cannot really justify its political supremacy on the grounds of better management or other technical skills. Rather, the common argument is that in a society as geographically dispersed and culturally disparate as Indonesia's, only the military has the authority, the cohesion and the coercive resources to keep the country together. There is certainly no other institution powerful or cohesive enough to govern the country.

Like Indonesia, Thailand is run by generals, who are also strongly anti-communist and American-trained. But these two characteristics, shared by several of the ASEAN countries' armed forces, do not, of themselves, guarantee identical results. The Thai military's role in politics, the economy and bureaucracy is less entrenched and all-powerful than in Indonesia.

The civilian—military dichotomy dates back to the days of King Trailok in the fifteenth century, who established parallel military and civil administrative structures, each headed by its prime minister. This dualism persisted until King Chulalongkorn abolished it in the late nineteenth century, though its legacies can be felt even today.

Even the 1932 'revolution' against absolute monarchy was split from the very start between the civilian and military factions. Since the mid-1950s, except for some short-lived democratic interregnums, the army has ruled supreme.

The dynamics of clique politics within the bureaucracy — dominated by military men — have not changed since the 1950s. The result is that development has become tangled in a bureaucratic morass which is hardly rational or efficient, but which reflects the complex patron—client networks in Thai military politics.

Development plans and bureaucratic agencies exist on paper, but in reality have little relevance to the needs of the country. As the 1978 World Bank report put it: 'There is little evidence that Thailand's development plans systematically guide or govern the activities of government affairs'.

Much of the blame must go to the military's continuing use of the bureaucracy as a playing-field on which to scramble for spoils.

On a broader level, one of the main criticisms of military-sponsored development plans was their failure to stimulate political participation, a factor which has retarded modernisation and exacerbated the gap between rich and poor.

But there are signs that the military may be modernising its own relationship to the political system. Thailand — one of the most *coup*-prone and military-controlled countries in Asia — in March 1980 witnessed as unprecedented, voluntary change of power from one general to another in line with popular will (though with considerable backroom politicking by various military factions). If this signifies, rather than an anomaly, the maturing of the military's political role, it may augur well for Thailand's modernisation. Prem's extension beyond his expected retirement as commander-in-chief of the Thai armed forces may, however, be the cause of further politicking.

Before they were catapulted to prominence as pillars of the martial law regime, the military in the Philippines remained in the relative detachment accorded them by an administration on the American model, insulated from life outside the barracks, and firmly under civilian control. Their orientation was basically professional, but since President Marcos brought them into the political arena, they have become politicised agents of the martial law government. With their new role under the Marcos government, officers have taken courses in business management, apparently in preparation for a shift from active military life to corporate concerns.

In many remote, insurgent-ridden areas, the army is the most palpable symbol of martial law, with almost unrestricted powers. Military abuses have created resentment among the rural populace, while for many soldiers the prospect of being embroiled in a no-win Vietnam-type war against fellow Filipinos, whether Muslim separatists or communist insurgents, is unattractive.

A secret organisation composed of young military officers from the Philippine Military Academy (PMA) surfaced during the 1978 national elections for representatives to the Interim Batasang Pambansa (National Assembly — IBP). They called for political reforms within the military, and for ridding the service of 'dirty generals'. These Young Turks, who say they subscribe to their PMA ideals, are now questioning their roles under the martial law government — whether as guardians of the republic and the Filipino people or as mere tools of a martial law dictatorship.

While Indonesian and Thai generals are active businessmen and politicians and the Philippine army upholds a controversial martial regime, the Malaysian and Singaporean officers are clearly told to stay in the officers' mess. Nevertheless, a common thread runs through the military in ASEAN as it does in other societies: it is a channel for upward mobility for poor youths, and provides management training and a modern outlook for a new, cohesive élite in some traditional societies. This trend has been reinforced by variants of youth training, national service and conscription adopted by all five ASEAN countries.

The Singapore Armed Forces' major non-defence role is in socialising a generation of multi-racial youths without a single national identity into a cohesive body. But as the rest of the society is already modern and totally urban, the military's role in providing management skills is negligible.

Across the causeway, the Malaysian army remains largely a Malay one, and thus it has not played any role in racial integration. On the other hand, any attempt by the army to play a political role has always been quickly slapped down. After the race riots of 1969, when there were allegations of Malay commanders showing racial prejudice, the government transferred officers or promoted them away from their posts. Ever since independence, Malaysia's civilian politicians have kept the army on a short leash, rotating generals on short terms of duty, and never allowing military commanders to make public statements without clearance from the civilian minister. No army officer has ever held political office.

The Rural Dilemma

Stark contrasts of rural development can be found between

the ASEAN countries and within them. Modern plantations with the latest technology coexist with tiny subsistence plots. Chemists, engineers, soil scientists and veterinarians bring their science to the labs of large-scale fruit and livestock enterprises, while for millions of rice farmers and other small-holders, access to credit, fertilisers, pesticides and other extension services remain election-year promises. Malnutrition and vitamin deficiency are evident even in areas which export fruit, vegetables and meat.

Overall, the region is a picture of progress and poverty intermixed. Much of this dualism is rooted in colonial heritages. The alien crops — sugar, rubber, maize and others which found their way via planters into the ASEAN countries — developed deep roots and are today essential contributors to the national economies.

ASEAN produces 85 per cent of the world's rubber, and possesses the largest reserves of tropical hardwoods. Malaysia is the world's largest producer of palm oil products, while the Philippines claims the production record for coconut oil and its by-products. The agricultural export sector — including both plantations and smallholders — is the largest employer in the region.

After independence, the ASEAN countries had little choice — or inclination, with world demand for its products high — but to continue along the agricultural export path. Starting from necessity, the export drive soon became a creed. As terms of trade for agricultural goods deteriorated, countries turned to crop diversification: Malaysia to palm oil to offset its dependence on natural rubber; Thailand to tapioca as rice exports dwindled; and the Philippines to pine-apples, bananas and other fruits, especially after the sugar market collapsed in 1976. With potential for processing into higher value-added finished goods, ASEAN's agricultural exports played an important role in boosting foreign-exchange earnings.

But while agricultural commodities were more lucrative than staple crops, and made agribusiness a major source of foreign investment, their dazzling performance obscured the fact that cash cropping did not alleviate, and in some cases worsened, the plight of the rural poor, many of whom became landless labourers. With national statistics showing steady agricultural growth, the urgency of land reform and the plight of the growing landless class were swept under the carpet.

Land reform legislation has relieved some agrarian discontent but is so riddled with loopholes and exemptions that no substantive land redistribution has taken place. In the Philippines, a 'radical' land reform programme has been whittled down to cover one-third of the original land area. Thailand's 'comprehensive land reform' programme, which includes outlays for village development, is hamstrung by funding problems. Indonesia has had land reform legislation since Sukarno's time, but it has been 'frozen' for security reasons.

Even more important than land reform legislation to protect tenants is the growing problem of landless labourers. Population pressures coupled with a diminishing land availability have pushed the man/land ratio downwards, to the half-hectare level in some countries. Continuing fragmention of land among small farmers on one hand, and concentration of land-ownership by plantations or wealthy land-owners on the other, have aggravated the problem. Forest land has been laid waste by slash-and-burn squatters and by logging profiteers. Erosion and siltation further exacerbate rural hardships.

In 1973, according to the International Labour Organisation (ILO), almost half of Java's rural households were virtually landless. These 30 million people did not even include the smallholders and tenants who 'have been reduced to *de facto* landless labourers through the modernisation of rice production'. There is not enough land for even subsistence farming for three-quarters of rural Java's population and the result is, the ILO says, 'a poor and worsening standard of nutrition'.[4]

In the Philippines, the corporate farming programme alone – designed to boost rice production – has pushed out 20,000 families from 70,000 hectares of farmland. Landless migrants account for up to one-third of the populations of Manila, Cebu and Davao, the three largest cities.

Virtually non-existent twenty years ago, Thailand's landless rural labourers now comprise 30 per cent of all households – almost double the urban population. Today, it is the fastest expanding income group – but with nowhere to go.

Malaysia's Felda (Federal Land Development Authority) settlement schemes cannot supply land to even half the annual increment of landless farmers, not to mention the existing backlog of 400,000 land-hungry peasants.

This looming problem for ASEAN in the coming decade of population pressure on land is not lightened by forecasts of massive food deficits. In 1972, the region was a net exporter of foodgrains, largely because of rice exports from Thailand. But by 1985 Thai rice exports will have dropped to less than half the 1972 level, while Indonesia's food deficit will have jumped six-fold. The Philippines was claimed to have a rice surplus for export since 1978, but that appears to be calculated on what it will earn in foreign exchange, compared to what poor Filipinos are able to pay for it.

At present the rural landless are an amorphous lot, unorganised and unaware of their potential weight. Attempts to organise the landless are seen as subversive to national security unless, as in the Philippines, the organisation is carried out through a government network.

The Development Spectrum

Of all developing sub-regions in Asia, and possibly even in the Third World in general, the ASEAN countries possess perhaps the greatest potential for rapid economic growth. Indonesia apart, the other countries have gone through, and by now largely abandoned, the import-substitution phase of light industries which characterised initial development efforts, and are now moving into medium and heavy industries. Singapore, of course, remains the anomaly; its role was defined early in its development history as that of an off-shore manufacturing and service centre for multinational companies, and in that somewhat limited role it has excelled. With no hinterland, natural resources or a large domestic market, it had few alternatives. And so Singapore has already distanced itself from the problems afflicting most of its neighbours, and has achieved standards of living and *per capita* GNP which will soon put it out of the ranks of developing nations. In comparative studies of ASEAN development, Singapore must continue to be the constant exception.

Singapore, aware of the advantages of international identity and preferential arrangements which its membership of ASEAN provides, is prepared to play down the differences between it and the other four members. As deliberate government moves to raise wage levels eliminate the labour-intensive industries in which Singapore's efficiency threatened its neighbours, Singapore is moving away from competition towards a more acceptable role of a services centre for the ASEAN region.

Singapore stands to gain from peace, stability and economic progress in ASEAN, in terms of support for its own identity as a commercial and financial centre, and as a recipient of investment and technology. It has been among the most vociferous of ASEAN countries in denouncing the Soviet influence in Southeast Asia as detrimental to the political, social and cultural systems of the ASEAN countries. It has seen its own prosperity as depending on theirs to a large extent, and its ideological outlook as compatible. As Foreign Minister S. Rajaratnam put it in 1979: 'The more real our regionalism becomes, the more solid become our political and economic defence lines.'[5]

Thus for Singapore, with no significant rural hinterland, the collective problems of ASEAN development are in a sense its own.

For the other ASEAN nations, possibly excepting Malaysia, economic development and the alleviation of poverty remain urgent priorities amid the promises of rapid growth. For if the social and economic imbalances in these societies worsen, there will arise an economic phenomenon which fast-growing Latin American nations have experienced, in which as one cynical observer has said of Brazil: 'the economy is doing great, but the people are not'.

The following four country case studies highlight some of the underlying problems facing ASEAN countries. By no means comprehensive or exhaustive, they are glimpses into the complex ASEAN reality.

THAILAND

For the past two decades, Western scholars have characterised Thai rural society as a 'loosely-structured social system' without social tensions or feudal heritages, and politicians claimed that the Thai farmer's love for nation, monarch and Buddhism could not be shaken. However, despite the tenacious reluctance of stereotypes to die, the image of the happy Thai farmer living in the rice bowl of Asia is no longer sustainable.

The majority of rain-fed subsistence rice farmers in the north and northeast, and to a lesser extent in the south, were left out of the economic boom of the 1960s. Their real incomes have either stagnated or declined in the past fifteen years. One-third of agricultural households — nine million people — are living in absolute poverty, and many millions more are barely above that line, while other income groups have grown very rich.[6]

Not only have successive governments been inactive in alleviating poverty but, according to a World Bank report, 'public sector activities tend to contribute to, rather than help reduce, welfare disparity among the country's population. In recent years it has become increasingly difficult to discern a sense of direction and purpose in public sector behaviour that is in any way comparable to its stated intentions and objectives.'[7]

The change in government in 1980 from General Kriangsak Chamanand to General Prem Tinsulanond was supposed to herald a new period of dynamic problem-solving, especially regarding long-delayed economic questions. But Boonchu Rojanasatien — the 'economic czar' of the new government — has proved unable to revitalise the bureaucracy, which now seems to exist in a world of its own. Unpopular but necessary decisions are stalled in political wrangling.

For over a decade, Thailand's economy has experienced an artificial boom, due mainly to American military spending which accounted for half the growth of gross national product in the 1960s.

Bangkok was transformed from a pleasant canal-lined capital into a sprawling 'primate' city (a metropolis amid underdevelopment) six times larger than the next largest city. Rural migrants flocked to run the massage parlours, taxis, tailors' shops and myriad other services catering for the Americans and the Thai *nouveaux riches,* so that by the 1970s one-third of Bangkok's 4.5 million people and up to half in other towns were made up of these migrants. And, as the price of 'modernisation', in 1973 there were estimated to be 400,000 drug addicts, 300,000 prostitutes, and 55,000 children under five who died of malnutrition.[8]

Less sensational but more problematic is the future of agriculture, which is still the cornerstone of the economy, though its share of the gross domestic product declined from 40 per cent in 1960 to 30 per cent in 1979.[9] Nearly three-quarters of all exports are agricultural products, and two-thirds of the labour force is in the rural sector. Much manufacturing activity depends on the processing of agricultural products, and rural household demand is a vital factor for consumer industries. The collection of primary commodities and distribution of consumer goods also account for a large part of the services sector.

Agricultural growth in the past two decades was on the momentum of two forces: the expansion of cultivated areas for rice, which almost doubled in the period, and the diversification of central farmers into cash crops such as tapioca, sugar and maize. In the provinces to the east and west of the alluvial Central Plains, more than half the farming households have abandoned rice growing for the more profitable cash crops. This was possible only because of the concentration of irrigation, transport and marketing infrastructures in provinces near Bangkok.

As a result, about 2.5 million farmers — 10 per cent of the national total — have doubled their real income since 1960 and earn twice the national average rural income, though in the process many have become tenants on land owned by urban investors.[10]

Cash cropping has also spread from the Central Plains to the lower fringes of the north and northeast, but no further. The major non-rice upland crop in the lower northeast is *kenaf* (jute), and in the mid-northeast tapioca cultivation has been adopted by more than half the farmers.

This has been the main source of the near doubling of their average real incomes since 1960, to a level about 45 per cent above the earnings of a farmer in the upper northeast, where the public services and infrastructure necessary for crop diversification are meagre. The lower north is now one of the major maize-producing regions in Thailand, resulting in a 75 per cent income rise for these cash croppers, so that they now enjoy real incomes about 20 per cent higher than the national rural average.

How the other half lives and farms, however, is another story. Literally half the population of the north and north-east — about 7 million people — have not been able to diversify at all, and continue to grow rice under rain-fed conditions, as did their forebears. Out of these, 40 per cent have holdings not large enough to produce even a small surplus, and have thus hardly benefited at all from the economic change over the past two decades.

In the rubber- and rice-producing south, holding sizes have changed only slightly, rice yields have stagnated, rubber yields are still extremely low, and upland areas remain under-utilised and badly managed. The Muslim provinces in the lower south are particularly economically depressed and the average real incomes of the farmers here are 25 per cent below the national rural average, and 65 per cent below that of the maize-producing provinces of the central region.[11]

The stagnation of real wages since the 1960s is not only in the countryside but also in the towns. The government has only recently legislated a minimum wage law, and, without non-market intervention, excess supply continually kept wages down. After declining in the 1960s owing to the economic boom, the incidence of urban poverty in the 1970s has remained unchanged at about 9–13 per cent.[12]

The impact has been political. In the 1973 riots against the Thanom regime, many obviously non-student youths, together with some vocational school students (who, unlike university students, also came from poor backgrounds) were at the forefront of the car-burnings, rock-throwings and other assaults against property. These same youths — unemployed, disenchanted with all authority — then became the recruits for the Red Gaurs, a paramilitary vigilante group organised covertly by members of the Internal Security Operations Command to disrupt student and labour rallies.

Since the military takeover in 1976, Thailand's new leaders seem to have realised the dangers of a pool of unemployed youths whose only ideology is that of frustration and disenchantment. As members of Red Gaurs or other rightist groups in the 1970s, they were instrumental in creating the general crisis which brought Tanin Kraivixien to power. However, their subsequent disenchantment with Tanin was utilised by his opponents to bring about his downfall.

Having tasted some measure of direct political power and violence in recent years, and ideologically capable of turning in either direction, this politically volatile underclass is unlikely to remain quiescent for long — martial law notwithstanding — unless the present regime can reverse a pernicious trend which the World Bank points to: 'There is little doubt that many households with capital or high level of education have benefited greatly, and in a few families great wealth has been accumulated'.[13]

Interest groups have never really existed in Thai politics, and in the vacuum a small coterie of soldier–politician cliques and their business clients determine economic policy on the principle of mutual back-scratching. The result is that public policy tends to be shaped by the interests of small, usually urban-based higher-income groups, rather than the declared social and economic priorities of the nation.

MALAYSIA

The 1980 World Development Report of the World Bank divided the Third World into the oil exporters and importers, with the former poised to grow faster than any other economies in the world. Indonesia and Malaysia are the only two energy exporters in Southeast Asia. Indonesia, already a member of OPEC, is saddled with enormous problems of poverty and population intertwined, with oil and gas as the only lifeline to keep the economy from becoming a South

Asian 'basket case'. Singapore, without its own oil, profits from refining petroleum for the region. The Philippines and Thailand struggle to develop alternative energy sources to make up for their almost total lack of oil. In Malaysia, however, oil and gas are the latest windfall to bless an economy which already ranks as the healthiest in ASEAN, apart from Singapore.

The reason that Malaysia is one of the largest holders of Japanese bonds, among other foreign assets, is that petroleum and gas revenues have grown faster than the country can absorb them. So Petronas keeps over half its M$4 billion annual revenue off-shore. But before too many years, Petronas will need every cent it possesses to finance its development programme and the planned petro-chemical industry.

The government now has so much money that it can boost public spending by 73 per cent above original Third Malaysia Plan (1976–80) estimates in order to reach the target of 8.4 per cent annual growth in gross domestic product. At the same time, the oil windfall will enable the expected debt servicing ratio to be halved, and foreign reserves to be doubled. Through disguised investment by the government, Malaysia now has the unique distinction of a 'private sector' dominated more by disguised public investment than by genuine private investors. As well, since Malaysia's oil and gas reserves are finite, the country is under the same dual pressure as all oil-producing countries: to discover more and to use oil revenues to develop alternative industries. Socio-economic objectives of the Third Plan, however, have lagged behind, with low-cost housing, for example, far behind construction targets. Regional income disparities are also increasing, with development efforts tending to drift towards those states best equipped to absorb them. Agricultural growth has been sluggish, and production growth for rubber, rice and palm oil have fallen below targets set in the Third Malaysia Plan.

A 'wealth-restructuring' programme of the New Economy Policy (NEP) was launched in the aftermath of the 1969 racial riots. The NEP's target for 1990 is to 'eradicate poverty irrespective of race', to redistribute national wealth, and to overcome the identification of race with certain occupations.

As a result, the officially encouraged – and subsidised – programme of greater *bumiputra* (sons of the soil) ownership of business equity has grown rapidly. The income growth of rural Malays, however has proceeded at a snail's pace compared with urban *bumiputra* share acquisitions.

In the past – and to a certain extent in the present – the problem was in selling the goals of the NEP's restructuring programme to those interests that felt most threatened. Fears that 'Ah Hing will be robbed to pay Ahmad' still exist among many Chinese investors, but there seems to be more confidence now that *bumiputra* share acquisition will not be through large-scale purchases of existing share capital.

The NEP has led to Malay quasi-state capitalism, through designated *bumiputra* institutions such as Pernas and MARA, banks and agencies owned by the federal or state governments. These organisations have been holding and acquiring share capital in trust for the entire Malay community, and are supposed to invest in projects which will benefit the poor Malays. In turn, shares of these institutions and other profitable corporations will be held by a national trust fund, Permodalan Nasional, which is still in the making. Discussed for many years, Permodalan is to be established in the Fourth Plan, as an enormous unit trust for *bumiputras,* with substantial investments in virtually every blue-chip Malaysian company. Whether it will be more successful than the many other government instrumentalities set up for similar purposes remains to be seen.

Not only in the proposed Permodalan, but in a wide array of *bumiputra* institutions and corporations set up to manage and utilise the newly acquired Malay wealth, a new breed of Malay bureaucrat–capitalists will emerge, handling the enormous funds that have been entrusted to them by, theoretically, the entire Malay community. The temptations and opportunities for personal aggrandisement and political abuse will be ever present, as recent scandals – especially the Bank Rakyat case which involved a powerful politician – have already shown.

This may well become the new Malay dilemma – how to manage and distribute the fruits of restructured national wealth among the entire Malay community, without at the same time fostering the rise of a new Malay élite and deepening class cleavages in the community. There are already signs of Malay class formation, an inevitable result of uneven economic growth. While extremes of wealth and poverty may persist, however, the prospects for growth of a broadly based middle class are better in Malaysia than in most other ASEAN countries.

Other infrastructure developments linking highly urbanised (and Chinese) Penang to largely rural and Malay Kedah, or better east—west routes linking the backward east coast to the Malaysian economic centres on the west, will inevitably spur the migration of Malays from the farms to the cities. It will alter the racial composition of the urban centres and therefore affect the configuration of political power, as well as creating economic and racial tensions.

Even as the Malaysian city changes with migration, the countryside remains an obstacle to rapid and equitable development. The MUDA irrigation scheme in northwest Malaysia brought the benefits of the Green Revolution to previously impoverished paddy farmers. With a price tag of US $180 million, the MUDA scheme is the government's main showpiece of rural development. And it has reaped results: three-quarters of the country's paddy farmers live below the official poverty line, compared with one-third for MUDA households.

Though small in numbers compared with the rice-farming peasantry in other ASEAN countries, Malaysia's paddy farmers are extremely important to the political élites. Their loyalties have been hotly contended for by the ruling and opposition Malay parties. The political volatility of the Malay peasantry has been shown in recent events; in early 1980 angry rice farmers in Kedah rioted over an apparently harmless scheme which changed their traditional rice subsidies from cash payments to a savings scheme. The government was stunned, and there were grim warnings that subversive elements were inciting the farmers.

Anxiety about falling real incomes was the main cause of protest. Official figures show that in real terms, a paddy farmer today earns 20—25 per cent less than he did five years ago. Inflation and scarcity have pushed up the cost of labour, harvesting machinery and fuel, while productivity gains have not kept up with often 60–100 per cent rises in the cost of inputs.

Paddy is not alone in its problems. Five years ago plummeting rubber prices, which fell 300 per cent in under a year, led to even greater protest marches in Baling, another district in the generally poor state of Kedah. Subsequently Malaysia campaigned for – and got – an international natural rubber agreement to stabilise the price of rubber and hence the incomes of smallholders.

Agriculture accounts for a quarter of GDP, nearly half of total employment and 42 per cent of total merchandise exports in 1979. But with the majority of the population dependent upon fluctuating commodity prices, the potential exists for unrest in other agricultural sectors. Palm oil smallholders have been lucky with very high prices in the past few years, and much rubber land has been replanted with oil palm. But prices started dropping by 20 per cent in the middle of 1980, and further price erosions could directly worsen the standard of living – an ominous situation in a society where expectations are rising.

The new policy will have to deal with some pressing problems. Anti-poverty measures have concentrated on rubber, oil palm and coconut smallholders, whose cash crops have benefited from the various smallholders' marketing, processing and credit co-operatives. But, as in other developing nations of Asia, the plight of the rice farmers, fishermen, and agricultural labourers has worsened – the MUDA showcase project notwithstanding. They account for around a third of Malaysia's poor households. It is to pre-empt any potential rural dissatisfaction with this state of affairs, as much as to stimulate agriculture from its malaise, that a 'new agricultural policy' will be incorporated in the next plan, due in 1981.

PHILIPPINES

In 1979 the Nobel-prizewinning economist Gunnar Myrdal said that the Philippines could become 'another Iran anytime'.

In 1980 a Wall Street research firm, First and Sullivan Inc., predicted that 'It is very unlikely that the Marcos regime will survive the next five years. . . a nationalistic leftist regime, an extensive civil war, and a repressive military regime are real possibilities.'[14] A recent World Bank study described Marcos's position as becoming increasingly 'precarious'.[15]

Predictions of this sort have become commonplace, almost fashionable. But it is difficult to gauge precisely the degree of political disaffection beneath the orderly veneer applied to the country during eight years of martial law. Prophets of the impending revolution have been vocal for the past decade, and yet despite the continuing insurgencies led by the Communist Party and the Muslim secessionists, Marcos has managed to hold onto power. In abandoning martial law in January 1981, he has at one stroke met the demands of his opponents and the wishes of the White House and the Vatican, without relinquishing his own power in any way.

Despite their attempts to coalesce into one united front in mid-1980, the 'legitimate' opposition groups led by 'Old Society' rivals to Marcos have not presented much of a challenge. The opposition cause was kept alight for eight years by the detention of ex-Senator Benigno Aquino, who would have been Marcos's principal rival for the presidency if martial law had not been declared. But Aquino was released in 1980 and went into exile — after an elaborate charade, designed to save faces on both sides. It is difficult to evaluate his recent claims that the Philippines is facing a 'gathering of storms' and a final confrontation with the Marcos system. Aquino has prophesied massive urban guerrilla warfare 'more vicious and more destructive than the country experienced during the 1950s', which would be fuelled by an escalation of rural insurgency and disenchanted idealistic youth.[16]

Aquino claimed knowledge of plans by urban guerrillas to destabilise the Marcos regime — including bombings, kidnappings, and assassinations. He disclosed no further details or evidence, but if the warnings are well-based, they would portend a new phase of armed resistance in the Philippines.

The radicalisation of erstwhile liberal groups has begun, though it may not represent a trend. The *Nagkakaisang Partidong Demokratiko at Sosyalista ng Philipinas* (United Demo-

cratic and Socialist Party of the Philippines — NPDSP), revealed in September 1979, is a loose organisation of socialist
and nationalist democrats which claims to have an armed
group called the *Sandigan ng Bayan* operating in limited areas
in Mindanao and Luzon. Late in 1980, bombs exploded in
government offices in Manila and in a department store
owned by Mrs Marcos. They may have been the work of new
armed groups not under the control of either the NPA or
MNLF.

While new militancy was displayed by students and
workers in a series of demonstrations in Manila and some of
its universities from mid-1980 onwards, the demonstrations
have yet to approach the scale of those of the early 1970s.
Yet the possibility that students will become more daring in
their open protests and more militant in their defiance of
martial law cannot be underrated — a mistake made by the
Thai military regime in 1973, when student demonstrations
snowballed into an overthrow of the government.

Even more significant, if warfare begins and is not quickly
squashed, there is a possibility that it could spill over from
the Philippines to herald a new phase of political change and
turmoil in the region, a kind of Latin Americanisation of
ASEAN, marked by increasing polarisation of social forces,
immobilisation of the political centre, and growing erosion of
the legitimacy of established political institutions.

Islamic fundamentalism in Malaysia and Indonesia has
both politically conservative and radical connections, and the
Buddhist Sangha in Thailand, despite signs of politicication in
the mid-1970s, remains neutral. But the Roman Catholic
Church in the Philippines has been in the forefront of social
criticism. In particular, the situation in the southern Philippines, racked by both Muslim and communist insurgencies,
and beset with economic problems, promises further radicalisation of the clergy. The Mindanao—Sulu Pastoral Conference (MSPC) has been one of the most militant voices within
the Church and the Church's harshest critic of the martial law
regime. 'Liberation theology' — a marriage of Marxism and
Christianity originating in Latin America — has found roots
in the Philippines. As political polarisation within Philippine
society increases, the tensions within the Church itself have

grown. Jaime, Cardinal Sin, acting as a weathervane of Church opinion, has in recent years swung towards the anti-martial law quarters.

The New Society and its successor, the New Republic, will stand or fall on its economic record, and that has been rather battered lately. The balance-of-payments deficit is the most serious in ASEAN, requiring emergency bail-outs from the IMF and World Bank, making the Philippines ASEAN's most indebted country. Virtually every leading sector — manufacturing, construction, agriculture, services — grew sluggishly in 1979, and fell short of targets.

Inflation in 1980 soared to over 25 per cent and unemployment was high. Real income for the average worker had declined by at least 10 per cent in the past decade. Foreign investors and local entrepreneurs, once considered Marcos's most dependable economic allies, were showing signs of unease. The outflow of investment capital from the country had noticeably increased, and new investments, local and foreign, had declined to a trickle.

The government has attributed the capital flight and the slowdown in new investments to worldwide recessionary trends and domestic inflation, the latter pushed up by oil prices. This is partially true, but it is also an attempt to play down the political controversy which surrounds foreign investment in the Philippines. Critics charge that the large multinationals encouraged Marcos to declare martial law, have been his strongest backers since, and have been granted preferential treatment over local businessmen. The government maintains that martial law provided the stability that attracts capital, which is a key ingredient for development.

Underlining this controversy is the fact that foreign investment has played a much more prominent role during martial law. In the two years prior to martial rule, annual foreign investments were less than domestic investments. But during the following two years, foreign investment expanded nearly three and a half times, while local investment grew by less than one and a half times. Since then, foreign investment has dominated local investment every year. On a cumulative source basis, from 1968 to 1971, total foreign investment amounted to 60 per cent of total domestic investment. But from the imposition of martial law to 1979, foreign investment has been 17 per cent greater than the cumulative local investment.[17]

As skilled technocrats, Marcos's economic engineers are trying their best to keep the economy running smoothly, but the problems seem to be outpacing their ability to select the levers and instruments with which to fine-tune the development strategy. Increasingly, basic questions about that strategy are being voiced by the 'liberal' opposition and the Church, which can produce a battery of statistics to prove that under martial law the economy may have grown but the people have suffered in terms of inflation and income distribution.

GNP has risen by 50 per cent since martial law was declared in 1972, but real wages fell by one-third and inflation-adjusted farming incomes today are only 60 per cent of what they were in 1974, according to official statistics.[18] According to the Ministry of Labour, the wages of nearly 90 per cent of rural and urban workers in 1977 were barely enough to meet subsistence needs. Up to a quarter of the population, according to a United Nations estimate,[19] cannot find enough work to earn a living, and thousands migrate annually from the poorest islands to Manila, Cebu and Davao, swelling the squatter, shantytowns to one-third of these cities' populations.

Bishop Julio Xavier Lebayen, one of the most outspoken Church leaders, has lamented that

'our experience in the Philippines has been that income distribution has worsened at a time when the main thrust of the government was, and still is, the intensification and diversification of exports. . . People can meet their needs only if they have money to pay. The poor have no money. They have needs but no wherewithal to meet them. That is why we export food while our people starve.'[20]

According to the semi-official Food and Nutrition Research Institute of the Philippines, in 1976, 70 per cent of the population were malnourished and 50 per cent were protein-deficient, while 40 per cent of deaths were caused by malnutrition. The UN's Food and Agriculture Organisation estimates average daily Filipino food intake to be only 100 calories above the Bangladesh average, and 270 calories below the minimum daily calorie requirement of 2,210 set by the World Bank. According to the Asian Development Bank, in 1976 the average daily calorie consumption in the Philippines was the lowest in Asia.[21]

The Ministry of Health reported in a survey that 85 per cent of schoolchildren suffer from protein—calorie malnutrition, and a US study says that half the Filipino children under four are malnourished — one of the highest rates in the world.[22]

The Cassandras of the Philippines are still in the political wilderness, but their prophecies cannot be dismissed as easily as before. 'To continue the present economic strategy is to sow the wind and sooner or later reap the whirlwind,' the Civil Liberties Union, a human rights organisation made up mainly of opponents of the government, warned Marcos in 1979.[23] Yet, as in Iran under the Shah, the path the Philippines has followed is that prescribed by the international financial institutions — reducing tariffs, opening industries to foreign investment, building up labour-intensive export manufactures, containing inflation wherever possible. If the prescription fails to cure the patient, it may be because, like the Iranians, Filipinos have not seen enough of the promised economic rewards to justify sacrificing their freedom to a dynasty.

INDONESIA

The New Order, nurtured for fourteen years by munificent foreign patrons and nourished by seemingly inexhaustible reserves of oil, enters its adolescence, not with promises of rapid growth but with prospects of stunted and stagnant development.

A decade of all-out petroleum exploitation has produced impressive GNP growth rates and numerous prestigious, capital-intensive industrial or infrastructural projects. Much of the oil bonus, however, has been squandered on 'white elephant' projects with few employment-creating effects, on consumption of luxury goods — many of them smuggled — by high-living élites, and on lining the pockets or overseas bank accounts of powerful generals and bureaucrats.

Agricultural development has been largely neglected in the past decade, though given lip service in the two previous national plans, and while GNP rates have risen, real agricultural wages have declined; three-quarters of Java's population do not have enough land for subsistence and massive food imports will be required in future years.

A UN International Labour Office survey states:

> Within the past decade or so, millions of Javanese have moved from mere poverty towards the perilous state of indigence, in which there is little or no access to work and food. . . what is far more disturbing, since it signifies permanence of the greater inequality and absolute poverty, is the suggestion that there has been a worsened distribution of land.[24]

As Indonesia's consortium of creditors, the Inter-Governmental Group on Indonesia (IGGI) met in 1979 in Amsterdam to consider the current year's aid commitments, they were advised by a confidential World Bank report that 'the high overall growth rates of the past decade will become more difficult to attain and the pressure on resources will increase significantly'. Simply in order to keep the economy afloat, the New Order is relying on foreign largesse more than ever, and piling up debts which — even after accounting for inflation — make the widely criticised borrowings during President Sukarno's 'old order' seem small by comparison. From 1974 to 1979, Indonesia's outstanding external debts have more than doubled from US $9.2 billion to US $19.5 billion. In seven years' time, the outstanding debt will again double.[25]

As long as Indonesia remains receptive to IGGI tutelage, however, the aid is likely to pour in. For what US President Richard Nixon observed, when the New Order was only a year old, remains essentially the same today: 'With its 100 million people [now 135 million] and its 3,000-mile area of islands containing the region's richest hoard of natural resources, Indonesia constitutes the greatest prize in the Southeast Asian area.'[26]

For the future, the industrialised nations have mapped out a new development strategy for Indonesia, the main feature being the great stress on 'export-oriented industrialisation' together with a gradual dismantling of import substitution policies and an abolition of all budgetary subsidies.

That 'export-oriented industrialisation' is seen as the engine of growth seems a little incongruous with the present reality, where the manufacturing sector employs only 8 per cent of the labour force, accounts for 5 per cent of total exports and 12 per cent of non-oil exports, and is clustered around Jakarta. Nevertheless, advocates claim that with the proliferation of export processing zones — populated by foreign multinationals and joint ventures taking advantage of cheap labour — manufactured exports can account for a quarter of total exports (roughly Malaysia's situation at present) within ten years.

'Indonesia has the largest remaining pool of inexpensive and relatively literate labour in East Asia,' a World Bank report[27] enthused, continuing:

Even before the recent devaluation, wages for unskilled labour were among the lowest in the world; lower than in Singapore, Hong Kong, South Korea and Taiwan. Labour is not unionised and government has largely refrained from intervening in the labour market... Indonesia also has a large number of potentially efficient seaports and relatively well-developed communications and other infrastructure.'

Export processing zones were born in Asia at the same time as the New Order, and in the dozen intervening years labour costs in the original 'cheap labour' countries of East Asia have escalated sharply, while Indonesia's have not. Just as multinationals are now eyeing the Subcontinent as a place to relocate some of their assembly plants, they are also looking at Indonesia. In addition, the policy of import substitution, which IGGI and the World Bank had one time favoured, has lost its attraction for foreign companies which invested in Indonesia to take advantage of a potentially enormous, protected domestic market. Because of widespread poverty, market demand remains low, and the Indonesian market for consumer goods is smaller than that of South Korea — which has a population only a quarter the size of Indonesia's.

Mismanagement of the economy is one of the most severe charges against Suharto, and his Achilles heel. Even before the Pertamina débâcle of 1975, which was a flashing danger signal of massive mismanagement of the country's petroleum resources, critical observers with some simple arithmetical calculations had warned that the oil-producing spree could not be long-lived. Under foreign encouragement, the New Order had adopted rapid oil exploitation as one cornerstone of its policy to 'liberalise the economy'. During the Sukarno years of 1960–66, annual growth in oil production had been a modest 2 per cent. But with the New Order's better 'investment climate' for foreign oil companies, annual crude oil output grew seven times the old rate at 15 per cent per year.

So long as the much-demanded 'sweet' (low sulphur and thus low polluting) crude flowed to Western and Japanese industries, via US oil companies, none of Indonesia's foreign patrons cautioned against the dangers of profligate oil production, even though the economy was becoming increasingly dependent on oil revenues. Only now that the crunch has come — and net oil exports account for over half the nation's exports and domestic revenue, 65 per cent of public investments and 13 per cent of GNP, and exceed the development budget — does the World Bank observe, with masterly understatement, that 'the economy is extremely exposed to oil sector developments'.[28]

During the past decade, the Indonesian peasantry and rural economy sank deeper into trouble. According to the UN's International Labour Office (ILO), by 1973 almost half of Java's rural households — more than 30 million people — were virtually landless, and this does not include the smallholders or tenants 'who have been reduced to *de facto* landless labourers through the modernisation of rice production'. Three-quarters of Java's farming families do not own enough land even for subsistence farming, and 'aggregate *per capita* food production data reveal a poor and worsening standard of nutrition'.[29]

The Javanese village network of patron–client relationships, while often a camouflage for rural exploitation and bonded labour, at least provided for what scholars have called 'shared poverty'. For example, the traditional practice of harvesting involved the farmer giving a fixed proportion of his harvest to fellow villagers who came to help, regardless of how many there were. The commercial revolution in rice production, however, has popularised another system, called *tebasan*. This involves the farmer pre-selling his crop to a trader, who then hires harvesters on a cash basis, which leads invariably to less employment.

Bonded labour is also increasing, as a large group of deficit-farmers or tenants become indebted to richer farmers who reaped the benefits of the new rice technology. While it increased inequalities, the so-called Green Revolution has managed to keep rice production growing by 3.5 per cent annually, but not enough to stem the rising tide of food imports. This is, however, only the food deficit reflected in market demand: the nutrition gap is actually several times higher.

Progress in other agricultural sectors has been equally dismal. Agricultural exports account for 80 per cent of non-oil exports and 35 per cent of total exports, but will take up very little of the slack left by declining oil exports. Although agricultural exports have risen in value terms owing to high world commodity prices, output of some key commodities such as rubber and tapioca has virtually stagnated through years of neglect.[30] But ecological problems are already arising, since restrictions on timber cutting and requirements on replanting are enforced only half-heartedly. (Much the same situation exists in Thailand and the Philippines.) Palm oil production is rising, because it comes largely from estates, where investment is higher than among smallholders.

The outlook for non-oil mineral exports is not much more encouraging. Although Indonesia is rich in mineral resources, and numerous projects have been undertaken to extract them, unfavourable world prices and rising investment costs have stalled their completion. Two large nickel-mining projects, in Sulawesi and Irian Jaya, have been postponed. Shell has cancelled a US$1.2 billion export-oriented coal mining project in Sumatra, and other projects remain uncertain.

Uncertain, too, is the key word for Indonesia's future. The giant of ASEAN is also the poorest member. Although the present élite appears firmly in control, there are increasing threats within the New Order. Until its massive problems of poverty and development are solved, Indonesia will find it difficult to claim its rightful position in the world community.

Insurgencies

The combined influences of economic inequity and external models have inspired insurgent movements against governments in ASEAN countries since before their independence. Of the three significant communist insurgencies in ASEAN countries today, the Maoist Community Party of the Philippines—New People's Army (CPP—NPA) has been the least affected by the Sino-Vietnamese conflict, continuing to grow while the others face serious ideological and survival problems. The Malayan Communist Party (MCP), traditionally hobbled by racial overtones — recruits are often young Chinese more angry over the pro-Malay government policies than ideologically motivated — and looking to China for guidance, has been demoralised by China's turn away from revolutionary ardour. Now that China consciously seeks to befriend the very same countries and national élites castigated by the MCP — 'American imperialism and the Hussein Onn fascist regime' — the MCP's rank and file are demoralised, and its supporters confused. The MCP is also racked with internal dissensions, and breakaway factions have formed, each trying to outdo the other in guerrilla warfare. Nevertheless, its running war against the Malaysian army on the Thai–Malaysian border continues with little change.

The Communist Party of Thailand (CPT) has also been gravely affected by the Sino–Vietnamese rift. Traditionally anti-Soviet and pro-China, the CPT could operate with direct support from both Vietnam and China in earlier days. But after the Sino–Vietnamese border skirmishes and Vietnamese invasion of Kampuchea, the CPT was forced to take a stand. It finally decided, after considerable disagreement among different factions, to condemn the Soviet Union and the Vietnamese. The result was the termination of Vietnamese arms supplies and the expulsion of CPT guerrillas from sanctuaries in Laos and Kampuchea in early 1979.

At the same time, the CPT's internal leadership became divided on ethnic lines – a Sino–Thai leadership with large Thai–Vietnamese rank-and-file. Furthermore, China decided around the same time to cease direct support for the CPT, viewing good relations with the Thai and other governments of ASEAN as more important goals in the conflict with Vietnam and the Soviet Union.

Faced with loss of logistics support and sanctuaries, the CPT has had to consider new tactics for survival. Like the NPA, the CPT has been a Maoist organisation, ideologically and in practice committed to rural insurgency and doctrines stressing the primacy of the peasantry in revolution. But unlike the NPA, the CPT's rural strongholds are less well established and without the support of urban-based opposition groups, its popular base and hence its survival are threatened. The CPT's front organisation, the Committee for Co-ordinating Patriotic and Democratic Forces (CCPDF), formed in the aftermath of the October 1976 military *coup* which forced thousands of progressive students, workers and intellectuals underground, was supposed to provide the popular base. But it nearly collapsed because of the unwillingness of groups like the Socialist Party of Thailand to accept CPT domination. Meanwhile thousands of students who 'entered the jungles' and the arms of the CPT in 1976 have defected back to the cities, disillusioned with what they feel are the obsolete, archaic stances of the CPT old guard. The CPT has now doctrinally accepted the necessity for urban struggle to go hand-in-hand with rural insurgency.

For the NPA, however, rural insurgency continues to grow, especially in Mindanao and the poorer islands of the Visayas, such as Samar. Because of its geographical isolation from the

Southeast Asian mainland, the NPA has never been as dependent on external support as the CPT and MCP. It is a factor which inhibited its growth but which may now be a source of resilience.

A few dozen hardcore NPA members launched their armed offensive in Davao in 1973, aiming to encompass areas of Mindanao not under MNLF influence. NPA squads then expanded to other provinces of Mindanao.

Today, a number of company-sized NPA units operate in these areas, and the government has conceded that areas around Davao City have become NPA territory. Yet the government presence is strong: there is now one soldier for every three civilians and the troops mount periodic offensives against the NPA and MNLF. Although the MNLF was founded earlier than the NPA, it launched its armed offensive on a large scale in 1973 and 1974. Both the NPA and the MNLF base their campaigns for mass support on the issues of land for the people and liberation from the existing socio-political system.

In the late 1950s, there was a massive influx of settlers from the Visayas and Luzon to Mindanao, long the promised land for poor migrants. The majority of the Visayan settlers ran into conflict with the local Muslims who held the area to be their ancestral lands. Landgrabbing on areas traditionally occupied by Muslims, non-Christian tribes and early Visayan settlers became prevalent in the 1960s when agribusiness swiftly expanded, led by transnational corporations. Vast tracts of timber concessions, pineapple and banana plantations, corporate rice and corn farming resulted in increasing landlessness. The situation provided opportunities for both the NPA and MNLF to gather support. But although the NPA now has some secure areas — 'liberated zones' — and areas of influence, its policy in Mindanao is not to engage in frequent offensives against government forces. In distant areas ambushes are made on isolated patrols to obtain arms. The NPA is hardpressed for weapons and ammunition, but it has been increasing its arms caches, sometimes even through arrangements with government soldiers who sell military supplies.

By its own reckoning, the NPA is active in forty-six of the country's seventy-seven provinces and is expanding. Vastly out-gunned, the NPA is still far from able to engage government forces in conventional warfare. But its guerrilla tactics have bogged down the Philippine army in several provinces. The CPP–NPA has been slowly drawing supporters, particularly among the victims of abuses by the armed forces, gaining credibility largely because of the erosion of more moderate opposition groups such as the National Union for Liberation (NUL). The inability of such groups of pre-martial law politicians to offer a clear alternative means of displacing Marcos short of armed struggle, coupled with massive Marcos victories against them in the 1978 National Assembly and 1980 local elections, has left them humiliated and helpless. UNIDO, the coalition of opposition groups formed in 1980, has refused to contest the elections planned for 1982.

The more determined of Marcos's opponents, including non-violent Catholic priests, have thus tended to downplay the CPP's ideological implications and instead, see it as the only viable route to toppling authoritarian rule. But the CPP–NPA has decided on a strategy of protracted struggle with decades rather than years as milestones, and its goal is the complete and profound transformation of Philippine society, not just the overthrow of Marcos. In this pursuit the CPP sees the moderate opposition groups as potential enemies. Furthermore, the NPA has clearly decided on a Maoist 'encirclement' strategy of guerrilla war, and dismisses urban guerrilla tactics.

The spate of urban bombings in 1980 probably represents therefore, the transformation of erstwhile moderate opposition groups into practitioners of urban guerrilla tactics, more than a new phase of NPA activity.

In spite of reports of a NPA–MNLF link-up, there is still no ideological alliance. There are prospects of joint operations in NPA and MNLF areas with common borders, but there has yet to be any joint operation on a significant scale. Co-operation has been based on territorial respect, and in areas with common borders the mutual use of training grounds and camps has been agreed. But if joint operations between the two insurgencies become a reality, the simmering Mindanao crisis could boil over. The MNLF, though presently subdued in its operations, could easily move on to the offensive, and its external support, mainly from Libya and other Middle East Islamic countries, is substantial. If the NPA can cash in on this, one of its major problems — arms supplies — could be eased considerably. The NPA is very far from offering itself as an alternative government. Indeed, if the Marcos regime fell, a violent interregnum with various opposition elements scrambling for power must be seen as likely. The ultimate winner of that scramble would need to have secured the support of the army: in the longer term the winner might indeed be the army itself.

The Armed Forces

The role of the armed forces in the ASEAN countries is in the process of rapid change.[31] From the time when the other four governments agreed with President Suharto that 'national resilience' was their individual responsibility, and that internal security their prime defence concern, none of the ASEAN countries' defence forces would have deterred an invader. Several factors, however, have changed that. The defeat of the United States in Vietnam in 1975 and its subsequent 'withdrawal' from Southeast Asia, Vietnam's alliances with the USSR and with Laos and Cambodia, the relative ease with which Vietnamese refugees entered ASEAN countries, the growing Soviet naval presence and the Vietnamese invasion of Kampuchea have combined to lead ASEAN governments to the conclusion that unarmed neutrality was not feasible. Each country had rapidly expanded its defence spending since 1976, more than doubling it in the case of Singapore, Malaysia and Thailand; each has ordered military equipment, aircraft and naval craft which are intended for external defence. At the same time, each has either introduced or is planning national conscription and training programmes to upgrade existing armed forces. Some commentators have been led by these developments to speculate that an ASEAN defence alliance is in prospect: that is repeatedly denied in formal ASEAN statements. It would also be erroneous to suppose that ASEAN is about to become another Switzerland: as Lee Kuan Yew has remarked: 'For at least ten years there is no combination of military forces in ASEAN that could check the Vietnamese army in any open conflict.'

The increase in defence capacity which new ASEAN arms purchases imply will not be translated into actual capacity perhaps for a decade. Much as the ASEAN countries are worried about external threats, they are not in agreement about where the worst threats come from: Indonesia and Thailand represent opposite poles, with one fearing China and the other Vietnam. What, then, is the purpose of arms expansion in ASEAN countries? Countries that have other pressing developmental objectives do not decide to devote a quarter of the national budget (as Thailand did in 1980) to defence for no good reason. In Thailand's case the need to give the appearance of capacity to deter Vietnam is paramount. In all the ASEAN countries, the aspiration for self-reliance applies to defence as it does to economic matters and foreign relations. In Malaysia, Indonesia and the Philippines and Singapore, however, governments are not under direct threat: and yet defence allocations have risen steadily since 1976 in relation to total government spending. The World Bank and IMF have drawn attention to the relative decline in amounts set aside – particularly in the Philippines, Indonesia and Thailand – for developmental purposes, for health, education and welfare. One implication is that where essential services spending is held back, the discontent of those who would benefit from it will increase. Hence, in order to maintain their hold on power, some ASEAN governments may see a need for more stringent internal security, discipline, national commitment – however it is described, it means increasing internal use of the armed forces to suppress dissent and insurgency and support the regime. The ASEAN countries watch events in South Korea, India, Iran and El Salvador with a concern sharpened by the fear that they could be repeated closer to home.

10

Conclusion:
East–West and North–South

Robyn Lim

The extent to which ASEAN is something more than the sum of its parts remains an open question. The officials, journalists and academics who have contributed to this book naturally approach it from their own experience, and ASEAN appears in different guises when viewed from different member countries. Contributors who are particularly familiar with one country sometimes found themselves seeing issues differently from their co-contributors whose experience of other countries is greater. Views also differed on the weight the ASEAN countries give to their associations with nations outside the region, and on the approaches they take to economic objectives. These disagreements were matters of emphasis rather than substance, but they illustrate the difficulty of trying to achieve a coherent 'focus on ASEAN'. As other commentators on ASEAN have noted, distinguishing the reality from the rhetoric is not always easy. ASEAN may well be, as Tan Sri M. Ghazali Shafie would have it, 'in its essence . . . merely a state of mind'.[1] But such a subjective definition is open to a range of interpretations. The experience of other regional economic associations among less developed countries does not make for excessive optimism about ASEAN's prospects.[2]

It is indisputable that there has been a 'meeting of minds' within ASEAN on important political questions. As both Irvines emphasise in their chapters, ASEAN is primarily a political association, notwithstanding the protestations of its founders that it is primarily for economic, social and cultural co-operation. The potential for intra-regional disputes disrupting the Association is much lower now than it was ten years ago. Neither the question of the future of Brunei nor the Philippine claim to Sabah appear likely to ruffle the surface of ASEAN consensus. The war in the southern Philippines has potential for attracting increased intervention by extra-regional powers such as Libya. To date, however, Indonesia and Malaysia have managed to reduce the likelihood of outside intervention either in the southern Philippines or in Southern Thailand. Relations between Singapore and its immediate neighbours have improved considerably, partly since the adoption of a less abrasive style by the Singapore leadership. Suspicions of possible Indonesian 'regional power chauvinism' may not be quite dead, but they are less significant than they were in the years immediately following Confrontation. An unintended outcome of Indonesia's invasion of East Timor in 1975 was that it highlighted for some observers the inefficiency of an important section of Indonesian armed forces.

The Indo-Chinese refugee crisis in 1978—9 created some strains among the members of ASEAN, partly because they were competing for resettlement places. Thailand felt that its plight was insufficiently acknowledged by its ASEAN partners. There was some resentment in Indonesia of the fact that refugees towed out to sea by Malaysians landed (if they did not drown) in the Indonesian Anambas and Natuna Islands. Singapore's extremely hard-line attitude, although well understood by the other ASEAN members, was not universally appreciated. In accepting 1,500 Khmer Muslim refugees, in addition to the estimated 120,000 Philippine Muslim refugees in Sabah, the Malaysian government was exposed to charges of discrimination on religious and ethnic grounds when it towed out to sea Indo-Chinese refugees who were predominantly ethnic Chinese. Yet, as Michael Richardson points out, ASEAN maintained a 'united front' on the refugee issue, partly as a result of the hardening of attitudes towards Vietnam in the latter half of 1979. That united front was very important in jolting the international community into recognition of the dimensions of the crisis.

ASEAN also maintained unity on the issue of the recognition of 'Democratic Kampuchea' after the Vietnamese invasion of Kampuchea in December 1978. Yet both Michael Richardson and Allan Gyngell point to the differing views within ASEAN, and within some ASEAN governments, on the question of whether China or Vietnam is the greater potential threat to the region. Thailand and Singapore are deeply suspicious of Vietnam. Opinion within the Indonesian government is divided, but misgivings about China remain entrenched. Despite some degree of internal strain, however, ASEAN was able not only to maintain an effective united voice at the UN and in other forums, but also to produce sufficient international support for its stance. That some resolution of the Kampuchean crisis has to be found is obvious: the nature of that solution will be much more difficult to define.

ASEAN has benefited from its heightened cohesiveness in its relations with external powers. The dialogue with the EC, for example, has recently moved beyond strictly economic issues. Allan Gyngell discusses the overtly political statements on Afghanistan and Kampuchea which emerged from the second ASEAN–EC Ministerial meeting in March 1980. While the hyperbole that characterises such occasions can easily lead to an exaggeration of these achievements,[3] it was clear that for both the EC and ASEAN, a new dimension had entered the relationship. Perhaps because the political characteristics of ASEAN are really apparent, there is a tendency for some observers to see this as extending to 'militarisation'. These suspicions are compounded by the fact that previous organisations such as SEATO and ASPAC were instruments of US foreign policy designed to help 'contain' China. A precursor of ASEAN, ASA, was vulnerable to criticism that it resembled SEATO. (Two of its members were members of SEATO and the third, Malaya, had a defence treaty with the UK, which was a SEATO member.) Malaysia and Singapore remain members of the Five-Power Defence Arrangements, and Thailand and the Philippines are signatories of the Manila Treaty. Like ASA, moreover, ASEAN is comprised of countries which are strongly anti-communist in their internal policies. 'Defence' issues are usually defined in terms of anti-communism. There are a number of bilateral military arrangements between member countries for the suppression of insurgency, smooth running mechanisms for the exchange of intelligence, and moves towards the standardisation of military equipment and training. Some Indonesian generals, notably General Panggabean, have consistently appealed for a more overtly military aspect of ASEAN co-operation. But none of this means that ASEAN is, or is about to become, a military alliance.

Those who level the 'military bloc' accusation at ASEAN indicate an inadequate understanding of the nature of Malaysian and, more particularly, Indonesian politics. The term 'military bloc' is automatically equated with SEATO in Indonesian minds. Despite urging from Japan and other countries, Indonesia was no more interested in joining ASPAC in the late 1960s than it had been interested in membership of ASA in 1961. Pressures in Indonesia for a more overly military ASEAN have successfully been resisted, notably by Adam Malik.[4] A pragmatic element is also present, as David Irvine emphasises. Given their military weakness *vis-à-vis* Vietnam, the consensus among ASEAN leaders is that there is not much point in provoking Vietnam if ASEAN has not sufficient bite to match its bark.

The charge that ASEAN is a military bloc also underrates the importance of some sensitive realities in the region. At the separation of Singapore from Malaysia in 1965, Singapore was denied access to jungle warfare training facilities in Johore and has had to seek them in Brunei, Taiwan and Australia. Notwithstanding close intelligence co-operation between the two countries, there is no prospect of Singapore troops training in Southern Malaysia, basically for communal reasons. Despite the urgings of the 'ASEAN hawks', the Association has successfully resisted moves towards militarisation. Since 1976, it has achieved a considerable degree of cohesion on political issues, both intra-regional and extra-regional. Yet this does not mean that no potentially divisive issue remains. Given the region's enormous diversity, as well as the fissiparous tendencies generated by colonialism, such expectations would be unrealistic. Competing territorial claims in the South China Sea are a possible source of trouble. All the ASEAN states except Thailand have now claimed 200-nautical-mile economic zones. These overlap with each other, as well as with those of outside powers. Communal and religious factors continue to have the potential to cause problems. The suspicion that Singapore acts as a 'Third China' is not quite buried, despite Singapore's constant reassurances on this point. The government's 'speak Mandarin' campaign directed at Singapore's Chinese community has raised eyebrows in Indonesia and Malaysia (with some Malaysians countering from time to time with suggestions that Malay—Indonesian should be the language of ASEAN). Singapore officials, however, have emphasised that the campaign does not affect non-Chinese, but its very existence does draw attention to Singapore's 'Chineseness'.

The apparent resurgence of 'fundamentalist' Islam will undoubtedly be very important in Southeast Asia, although its implications are hard to forecast. The *Dakwah* (missionary) movement has a clear anti-Western orientation; it also has a potentially anti-Chinese bias. How important *Dakwah* may become is difficult to judge, but it is of considerable concern to the Malaysian government in particular.[5] The currents of revived Islam also swirl around the Southern Philippines. The continuing, if largely unreported war there raises the possibility of outside involvement, although both Indonesia and Malaysia have helped prevent such intervention on any significant scale. As Fifield has noted,[6] the Sabah claim is 'dead but not buried'. President Marcos promised to drop it at the Bali Summit in 1976, but the Malaysians have apparently insisted on a redrafting of the 1973 Philippine constitution, specifically to exclude Sabah. The Malaysian Prime Minister has yet to visit the Philippines. The Sabah question does not seem to be a major issue at the moment, but there is always an element of volatility in Philippine politics. Presumably a third ASEAN Summit Meeting should be held in the foreseeable future. Before it can be held in Manila, some 'final solution' to the Sabah issue must be on the pre-Summit agenda.

The Third Summit will probably not be held until more concrete economic achievements can be demonstrated. Progress on the economic front, where real financial commitments have to be made and risks taken, has been much slower than on political issues. As David Irvine and Dr Castro both indicate, the communist victories in Indo-China had a galvanising effect on ASEAN. The economic co-operation projects recommended in the Kansu/Robinson Report of 1972 were revived and put forward at the Bali Summit. But their implementation has been slow. Of the joint industrial projects, only the Indonesian and Malaysian projects appear likely to go ahead in their original form; they would probably have done so anyway if ASEAN did not exist. Experience in other regional groupings of less developed countries seems to indicate that without joint regulation of technology and capital imports, it is unlikely that a policy of industrial allocation among economically disparate states will succeed. In the absence of such agreement, other corrective mechanisms cannot operate in order to promote a more equitable distribution of costs and benefits among integration partners.[7] To date, the only attempt at such regulation in a Third World regional association is Decision 24 of the ANDEAN Pact.[8] The results of this attempt to regulate foreign investment and technology transfer have been less impressive than the signatories of the agreement would have hoped. Deep philosophical differences between ASEAN governments impinge on these questions. Given their very different sizes, historical experience and resource endowments, it is not surprising that Indonesia and Singapore often represent opposite poles in ASEAN thinking. In general, Indonesia takes a much more restrictive approach to foreign investment, on paper at least, than does Singapore.

If one of the long-term goals of regional co-operation is to enable the ASEAN countries to achieve more self-reliant economic growth, some attempt to regulate the activities of multinational corporations is inevitable. French-Davis warns:

When liberalization of reciprocal trade within an integration process is not accompanied by coordinated industrial development policies and uniform treatment of foreign investment, integration can tend to weaken the position of the developing country *vis-à-vis* the giant multinational corporations. Indeed the gamut of options open to foreign enterprises is expanded with integration, for now by investing in any one country the enterprise has access to the markets of all the member countries. Thus the corporation is in the position of picking the country offering the greatest privileges.[9]

Dr Castro's discussion of the demise of the 'ASEAN car' idea indicates the difficulties inherent in the inter-relationship between multinational corporations and ASEAN complementation schemes. Other regional observers also feel that in general the multinationals have resisted the complementation schemes since they conflict with the plans the corporations already have for industrial development in each of the member countries.[10] The ASEAN governments have also been unable to agree on how much foreign equity is to be allowed in the complementation projects if they have government support. It is also clear, as the same chapter points out, that on questions such as the rate of tariff reductions in ASEAN, the private sector wants to move ahead at a faster rate than some of the governments are prepared to accept. Another sensitive issue is the fact that 'overseas Chinese' interests are heavily represented in ASEAN private sector bodies. Attempts by the Indonesian and Malaysian governments to promote 'indigenous' economic interests in ASEAN complementation schemes complicate relations between those governments and the ASEAN private sector. As Lee Kuan Yew has pointed out (see Chapter 3), so far ASEAN has found it easier to take economic decisions relating to negotiating as a group with dialogue countries than to tackle some of the difficult decisions on preferential tariffs. Japanese and Australian responses to ASEAN's bloc approach, which are juxtaposed in the chapters by Alan Rix and Frank Frost, demonstrate in different ways the success of ASEAN's technique. ASEAN has undoubtedly achieved an impressive degree of cohesion on political issues. It is still an unanswered question whether its political fabric will be able to cope with the internal strains created by the process of economic integration.

In its relations with extra-regional powers, ASEAN is confronted with the major cleavages in world politics – the East–West and North–South conflicts. Although they are in common usage, neither term is very accurate. The 'East–West' conflict has of course been complicated by the fact that China has now emerged as a *de facto* ally of the United States. Economic rivalry between the US, Japan and the EC also clouds the picture. But increased tension between the

US and the USSR over such issues as the Soviet invasion of Afghanistan has raised the temperature of superpower rivalry in Southeast Asia and the Indian Ocean. Vietnam has apparently given the Soviet Union easy access to the former US bases at Danang and Cam Ranh Bay. Since the beginning of the Iranian crisis in 1979, the waterways of the Indonesian archipelago, especially the Straits of Makassar, Lombok and Ombai-Wetar, have become even more important to the US, as well as to Japan and to the USSR. The American bases in the Philippines[11] remain crucial for US strategic interests in the region. While an 'over-the-horizon' US presence may have been preferred three or four years ago, significant changes have recently occurred. As Allan Gyngell points out, the Thais have sought reassurances from the United States on the nature of US commitments to Thailand. Rhetoric aside, the Philippines shelters under the US umbrella. Singapore has never made any secret of its preference for a strong US economic and security role in the region, and has urged Japan to take its share of the task of defence.

Currents leading ASEAN towards a more overtly pro-American stance, however, encounter strong counter-currents in Indonesia and Malaysia. While some influential groups in both countries favour a close relationship with the United States, a strong commitment to the ideal of non-alignment remains. In Indonesia, President Suharto is begining to take on the mantle of Sukarno for his own domestic purposes, but the foreign policy implications are also significant. Indonesia is proud of its history as a leading member of the non-aligned movement, even if its invasion of East Timor made for some problems with its NAM colleagues. The world-views of the current Indonesian leadership were forged in the anti-colonial struggle of 1945—9, during which it became apparent that both superpowers were prepared to sacrifice Indonesian interests when it was politic to do so. Despite the strong tilt to the West after 1966, Franklin Weinstein states: 'It is fair to conclude. . . that despite their genuine admiration, the Indonesian leaders retain a strong belief that the US is a country which exploits its own downtrodden and seeks to dominate other countries as well. Few see it as a country that can be relied on to assist Indonesia.[12] Similarly, Harold

Crouch has pointed out that army officers have always been conscious of Indonesia's potential as a 'significant regional power' and have tended to regard the involvement of the great powers in the region as a hindrance to the fulfilment of their aspirations. In the short term, Indonesia may have welcomed the involvement of American military forces in the region, but their presence 'has been seen as a temporary necessity while Indonesia builds up her own military power'.[13]

There are conflicting attitudes towards Vietnam within Indonesia. On the one hand, many Indonesians feel a bond with Vietnam, since Indonesia and Vietnam were the only countries in the region to achieve independence by armed struggle against colonialism. (Only the Filipinos seem to remember that theirs was the first, if unsuccessful, revolution against colonialism.) Throughout the second Indo-China war, Indonesia continued to recognise Hanoi and to permit the South Vietnamese National Liberation Front to maintain an office in Jakarta. There is a degree of admiration for Vietnam's stamina in sustaining a thirty-year war. On the other hand, Vietnam and Indonesia are clear rivals for regional hegemony. Signs of a tougher attitude towards Vietnam have begun to emerge in Jakarta recently, mainly owing to Vietnam's resistance to ASEAN attempts to reach a settlement on Kampuchea. But all the ASEAN governments are aware that Vietnam must eventually be accommodated within the Southeast Asian state system if there is to be any chance of weaning Hanoi away from the Soviet Union. The American treatment of Vietnam as an international pariah is hardly the way to achieve that objective.

The ASEAN countries are acutely aware of their sensitive strategic position and realise that all the great powers have interests in the region. But they are nonetheless determined that those great powers should not fight proxy wars on ASEAN soil or in ASEAN waterways. This determination has been strengthened by events of the second and third Indo-China wars. In the West, the continuing significance of Nixon's 'Vietnamisation policy' is often overlooked. By implying that it was preferable for South Vietnamese troops to die instead of Americans, it reinforced existing suspicions in Asia that Westerners regard Asian lives as less valuable than Caucasian lives. Despite the political and ideological differences between Asian countries during the second Indo-China war, 'the common denominator that cut across so many variations of ideology and special interest was a sense of racial anger in the face of the largely unrestrained application of white, Western power'.[14] Soviet attitudes towards Asians, especially ethnic Chinese, are also frequently seen as racist; this reinforces the belief that both superpowers are not averse to fighting proxy wars in Asia.

While China might not be accused of the same racist attitudes, its attack on northern Vietnam in February 1979 indicates that it is capable of traditional 'great power chauvinism' towards weaker states. The closer relationship between the US and China during the Carter Administration has not been entirely welcomed by Indonesia and Malaysia. Although Malaysia set the pace in ASEAN by recognising China in 1974, and Indonesia has not yet defrosted its relations with Beijing, the two countries share a suspicion of China's long-term intentions in the region. As Michael Richardson points out, the Malaysians were publicly critical of China for helping to panic the ethnic Chinese in northern Vietnam in 1979. The fact that China appeared to be championing the interests of the Chinese in Vietnam caused considerable disquiet in Jakarta and Kuala Lumpur, despite reassurances from Beijing that this was a 'special case'. In addition, the communist parties in ASEAN countries are almost entirely pro-China. China's support for them may be only verbal, but it causes irritation in Jakarta and Kuala Lumpur in particular. China's extensive territorial claims in the South China Sea also cause some concern in ASEAN, as indeed do those of Vietnam. The deep-seated suspicion of Vietnam in the region should not be underrated. Yet those inclined to a simplistic 'Cold War' analysis exaggerate the degree to which the ASEAN identifies with and supports US policy in Southeast Asia. It is nevertheless difficult to pinpoint exactly where ASEAN stands on East—West issues, and what impact the election of Ronald Reagan as US President may have on these questions.

There is also considerable scope for disagreement on the

question of ASEAN's position in the North–South conflict. The contributors to the recent Council on Foreign Relations volume on Southeast Asia could reach no consensus on this issue.[15] It is an interesting question whether the ASEAN countries, Indo-China and Burma will ever be able to over-come their ideological differences in order to forge a regional entity able to present a united front against developed count-ries. The ASEAN countries are not radical members of the Group of 77. Their development strategies are dependent on high levels of foreign investment, which can only come from the West and Japan. As Allan Gyngell has noted, the dialogues ('the dentist's chair approach') with developed countries have achieved more than any single ASEAN country could have expected to gain. Yet there are major areas of dissatisfaction. After accepting the advice of Western economists, World Bank officials – and their own Western-trained planners – that they should begin to concentrate on export-led industrialisation, by 1974–5 the ASEAN count-ries found that markets for their products were not growing as rapidly as they had hoped. They were coming up against protectionist barriers in the developed countries. Neither Japan, the EC nor the US has met ASEAN requests for a Stabex scheme along the lines of the Lomé convention. As a member of OPEC, Indonesia continues to be denied access to the United States' GSP. The emotional influence of the call for a New International Economic Order (NIEO) is also im-portant, even if underrated by many First World economists. Like other parts of the Third World, Southeast Asia was carved up by the former colonial powers according to histor-ical accident or their own convenience. The economies of the ASEAN countries became closely integrated with those of the metropolitan powers – one reason for the level of intra-regional trade remaining so low. Many of the current ASEAN leaders are old enough to remember the arrogance of some of the former colonial masters. A strong sense of identification with the G77, and a tendency to seek Third World credentials, is understandable. Underlying the call for a NIEO is the strong belief that the West and Japan have enriched them-selves at the expense of the Third World, and are continuing to do so. On specific issues of concern to some ASEAN countries, there are strong philosophical differences with the US and Japan. Indonesia, supported by the Philippines, insists on the archipelagic principle in Law of the Sea conferences, a position at odds with those of the US and Japan as well as that of the USSR.

ASEAN does include one Newly Industrializing Country (NIC). Singapore, having no alternative but to remain in ASEAN, would resist any divide and rule tactics on the part of developed countries aimed at splitting off the NICs from the poorer members of the Third World. Singapore is sometimes suspected of voting for G77 resolutions which adversely affect its own economic interests. The Singapore government is well aware of these sensitivities, and is at pains to point out that its 'Second Industrial Revolution' will be beneficial to ASEAN. Instead of trying to restrain wages and having to rely on foreign workers, Singapore is trying to move into more technologically advanced production. It can, according to Mr Lee, play a role similar to that of the Swiss in Europe, and will invest more heavily in neighbouring labour-abundant economies such as Malaysia and Indonesia. Yet there is always some tension between Singapore's 'global city' role and its membership of ASEAN. To some extent, Singapore's decision to invest in labour-intensive economies outside ASEAN, notably Sri Lanka, reflects its impatience with the slow progress of economic integration in ASEAN. On the other hand, ASEAN finds Singaporean outspokenness very useful in drawing attention to North—South issues. At the Commonwealth Heads of Government Regional meeting in New Delhi in September 1980, for example, Mr Lee minced no words in attacking Australian protectionism. Singapore's Ambassador to the UN, Professor Tommy Koh, has also been a highly effective spokesman for ASEAN positions on North—South issues.

The North—South 'dialogue' has focused attention on inequality between states. Such emphasis on equality has an inherent domestic radicalism for all Third World countries. Regimes which advocate greater equality between states but do nothing about inequality at home are vulnerable to charges of hypocrisy. The East—West rivalry also gives added importance to questions of equitable growth in ASEAN countries. David Irvine's chapter emphasises Indonesia's concept of 'regional resilience' based on 'national resilience'. The ASEAN countries are well aware that they are in a race with Vietnam to show that non-communist economies are more capable of providing for the needs of their people than communist countries. They realise that Vietnam's invasion of Kampuchea, as well as its economic troubles, have given them a breathing space. There is no lack of agreement about the need for greater equality and social justice. But, as Ho Kwon Ping's chapter indicates, the translation of such talk into effective policies is much more difficult. The tendency to blame all indications of social unrest on 'subversion' sometimes diverts attention from the real underlying causes.

Political stability is obviously a crucial factor in economic development. Since the fall of the Shah, predicting political instability in Third World countries has become a growth industry. Political science is, however, a discipline less amenable to quantification than economics. Assessing the future political stability of ASEAN countries is not easy. Even ASEAN's most vehement critics would have to concede that, with the exception of Thailand (where in any case the monarchy provides an important element of stability), the ASEAN countries have enjoyed remarkably stable political leadership. The fact that Lee Kuan Yew, Rajaratnam, Marcos, Romulo, Suharto, Adam Malik and Ghazali Shafie have been in government positions for such a long period has been a crucial element in achieving greater cohesion in ASEAN. Yet political stability in the 1980s will hinge on two crucial issues – the question of succession and the legitimacy of governments. Within the next decade, most of the present leadership will change. In the Philippines, there is no clear procedure for choosing Marcos's successor. Whoever hopes to become president would presumably need the support of a significant section of the armed forces. In Indonesia, political unrest will probably gather momentum towards the elections in 1982, but there is less likelihood of the upheaval to which the Philippines is exposed. The contrast between the Philippines and Indonesia on the one hand, and Singapore on the other, is startling. With typical thoroughness, Singapore is going through a unique process of choosing its second generation leadership. Whether those leaders will be of the calibre of their predecessors remains to be seen. But in ASEAN countries generally, it is doubtful if the extraordinary stability of leadership of the 1970s can be maintained in the next decade. An important aspect of stability is whether governments are seen as legitimate. It is often assumed that the conduct of elections is a test of legitimacy. Those countries whose election results are less obviously predetermined than others are regarded as possessing more legitimacy.

This is a rather simplistic view. There is a sense in which the Malaysian and Singaporean governments can be regarded as more legitimate than those of the other ASEAN countries, but not necessarily because of their electoral procedures. A more important test is that of the degree of corruption. Corruption is 'not so much a breach of abstract moral or ethnical standards as it is of the national effort to rise up from deprivation'.[16] The extent to which leaders are believed to personify 'self-sacrificing dedication to the national cause', according to Harrison, is the critical test of legitimacy in Asia.[17] Elusive though such a test sometimes is, it marks the crucial distinction between the governments of Lee Kuan Yew and Ferdinand Marcos. Mr Lee's stern moralising may be irritating to some Western observers, but it is a significant element in Sinagpore's economic success. Malaysia has not been as effective as Singapore in controlling corruption, but it is clearly not in the same league as the other three ASEAN countries. Pauker makes a gloomy prediction for the political systems of ASEAN: 'Noncommunist Southeast Asia may be heading for the same nefarious treadmill from which Latin America has been unable to escape after a century and a half of political independence within a Western sphere of influence, namely the alternation of civilian and military authoritarian regimes.'[18] This may be dismissed as an excessively Western view, and irrelevant to Malaysia and Singapore. Yet it is demonstrable that a high degree of corruption mixed with authoritarianism is a potentially unstable brew in any society. If 'regional resilience' based on 'national resilience' is to be achieved, the ASEAN countries will need to bend their political will to implementing not only economic co-operation within the Association but, more importantly, effective national programmes for reducing poverty and inequality. Regional schemes and rhetoric are easier to produce than solutions to such difficult and pressing problems, especially for Thailand, the Philippines and Indonesia.

Also at the axis of the 'East–West' and 'North–South' issues is the question of possible ASEAN membership in a wider Pacific grouping. Proponents of various 'Pacific Community' proposals have been treading the academic conference circuit for more than a decade. Recently such proposals have enjoyed more official attention. The OPTAD idea proposed by Patrick and Drysdale[19] has been discussed by the Asia and Pacific Subcommittee of the US Senate Foreign Relations Committee. At UNCTAD V in May 1979, and during his visit to Australia in February 1980, the late Japanese Prime Minister Ohira held discussions on the 'Pacific Community' with his Australian counterpart. Several conferences have recently been held, involving officials, academics and business people, notably by the Centre for International and Strategic Studies in Bali in January 1980, and at the Australian National University in Canberra in September 1980. A Japanese Study Group report to government on the concept has been published. Yet major issues remain unresolved, including those of membership, and whether the 'Pacific Community' should be established on a government or non-government basis. Since the ANU seminar, it appears likely that a continuing process of unofficial consultations will take place, leading to governmental involvement at some stage in the future, if that is what regional countries decide they want.

Much of the impetus for the concept comes from the need perceived by economists to improve consultation, regularise economic planning and reduce tension on economic issues between Japan and the US and between Japan and the Asian NICs. Also of significance is Japan's recent turn from an 'omni-directional' foreign policy towards greater concentration – which Alan Rix has documented – on a more positive foreign policy role in Asia. Recent crises in the Middle East have accentuated Japanese anxiety about the availability of resources, especially energy. The Japanese government is, however, very sensitive to accusations that the Pacific Com-

munity may be a smokescreen for Japan's increasing exploitation of the Southeast Asian region. The Philippine government, for instance, has occasionally made explicit statements
about Japanese exploitation which indicate that the memory
of the Co-Prosperity Sphere is not quite dead. Philippine
rhetoric, if it seems to be directed towards a domestic audience, is not always taken too seriously by other ASEAN
governments. But Japanese sensitivities about ASEAN reservations have made Japan reluctant to lead in moves to establish a Pacific Community. Former Japanese Foreign Minister
Okita, whose academic work has been important in the development of the Pacific Community concept, has indicated
that if the ASEAN countries opposed it, it would not mater-
ialise.[20]

There is as yet no 'ASEAN view' of a Pacific Community.
Early in 1980, Singaporean officials were openly in favour of
the concept, but later seemed to realise that too much
enthusiasm might be counterproductive – as did its supporters in other ASEAN countries. Malaysia and Indonesia have
made explicit their distaste for any security-related proposal
which might lock ASEAN into an arrangement with the US.
This has been put clearly by Tan Sri M. Ghazali Shafie: 'A
Pacific Community concept that promises little beyond the
freezing of the present international division of labour and
the entrenchment of the current political and military divisions of the developed North will be quite distasteful to
ASEAN.'[21] It is not clear whether these objections would
apply to an arrangement which included Japan but excluded
the United States. General Ali Murtopo, for instance, in the
early 1970s suggested an Indonesian–Japanese–Australian
triangular *entente* to maintain regional stability.[22] The motivation was apparently that such a relationship could 'balance'
the rapid improvements in Japan's relationship with China
which were a consequence of the Nixon–Kissinger changes in
US–China policy. Any such proposal in the present climate
would presumably have to include Indonesia's ASEAN partners and would be unlikely to have a defence emphasis. Other
members of ASEAN, however, might be more inclined to
believe that the dangers of Japanese economic domination
impel ASEAN towards favouring US participation as a

counterweight in any Pacific Community arrangement. Even if security-related concepts are eschewed, difficult questions remain. The pressures which pull ASEAN towards stronger identification with the 'Southern' countries will tend to counteract the pressures from those who see net economic benefits for ASEAN in membership in a wider Pacific grouping. If Japan is unable or unwilling to deliver its pledges to ASEAN under the Fukuda Doctrine, for example, the result might be diminished ASEAN interest in becoming a partner with Japan in any wider regional arrangement. A resolution of the Kampuchean issue could also lead to an expanded ASEAN which would include the Indo-China states and Burma (in addition to Brunei, which on present indications will join ASEAN when it becomes independent in 1983). Such an arrangement could be expected to have strong supporters in Jakarta and Kuala Lumpur. It would, moreover, have the attraction of being a grouping whose membership was confined to Southeast Asian countries.

The Pacific Community concept raises other issues, such as the bureaucratic demands created by a wider grouping. It is also unclear at this stage what ASEAN could expect to get out of its membership. Above all, the major consideration is that since 1976 ASEAN has been able to achieve a significant degree of cohesion, even if progress on economic co-operation has been slow. Advocates of a 'Pacific Community' may be able to marshal convincing arguments to show the economic benefits to ASEAN of membership in such a grouping. But they may not be able to convince ASEAN governments, at least for some years to come, of the wisdom of exposing to dilution or external competition the ASEAN political solidarity which has taken so much time and effort to achieve.

Statistical Tables

TABLE 4.1 *ASEAN: Area and Population*
1978

	Area ('000 sq. km.)	Population (mid-1978) millions	Population density (per sq. km.)	Average population growth (%) 1960-70	Average population growth (%) 1970-78	Population projected to AD 2000
Indonesia	2,027	136.0	67	2.2	1.8	204
Malaysia	330	13.3	40	2.9	2.7	20
Philippines	300	45.6	152	3.0	2.7	75
Singapore	0.6	2.3	3,833	2.4	1.5	3
Thailand	514	44.5	86	3.0	2.7	68
ASEAN	3,172	241.7	176			370

Source: World Bank, World Development Indicators – Annex to *World Development Report, 1979* (Washington, DC, 1980).

TABLE 4.2 *ASEAN: Gross National Product and Food Production*
1978

	GNP per capita 1978 US $	Average annual growth, 1960-78 %	Average annual inflation rates 1960-70 %	Average annual inflation rates 1970-78 %	Index of food production per capita Av. 1976-8
Indonesia	360	4.1	–	20.0	100
Malaysia	1,090	3.9	-0.3	7.2	110
Philippines	490	2.6	5.8	13.4	115
Singapore	3,290	7.4	1.1	6.1	112
Thailand	510	4.6	1.9	9.1	122

Source: World Bank, World Development Indicators – Annex to *World Development Report, 1979* (Washington, DC, August 1980).

TABLE 4.3 ASEAN: Gross Domestic Product
1978

(A) *Percentage Growth Rates of GDP by Sector*

	GDP		Agriculture		Industry		Manufacturing		Services	
	1960–70	1970–78	1960–70	1970–78	1960–70	1970–78	1960–70	1970–78	1960–70	1970–78
Indonesia	3.5	7.8	2.5	4.0	5.0	11.2	3.3	12.4	8.0	8.7
Malaysia	6.5	7.8	—	5.0	—	9.6	—	12.3	—	8.4
Philippines	5.1	6.3	4.3	4.9	6.0	8.6	6.7	6.8	5.2	5.4
Singapore	8.8	8.5	5.0	1.5	12.6	8.5	13.0	9.2	7.7	8.6
Thailand	8.2	7.6	5.5	5.6	11.6	10.2	11.0	11.5	9.0	7.4

(B) *Percentage Distribution of GDP by Sector*

	Agriculture		Industry		Manufacturing		Services	
	1960	1978	1960	1978	1960	1978	1960	1978
Indonesia	54	31	14	33	8	9	32	36
Malaysia	37	25	18	32	9	17	45	43
Philippines	26	27	28	35	20	25	46	38
Singapore	4	2	18	35	12	26	78	63
Thailand	40	27	19	27	13	18	41	46

Source: World Bank, World Development Indicators — Annex to *World Development Report,*
1980 Washington, DC, August 1980).

TABLE 4.4 ASEAN Exports and Imports by General Commodities
1978/79
(Percentage of total)

ASEAN Country	Indonesia 1979		Malaysia 1979		Philippines 1978		Singapore 1979		Thailand 1978	
General commodities	Imports	Exports	Exports	Imports	Exports	Imports	Imports	Exports	Imports	Exports
0. Food and Live Animals	14.4	7.7	4.5	12.0	20.1	6.7	6.6	5.4	3.0	49.0
1. Beverages and Tobacco	0.3	0.4	—	1.1	1.0	0.9	0.5	0.4	1.0	1.4
2. Raw Materials (not fuels)	5.1	19.6	37.2	5.0	24.4	5.0	8.1	14.3	6.4	15.1
3. Mineral Fuels	11.1	65.2	17.9	12.0	0.3	21.2	25.2	24.0	21.2	0.1
4. Animal/Vegetable Oil/Fats	—	1.4	12.4	—	18.6	—	2.2	2.8	0.3	—
5. Chemicals	14.1	0.4	0.5	10.3	1.8	11.3	5.7	3.7	13.7	0.5
6. Basic Manufactures	19.3	3.6	13.7	17.2	9.1	14.8	15.0	9.1	17.1	20.6
7. Machinery and Transport Eqpt.	31.9	0.7	10.5	36.9	2.1	27.5	29.4	26.5	30.8	3.3
8. Miscellaneous Manufactures	3.0	0.5	2.5	4.6	9.8	2.6	5.9	6.9	2.8	6.7
9. Goods not Classified	0.8	0.4	0.6	0.6	12.8	9.7	1.3	6.9	3.6	3.2
Total Value (US $ Millions)	7,183	15,590	11,078	7,830	3,349	5,143	17,638	14,233	5,314	4,085

Source: United Nations, *Yearbook of International Trade Statistics 1979*, vol. 1 (New York, 1980).

TABLE 4.5 *ASEAN Countries' Trade by Country 1979*
(Percentage trade with specified partners)

ASEAN country Trade with:	Indonesia		Malaysia		Philippines		Singapore		Thailand[a]	
	Imports	Exports	Imports	Exports	Imports	Exports	Imports	Exports	Imports	Exports
Indonesia	–	–	1.0	0.2	3.0	1.0	11.1[b]	3.7[b]	0.5	1.7
Malaysia	0.5	0.4	–	–	1.5	1.2	14.1	14.3	1.3	5.2
Philippines	0.7	1.1	0.6	1.1	–	–	0.4	1.6	0.1	0.5
Singapore	7.6	12.6	9.2	17.4	1.3	1.4	–	–	4.1	8.1
Thailand	3.0	0.2	3.6	1.3	0.2	0.4	2.8	4.3	–	–
Total ASEAN	11.8	14.3	14.4	20.0	6.0	4.0	28.4	23.9	6.0	15.5
Japan	29.3	46.1	22.4	23.4	22.8	26.4	17.0	9.6	31.0	20.3
EEC (9)	14.7	7.5	17.5	17.7	13.9	20.2	11.3	13.2	13.9	26.3
United States	14.3	20.3	15.0	17.3	22.9	30.2	14.3	13.8	13.9	11.0
Australia	3.1	1.2	6.1	1.8	3.4	2.0	2.2	3.7	2.3	0.9
Others	26.8	10.6	24.6	19.8	31.0	17.2	26.8	35.8	33.0	26.0
Total Value (US $ Millions)	7,183	15,590	7,830	11,078	6,141	4,601	17,638	14,233	5,314	4,085

(a) Data for 1978. (b) Singapore does not report trade with Indonesia. Indonesia's reported trade with Singapore has been used.
Source: United Nations, *Yearbook of International Trade Statistics 1979*, vol. 1 (New York, 1980).

TABLE 7.1 *Australia–ASEAN Trade: 1973/74 to 1978/79 p: Summary*
$' 000 f.o.b.

	1973/74	1974/75	1975/76	1976/77	1977/78	1978/79
Exports	502,776	727,235	659,652	772,201	856,771	1,089,118
Imports	194,357	244,695	317,022	431,069	556,857	641,876
Balance (+)	308,419	482,540	342,630	341,132	299,914	447,242

TABLE 7.2 *Australia–ASEAN Trade, by Country*

A $ million

Indonesia	1973/74	1974/75	1975/76	1976/77	1977/78	1978/79
Australian Exports	107.6	177.5	161.6	180.6	196.3	217.6
Australian Imports	16.6	18.7	25.6	50.2	84.1	99.2
Balance	+91.0	+158.8	+136.0	+130.4	+112.2	+118.4

A $ million

Malaysia	1973/74	1974/75	1975/76	1976/77	1977/78	1978/79
Australian Exports	117.6	194.4	172.7	224.6	214.8	330.5
Australian Imports	69.5	58.8	82.1	113.4	120.5	152.6
Balance	+48.1	+135.6	+90.6	+111.2	+94.3	+177.9

A $ million

The Philippines	1973/74	1974/75	1975/76	1976/77	1977/78	1978/79
Australian Exports	79.2	99.7	93.5	118.5	130.5	165.8
Australian Imports	16.2	24.1	27.9	43.9	56.8	76.9
Balance	+63.0	+75.6	+65.6	+74.6	+73.7	+88.9

A $ million

Singapore	1973/74	1974/75	1975/76	1976/77	1977/78	1978/79
Australian Exports	147.7	206.2	185.3	183.5	240.7	263.8
Australian Imports	82.1	126.9	160.3	196.3	264.9	277.7
Balance	+65.6	+79.3	+25.0	−12.8	−24.2	−13.9

A $ million

Thailand	1973/74	1974/75	1975/76	1976/77	1977/78	1978/79
Australian Exports	50.6	49.4	46.4	65.0	74.5	112.8
Australian Imports	9.9	16.1	21.7	25.6	30.5	35.4
Balance	+40.7	+33.3	+24.7	+39.4	+44.0	+77.4

Source: Department of Trade and Resources, Australia

Notes and References

Chapter 2

1. Bernard K. Gordon, *Toward Disengagement: A Strategy for American Foreign Policy* (Prentice-Hall, 1969), p. 113.

2. Ibid., pp. 113–17.

3. *Antara News Bulletin*, 11 August 1967.

4. 'A New Era of Regional Co-operation', address to the Foreign Correspondents' Club, Johore Bahru, 23 June 1966.

5. 'Regional Co-operation in International Politics', pp. 161–2, in *Regionalism in Southeast Asia*, Centre for Strategic and International Studies, Jakarta, proceedings of a conference held in Jakarta, 22–5 October 1974.

6. *Antara News Bulletin*, 15 December 1966.

7. *Asian Almanac*, p. 2271.

8. UPI, Tokyo, 5 March 1968.

9. See, for example, 'A Policy of Regional Co-operation', in *Foreign Affairs Bulletin* (Thailand), August–September 1968, pp. 1–4.

10. Cited in Lela Garner Noble, 'The National Interest and the National Image: Philippine Policy in Asia', in *Asian Survey*, June 1973, p. 568.

11. Barbara Pace *et al.*, 'Regional Co-operation in Southeast Asia: The First Two Years of ASEAN 1967–1969', Research Analysis Corporation RAC-R-98-2, October 1970, p. 42.

12. *Foreign Affairs Malaysia*, 1, 7 and 8, p. 49.

13. Zainal Abidin A. Wahid, 'The Problem of Security in Southeast Asia: Is Neutralisation the Answer?', in *Nusantara*, January 1972, pp. 137–8.

14. 'Malaysia's Foreign Policy', in *Foreign Affairs Malaysia*, September 1971, pp. 24–9.

15. 'Neutralization of Southeast Asia', in *Pacific Community*, October 1971.

16. 'Indonesia and the World', Dyason Memorial Lectures 1967, Australian Institute of International Affairs.

17. 'Prospects of a New Pax Asiana', Dillingham Lectures 1969, East–West Center, Honolulu, Hawaii, delivered 9 October 1969.

18. *Foreign Affairs Bulletin* (Thailand), October–November 1971, p. 88.

19. 'Towards a New Era in Asia', in *Solidarity*, March 1972.

20. 'Southeast Asia in Transition', Dyason Memorial Lectures 1973, Australian Institute of International Affairs.

21. *Asian Almanac*, p. 5440.

Chapter 3

1. Joint Communiqué of the Seventh ASEAN Meeting, Jakarta, 7–9 May 1974, quoted in *10 Years ASEAN* (Jakarta, 1978), p. 279.

2. *Siaran Akhbar* (Malaysian Information Service Bulletin), Kuala Lumpur, 22 October 1974.

3. Laurence D. Stifel, 'ASEAN Cooperation and Economic Growth in Southeast Asia' in *Asia, Pacific Community*, Spring–Early Summer 1979, pp. 126–7.

4. Arnfinn Jorgensen-Dahl, 'ASEAN 1967–76, Development or Stagnation', in *Pacific Quarterly*, 7, 4, July 1976, p. 534.

5. *10 Years ASEAN*, op. cit., 281.

6. *Regionalism in Southeast Asia* (Papers presented at the First Conference of ASEAN Students of Regional Affairs; Jakarta, 22–5 October 1974), Jakarta, 1975, p. 8.

7. Ibid., p. 80.

8. Ibid., p. 8.

9. Ali Moertopo, 'Future Indonesian–US Relations: A View from Jakarta', *Pacific Community*, 7, 4, July 1976, p. 582.

10. Harvey Stockwin, *Far Eastern Economic Review (FEER)*, Hong Kong, 5 March 1976.

11. *The Straits Times* (Singapore), 30 October 1975.

12. Stifel, op. cit., pp. 126–7.

13. Michael Richardson, *The Age* (Melbourne), 10 October 1975.

14. Stockwin, *FEER*, 12 March 1976.

15. Richardson, *The Age*, op. cit.

16. Ibid.

17. *Antara Newsagency Bulletin* (Jakarta), 12 January 1976.

18. A. P. Renouf, *The Frightened Country* (Melbourne, 1979), p. 21.

19. Stockwin, *FEER*, 5 March 1976.

20. *10 Years ASEAN*, op. cit., p. 93.

21. Ibid., p. 98.

22. Ibid., p. 99.

23. Ibid., p. 104.

24. The text of this Agreement can be found in *10 Years ASEAN*, op. cit., pp. 125–32.

25. H. H. Indorff, 'ASEAN: Problems and Prospects', Occasional Paper no. 38 (December 1975), Institute of Southeast Asian Studies (Singapore), pp. 45–7.

26. *Kompas* (Jakarta), 1 August 1977.

27. Adam Malik's Opening Statement to the ASEAN Ministers at the Tenth Annual Ministerial Meeting in Singapore on 5–8 July 1977. This statement, together with those of the other Foreign Ministers, were obtained from transcripts distributed to the Press during the meeting.

28. Dharsono's appointment was formally terminated at the request of the Indonesian Government and with the consent of the other four member Governments on the grounds that the Secretary-General should not engage in domestic politics – as Dharsono had done in Indonesia in late 1977 and early 1978.

29. *FEER*, 28 December 1979.

30. *FEER*, 1 February 1980.

Chapter 4

1. This Chapter draws on material prepared for the Tenth Pacific Trade and Development Conference, held at the Australian National University, in Canberra, in March 1979. Proceedings appear in Ross Garnaut (ed.), *ASEAN in a Changing Pacific and World Economy* (Canberra: ANU Press, 1980).

2. Mari Pangestu, 'The ASEAN Economies: A Comparative Assessment of the Pattern of Trade and Direct Foreign Investment and Implications for Economic Cooperation', *World Review*, 19, 3, University of Queensland Press, August 1980, p. 18. See also: L. D. Stifel, 'ASEAN Cooperation and Economic Growth in S. E. Asia', *Asia Pacific Community*, Spring–Early Summer 1979, pp. 125–6.

3. Pangestu, op. cit., p. 17.

4. Ibid., p. 21. See also Garnaut (ed.), op. cit., for a fuller treatment.

5. Pangestu, op. cit., p. 21.

6. 'Economic Cooperation Among Member Countries of the Association of South East Asian Nations', Report of a United Nations Team, *Journal of Development Planning*, no. 7, United Nations, New York, 1974.

7. Ibid., p. 249.

8. Ibid., p. 52.

9. Ibid., p. 250.

10. Article 7 (see Appendix B).

11. Article 5 (see Appendix C).

12. John Wong, *ASEAN Economies in Perspective: A Comparative Study of Indonesia, Malaysia, the Philippines, Singapore and Thailand* (1979), p. 38.

13. Report of a United Nations Team, op. cit., p. 50.

14. Ibid., p. 54.

15. Hirono Ryokichi, 'Towards Increased Intra-ASEAN Cooperation', *Asia Pacific Community*, 3, Winter 1978, p. 108.

16. H. W. Arndt and Ross Garnaut, 'ASEAN and the Industrialisation of East Asia', *Journal of Common Market Studies*, XVII, 3 (March 1979).

17. At a meeting in Kuala Lumpur in April 1981, after this chapter was written, ASEAN Energy Ministers set up their own Committee on Energy Cooperation (COEC).

18. A fuller treatment of ASEAN banking and finance can be found in Michael T. Skully, *ASEAN Regional Financial Co-operation, Developments in Banking and Finance*, Institute of Southeast Asian Studies, Singapore, Occasional Paper no. 56, 1979.

Chapter 6

1. For the period 1970–79 annual average economic growth rates for the ASEAN countries ranged from 6.1 per cent to 9.2 per cent.

2. See particularly L. Niksch, *ASEAN: An Emerging Challenge in US Policy Towards Asia*, November 1978, p. 81.

3. *Asian Wall Street Journal*, 6 March 1978.

4. Speech by Vice-President Mondale, East–West Center, Honolulu, 10 March 1978.

5. For an account of the early problems in establishing the ASEAN–Canada dialogue see A. Douglas Small, 'The Developing Relationship between Canada and ASEAN', *International Perspectives*, March/April 1978.

6. The question of whether ASEAN should accord some form of associate status to Papua New Guinea, whose observer had attended several dialogue

meetings following the annual meetings of ASEAN Foreign Ministers, was under discussion in 1980 and 1981. Along with this, the status of Brunei, due for independence in 1983, and of Sri Lanka, which in April 1981 sought an association with ASEAN, were under consideration by ASEAN Foreign Ministers in mid–1981.

7. Quoted in Frank Frost, *Vietnam and ASEAN*, unpublished paper, 1979.

8. Russell H. Fifield, *National and Regional Interests in ASEAN: Competition and Co-operation in International Politics*, ISEAS, Singapore, 1979.

9. For a full treatment of this subject see John Funston, 'The Third Indochina War and Southeast Asia', *Contemporary Southeast Asia*, December 1979. Also *Far Eastern Economic Review (FEER)*, 19 December 1980.

10. See, for example, *FEER*, 9 May 1980, p. 12.

11. *FEER*, 16 November 1979.

12. *FEER*, 8 September 1980.

13. *FEER*, 8 September 1980.

14. See Chee-meow Seah, 'Major Powers in the Search for a New Equilibrium in Southeast Asia', *Asian Pacific Community*, no. 7, Winter 1980.

15. Lee Kuan Yew, speech in Orlando, Florida, USA, 5 October 1978.

Chapter 7

1. *Daily Mirror* (Sydney), 29 April 1969.

2. 'Southeast Asia: The Neutralisation Proposals', *Current Notes on International Affairs*, 43, 10, October 1972, pp. 498–504.

3. Speech to Thai–Australian Association, Bangkok, 1 February 1974, in *Australian Foreign Affairs Record*, 45, 2, February 1974, p. 76.

4. *Australian Financial Review*, 19 January 1976.

5. Department of Trade and Resources, 'Submission to Standing Committee on Foreign Affairs and Defence' (Canberra, 1980), p. 1.

6. Ibid., p. 4.

7. Ibid., p. 5.

8. C. T. Edwards, 'Australia and Asia: Emerging Economic Challenges', in *Recent Changes in Asia: Australian Responses*, Centre for Continuing Education, Australian National University, Canberra, 1977, pp. 23–4; Industries Assistance Commission, *Annual Report 1976– 77*, pp. 22–38; Bureau of Industry Economics, 'Industrialisation in Asia: Some Implications for Australian Industry', Canberra 1978.

9. C. T. Edwards, 'Current Issues in Australian-ASEAN Trade Relations' in *Southeast Asian Affairs 1979*, Singapore, 1979, pp. 30–44.

10. *Far Eastern Economic Review*, 10 June 1977.

11. *Australian Financial Review*, 22 November 1978.

12. Cf. Prime Minister Fraser's 'Address to Second ASEAN Trade Fair, Melbourne', 4 August 1980.

13. 'Speech by Tengku Razaleigh Hamzah, Minister of Finance, Malaysia, to the First ASEAN–Australia Business Conference on Tuesday 24th June 1980', pp. 7–8.

14. *Far Eastern Economic Review*, 31 October–6 November 1980.

15. On the ICAP issue, see Robyn Lim, 'Current ASEAN-Australian Relations', *Southeast Asian Affairs 1980*, Singapore, 1980, pp. 37–53; and *Far Eastern Economic Review*, 23 February, 2 March, 9 March, 30 March, 18 May, 25 May 1979.

16. *Far Eastern Economic Review*, 9 March 1979.

17. On the refugee issue, see especially Nancy Viviani, 'Australian Government Policy on the Entry of Vietnamese Refugees in 1975', and Viviani and

Joanna Lawe-Davies, 'Australian Government Policy on the Entry of Vietnamese Refugees', Centre for the Study of Australian–Asian Relations, Griffith University, 1980.

18. Frank Frost and Carlyle A. Thayer, 'Australia and Vietnam 1950–1980', in *Dyason House Papers*, 6, 3, March 1980, pp. 1–12.

19. Report of the Committee on Australia's Relations with the Third World, *Australia and the Third World*, Canberra 1979, p. 125.

20. Ibid., p. 127.

21. Business Times (Kuala Lumpur), 29 April 1981.

Chapter 8

1. Yano Tōru, *Nihon no 'nanshin' to tōnan ajia* (Japan's 'advance to the South' and Southeast Asia), Tokyo, *Nihon Keizai Shimbunsha,* 1975.

2. Yoshida Shigeru, *The Yoshida Memoirs* (London: Heinemann, 1961), p. 9.

3. Yoshida himself has written to this effect. See *The Yoshida Memoirs*, ibid., pp. 123–4, where he writes that 'the economic development of Asia was the best means of defending the freedom and peace of Asia'.

4. Edgar C. Harrell, *Japan's Postwar Aid Policies*, unpublished PhD dissertation, Columbia University, 1976, p. 4.

5. Lawrence Olson, *Japan in Postwar Asia* (London: Pall Mall Press, 1970), Chapter II.

6. Ibid., p. 66.

7. Immediately after the establishment of ASEAN, the Ambassador Kai said at Kuala Lumpur Airport, while leaving for Canberra, that Japan would consider the proposition seriously, if Japan were invited to join ASEAN. But Prime Minister Sato told the Press in Singapore that there now were too many regional organisations, although he was in favour of establishing such organisations. At the end of his tour, Mr Sato said that it was misleading to think of Asia as one cohesive region; indeed he found varieties among Asian countries. Ikema Makoto, 'Japan's Economic Relations with ASEAN' paper presented to the Tenth Pacific Trade and Development Conference, ANU, Canberra, March 1979.

8. Lawrence Krause, 'Direct Foreign Investment in ASEAN by Japan and the United States' paper to Tenth Pacific Trade and Development Conference, Canberra, March 1979; and Yoshihara Kunio, *Japanese Investment in Southeast Asia*, Honolulu, The University Press of Hawaii, 1978.

9. *Asahi Shimbun* (hereafter *Asahi*), 8 August 1967.

10. *Nihon Keizai Shimbun* (hereafter *Nikkei*), 9 August 1967.

11. *Asahi*, 5 August 1968.

12. *Asahi*, 26 and 30 September 1967.

13. Colin Barlow, *The Natural Rubber Industry* (Kuala Lumpur: Oxford University Press, 1978), p. 111.

14. Lim Swee Aun, *Rubber and the Malaysian Economy*, Ohio University, 1969, p. 30.

15. Irfan ul Haque, *Analysis of Natural Rubber Market*, IBRD Economic Staff Working Paper, no. 133, August 1972.

16. Lim Teck Ghee, in Institute of Southeast Asian Studies, *Japan as an Economic Power and its Implications for Southeast Asia* (Singapore: Singapore University Press, 1974), p. 92.

17. Yoshihara Kunio, in *Japan as an Economic Power*, op. cit., p. 105.

18. Wakaizumi Kei, 'Tanaka's Approach to Summit Diplomacy', in *Pacific Community*, 5, 2, January 1974, p. 284.

19. *Nikkei*, 26 February 1976.
20. At a speech at the National Press Club in Washington.
21. H. W. Arndt and Ross Garnaut, 'ASEAN and the Industrialization of Southeast Asia', *Journal of Common Market Studies*, XVII, 3, March 1979, p. 199.
22. See Jenny Corbett and Ross Garnaut, 'Japan and the Resource-rich Developing Countries', *Australia–Japan Economic Relations Research Paper* no. 25, Canberra, February 1975.
23. *Nikkei*, 23 January 1977.
24. See Chapter 4 of this volume.
25. See *Nikkei*, 20 January 1977, *Asahi*, 21 January 1977 and *Mainichi Shimbun*, 26 January 1977.
26. *Asahi*, 18 July 1977.
27. *Yomiuri Shimbun*, 5 August 1977.
28. For a full text of the speech, see *Japan Times Weekly*, 27 August 1977.
29. *Asiaweek*, 22 February 1980.
30. *Asian Wall Street Journal*, 23 January 1979.

Chapter 9

1. Keith Buchanan, 'South-East Asia', *The Far East and Australasia 1975–76*, (London: 1975), Europa Publications, pp. 139–57.
2. Ibid.
3. Ho Kwon Ping and Cheah Cheng Hye, 'The Arming of ASEAN', *Far Eastern Economic Review (FEER)*, 24 October 1980, p. 36.
4. Ho Kwon Ping, 'The Landed and the Landless', *FEER*, 13 July 1979, p. 46.
5. Quoted in Lau Teik Soon, 'The Role of Singapore in Southeast Asia', *World Review*, 19, 3, University of Queensland, August 1980.
6. *Thailand: Towards a Development Strategy of Full Participation*, World Bank, Washington, 5 May 1978, pp. 27–54.
7. Ibid.
8. Ho Kwon Ping, 'Thailand's Broken Rice Bowl', *FEER*, 1 December 1978, pp. 40–44.
9. Ibid.
10. World Bank, op. cit.
11. Ibid.
12. Ibid.
13. Ibid.
14. *Asian Wall Street Journal*, 20 August 1980.
15. Ibid.
16. Sheilah Ocampo, 'The Prophet of Doom and Violence', *FEER*, 15 August 1980, pp. 8–9.
17. Ho Kwon Ping, 'The Mortgaged New Society', *FEER*, 19 June 1979, pp. 51–6.
18. Ibid.
19. Ibid.
20. Ibid.
21. Ibid.
22. Ibid.
23. Ho Kwon Ping, 'Back to the Drawing Board', *FEER*, 27 April 1979, pp. 86–93.

24. Ibid.
25. Ibid.
26. *Indonesia: Growth Patterns, Social Progress and Development Prospects*, World Bank, Washington, 20 February 1979.
27. Ibid.
28. *FEER*, 27 June 1979.
29. Ibid.
30. *FEER*, 24 October 1980.
31. Ibid.

Chapter 10

1. Tan Sri M. Ghazali Shafie, 'Towards a Pacific Basin Community – A Malaysian Perception', Conference on New Foundations for Asian and Pacific Community, Pattaya, 12 December 1979.
2. See Constantino Vaitsos, 'Crisis in Regional Cooperation (Integration) among Developing Countries: A Survey', *World Development*, no. 6, 1978.
3. See Philip Bowring, 'A Negative View of the "Historic" ASEAN–EC Accord', *Asian Wall Street Journal*, 12 March 1980.
4. See Harold Crouch, *The Army and Politics in Indonesia* (Cornell, 1978), pp. 330–43.
5. See Sharon Siddique, 'Contemporary Islamic Developments in ASEAN', *Southeast Asian Affairs* (Singapore), 1980; and Carl A. Trocki, 'Islam: Threat to ASEAN Regional Unity?', *Current History*, April 1980.
6. Russell H. Fifield, 'ASEAN: Image and Reality', *Asian Survey*, XIX, 12, December 1979, p. 1203.
7. Lynn K. Mytelka, *Regional Development in Global Economy: The Multinational Corporation, Technology, and Andean Integration* (New Haven and London: Yale University Press, 1979), p. 21.
8. The ANDEAN Pact consists of Bolivia, Colombia, Ecuador, Peru and Venezuela. For details of Decision 24, see Roger W. Fontaine, 'The ANDEAN Pact: A Political Analysis', Washington Papers, Sage, 1977; and Mytelka, op. cit.
9. Ricardo French-Davis, 'The ANDEAN Pact: A Model of Economic Integration for Developing Countries', *World Development*, 5, 1/2, 1977, p. 144.
10. David Sycip, in *ASEAN and the Multinational Corporations* Singapore: ISEAS, 1977), p. 90.
11. Since the renegotiation of the bases agreement in December 1978, the bases are officially 'Philippine' bases.
12. Franklin B. Weinstein, *Indonesian Foreign Policy and the Dilemma of Dependence: from Sukarno to Suharto* (Cornell, 1976), p. 82.
13. Crouch, op. cit., p. 343.
14. Selig S. Harrison, *The Widening Gulf: Asian Nationalism and American Policy* (Free Press, 1978), p. 429.
15. Guy G. Pauker, Frank H. Golay and Cynthia H. Enloe, *Diversity and Development in Southeast Asia: The Coming Decade* (1980's Project Council on Foreign Relations, McGraw-Hill, 1977), p. 76.
16. Harrison, op. cit., p. 28.
17. Ibid.
18. Pauker, in Pauker, Golay and Enloe, op. cit., p. 43.

19. Organization for Pacific Trade and Development. See Peter Drysdale and Hugh Patrick, 'Evaluation of a proposed Asian–Pacific Regional Economic Organisation', Australia–Japan Economic Relations Research Project, Research Paper no. 61, July 1979.

20. *Far Eastern Economic Review*, 21 December 1979.

21. Tan Sri M. Ghazali Shafie, op. cit.

22. Charles E. Morrison and Astri Suhrke, *Strategies of Survival: the Foreign Policy Dilemmas of Smaller Asian States* (University of Queensland, 1978), p. 218.

Appendix A

The ASEAN Declaration
(Bangkok Declaration, 1967)

The Presidium Minister for Political Affairs/Minister for Foreign Affairs of Indonesia, the Deputy Prime Minister of Malaysia, the Secretary of Foreign Affairs of the Philippines, the Minister for Foreign Affairs of Singapore and the Minister of Foreign Affairs of Thailand:

MINDFUL of the existence of mutual interests and common problems among the countries of South East Asia and convinced of the need to strengthen further the existing bonds of regional solidarity and co-operation;

DESIRING to establish a firm foundation for common action to promote regional cooperation in South East Asia in the spirit of equality and partnership and thereby contribute towards peace progress and prosperity in the region;

CONSCIOUS that in an increasingly interdependent world, the cherished ideals of peace, freedom, social justice and economic well being are best attained by fostering good understanding, good neighbourliness and meaningful cooperation among the countries of the region already bound together by ties of history and culture;

CONSIDERING that the countries of South East Asia share a primary responsibility for strengthening the economic and social stability of the region and ensuring their peaceful and progressive national development, and that they are determined to ensure their stability and security from external interference in any form or manifestation in order to preserve their national identities in accordance with the ideals and aspirations of their peoples;

AFFIRMING that all foreign bases are temporary and remain only with the expressed concurrence of the countries concerned and are not intended to be used directly or indirectly to subvert the national independence and freedom of States in the area or prejudice the orderly processes of their national development;

DO HEREBY DECLARE:

FIRST, the establishment of an Association for Regional Cooperation among the countries of South East Asia to be known as the Association of South East Asian Nations (ASEAN).

SECOND, that the aims and purposes of the Association shall be:
1. To accelerate the economic growth, social progress and cultural development in the region through joint endeavours in the spirit of equality and partnership in order to strengthen the foundation for a prosperous and peaceful community of South East Asian nations;
2. To promote regional peace and stability through abiding respect for justice and the rule of law in the relationship among countries of the region and adherence to the principles of the United Nations Charter;
3. To promote active collaboration and mutual assistance on matters of common interest in the economic, social, cultural, technical, scientific and administrative fields;
4. To provide assistance to each other in the form of training and research facilities in the educational, professional, technical and administrative spheres;
5. To collaborate more effectively for the greater utilization of their agriculture and industries, the expansion of their trade, including the study of the problems of international commodity trade, the improvement of their transportation and communication facilities and the raising of the living standards of their peoples;
6. To promote South East Asian studies;
7. To maintain close and beneficial cooperation with existing international and regional organisations with similar aims and purposes, and explore all avenues for even closer cooperation among themselves.

THIRD, that, to carry out these aims and purposes, the following machinery shall be established:

(a) Annual Meeting of Foreign Ministers, which shall be by rotation and referred to as ASEAN Ministerial Meeting. Special Meetings of Foreign Ministers may be convened as required;

(b) A Standing Committee, under the chairmanship of the Foreign Minister of the host country or his representative and having as its members the accredited Ambassadors of the other member countries, to carry on the work of the Association in between Meetings of Foreign Ministers;

(c) Ad Hoc Committees and Permanent Committees of specialists and officials on specific subjects;

(d) A National Secretariat in each member country to carry out the work of the Association on behalf of that country and to service the Annual or Special Meetings of Foreign Ministers, the Standing Committee and such other committees as may hereafter be established.

FOURTH, that the Association is open for participation to all States in the South East Asian Region subscribing to the aforementioned aims, principles and purposes.

FIFTH, that the Association represents the collective will of the nations of South East Asia to bind themselves together in friendship and cooperation and, through joint efforts and sacrifices, secure for their peoples and for posterity the blessings of peace, freedom and prosperity.

DONE in Bangkok this Eighth Day of August in the Year One
Thousand Nine Hundred and Sixty-Seven.

For Indonesia
(Sgd.) ADAM MALIK
Presidium Minister for
Political Affairs/Minister for Foreign Affairs

For Malaysia
(Sgd.) TUN ABDUL RAZAK
Deputy Prime Minister
Minister of Defense and
Minister of National
Development

For the Philippines
(Sgd.) NARCISO RAMOS
Secretary of Foreign Affairs

For Singapore
(Sgd.) S. RAJARATNAM
Minister for Foreign Affairs

For Thailand
(Sgd.) THANAT KHOMAN
Minister of Foreign Affairs

Appendix B

Treaty of Amity and Co-operation in Southeast Asia (1976)

PREAMBLE

The High Contracting Parties:

CONSCIOUS of the existing ties of history, geography and culture, which have bound their peoples together;

ANXIOUS to promote regional peace and stability through abiding respect for justice and the rule of law and enhancing regional resilience in their relations;

DESIRING to enhance peace, friendship and mutual cooperation on matters affecting Southeast Asia consistent with the spirit and principles of the Charter of the United Nations, the Ten Principles adopted by the Asian—African Conference on Bandung on 25 April 1955, the Declaration of the Association of Southeast Asian Nations signed in Bangkok on 8 August 1967, and the Declaration signed in Kuala Lumpur on 27 November 1971;

CONVINCED that the settlement of differences or disputes between their countries should be regulated by rational, effective and sufficiently flexible procedures, avoiding negative attitudes which might endanger or hinder cooperation;

BELIEVING in the need for cooperation with all peace loving nations, both within and outside Southeast Asia, in the furtherance of world peace, stability and harmony;

SOLEMNLY AGREE to enter into a Treaty of Amity and Cooperation as follows:

CHAPTER I

Purpose and Principles

Article 1

The purpose of this Treaty is to promote peace, everlasting amity and cooperation among their peoples which would contribute to their strength, solidarity and closer relationship.

Article 2

In their relations with one another, the High Contracting Parties shall be guided by the following fundamental principles:

a. Mutual respect for the independence, sovereignty, equality, territorial integrity and national identity of all nations;

b. The right of every State to lead its national existence free from external interference, subversion or coercion;

c. Non-interference in the internal affairs of one another;

d. Settlement of differences or disputes by peaceful means;

e. Renunciation of the threat or use of force;

f. Effective cooperation among themselves.

CHAPTER II
Amity
Article 3

In pursuance to the purpose of this Treaty the High Contracting Parties shall endeavour to develop and strengthen the traditional, cultural and historical ties of friendship, good neighbourliness and cooperation which bind them together and shall fulfil in good faith the obligations assumed under this Treaty. In order to promote closer understanding among them, the High Contracting Parties shall encourage and facilitate contact and intercourse among their peoples.

CHAPTER III
Cooperation
Article 4

The High Contracting Parties shall promote active cooperation in the economic, cultural, technical, scientific and administrative fields as well as in matters of common ideals and aspirations of international peace and stability in the region and all other matters of common interest.

Article 5

Pursuant to Article 4 the High Contracting Parties shall exert their maximum efforts multilaterally as well as bilaterally on the basis of equality, nondiscrimination and mutual benefit.

Article 6

The High Contracting Parties shall collaborate for the acceleration of the economic growth in the region in order to strengthen the foundation for a prosperous and peaceful community of nations in Southeast Asia. To this end, they shall promote the greater utilisation of their agriculture and industries, the expansion of their trade and the improvement of their economic infrastructure for the mutual benefit of their principles. In this regard, they shall continue to explore all avenues for close and essential cooperation with other States as well as international and regional organisations outside the region.

Article 7

The High Contracting Parties, in order to achieve social justice and to raise the standards of living of the peoples of the region, shall intensify economic cooperation. For this purpose, they shall adopt appropriate regional strategies for economic development and mutual assistance.

Article 8
The High Contracting Parties shall strive to achieve the closest co-operation on the widest scale and shall seek to provide assistance to one another in the form of training and research facilities in the social, cultural, technical, scientific and administrative fields.

Article 9
The High Contracting Parties shall endeavour to foster cooperation in the furtherance of the cause of peace, harmony and stability in the region. To this end, the High Contracting Parties shall maintain regular contacts and consultations with one another on international and regional matters with a view to coordinating their views, actions and policies.

Article 10
Each High Contracting Party shall not in any manner or form participate in any activity which shall constitute a threat to the political and economic stability, sovereignty, or territorial integrity of another High Contracting Party.

Article 11
The High Contracting Parties shall endeavour to strengthen their respective national resilience in their political, economic, socio-cultural as well as security fields in conformity with their respective ideals and aspirations, free from external interference as well as internal subversive activities in order to preserve their respective national identities.

Article 12
The High Contracting Parties in their efforts to achieve regional prosperity and security, shall endeavour to cooperate in all fields for the promotion of regional resilience, based on the principles of self confidence, self reliance, mutual respect, cooperation and solidarity which will constitute the foundation for a strong and viable community of nations in Southeast Asia.

CHAPTER IV
Pacific Settlement of Disputes
Article 13
The High Contracting Parties shall have the determination and good faith to prevent disputes. In case disputes on matters directly affecting them should arise, especially disputes likely to disturb regional peace and harmony, they shall refrain from the threat or use of force and shall at all times settle such disputes among themselves through friendly negotiations.

Article 14
To settle disputes through regional processes, the High Contracting Parties shall constitute, as a continuing body, a High Council comprising a Representative at ministerial level from each of the High Contracting Parties to take cognizance of the existence of disputes or situations likely to disturb regional peace and harmony.

Article 15
In the event no solution is reached through direct negotiations, the High Council shall take cognizance of the dispute or the situation and shall recommend to the parties in dispute appropriate means of settlement such as good offices, mediation, inquiry or conciliation. The High Council may however offer its good offices, or upon agreement of the parties in dispute, constitute itself into a committee of mediation, inquiry or conciliation. When deemed necessary, the High Council shall recommend appropriate measures for the prevention of a deterioration of the dispute or the situation.

Article 16
The foregoing provisions of this Chapter shall not apply to a dispute unless all the parties to the dispute agree to their application to that dispute. However, this shall not preclude the other High Contracting Parties not party to the dispute from offering all possible assistance to settle the said dispute. Parties to the dispute should be well disposed towards such offers of assistance.

Article 17
Nothing in this Treaty shall preclude recourse to the modes of peaceful settlement contained in Article 33 (1) of the Charter of the United Nations. The High Contracting Parties which are parties to a dispute should be encouraged to take initiatives to solve it by friendly negotiations before resorting to the other procedures provided for in the Charter of the United Nations.

CHAPTER V
General Provisions
Article 18
This Treaty shall be signed by the Republic of Indonesia, Malaysia, the Republic of the Philippines, the Republic of Singapore and the Kingdom of Thailand. It shall be ratified in accordance with the constitutional procedures of each signatory State.

It shall be open for accession by other States in Southeast Asia.

Article 19
This Treaty shall enter into force on the date of the deposit of the fifth instrument of ratification with the Governments of the signatory States which are designated Depositories of this Treaty and of the instruments of ratification or accession.

Article 20
This Treaty is drawn up in the languages of the High Contracting Parties, all of which are equally authoritative. There shall be an agreed common translation of the texts in the English language. Any divergent interpretation of the common text shall be settled by negotiation.

IN FAITH THEREOF the High Contracting Parties have signed the Treaty and have hereto affixed their Seals.

DONE in Denpasar, Bali, on the twenty fourth day of February in the year One thousand nine hundred and seventy six.

For the Republic of Indonesia
(Sgd.) SOEHARTO
President

For Malaysia
(Sgd.) DATUK HUSSEIN ONN
Prime Minister

For the Republic of the Philippines
(Sgd.) FERDINAND E. MARCOS
President

For the Republic of Singapore
(Sgd.) LEE KUAN YEW
Prime Minister

For the Kingdom of Thailand
(Sgd.) KUKRIT PRAMOJ
Prime Minister

Declaration of ASEAN Concord (1976)

A COMMON BOND EXISTING AMONG THE MEMBER STATES OF THE ASSOCIATION OF SOUTHEAST ASIAN NATIONS,

The President of the Republic of Indonesia, the Prime Minister of Malaysia, the President of the Republic of the Philippines, the Prime Minister of the Republic of Singapore, and the Prime Minister of the Kingdom of Thailand,

REAFFIRM their commitment to the Declarations of Bandung, Bangkok and Kuala Lumpur, and the Charter of the United Nations;

ENDEAVOUR to promote peace, progress, prosperity and the welfare of the peoples of member states;

UNDERTAKE to consolidate the achievements of ASEAN and expand ASEAN cooperation in the economic, social, cultural and political fields;

DO HEREBY DECLARE:

ASEAN cooperation shall take into account, among others, the following objectives and principles in the pursuit of political stability:

1. The stability of each member state and of the ASEAN region is an essential contribution to international peace and security. Each member state resolves to eliminate threats posed by subversion to its stability thus strengthening national and ASEAN resilience.

2. Member states, individually and collectively, shall take active steps for the early establishment of the Zone of Peace, Freedom and Neutrality.

3. The elimination of poverty, hunger, disease and illiteracy is a primary concern of member states. They shall therefore intensify cooperation in economic and social development, with particular emphasis on the promotion of social justice and on the improvement of the living standard of their peoples.

4. Natural disasters and other major calamities can retard the pace of development of member states. They shall extend within their capabilities, assistance for relief of member states in distress.

5. Member states shall take cooperative action in their national and

regional development programmes, utilising as far as possible the resources available in the ASEAN region to broaden the complementariness of their respective economies.

6. Member states, in the spirit of ASEAN solidarity, shall rely exclusively on peaceful processes in the settlement of intraregional differences.

7. Member states shall strive, individually and collectively, to create conditions conducive to the promotion of peaceful cooperation among the nations of Southeast Asia on the basis of mutual respect and mutal benefits.

8. Member states shall vigorously develop an awareness of regional identity and exert all efforts to create a strong ASEAN community, respected by all, and respecting all nations on the basis of mutually advantageous relationships, and in accordance with the principles of self determination, sovereign equality and non-interference in the internal affairs of nations.

AND DO HEREBY ADOPT:

The following programme of action as a framework for ASEAN cooperation.

A. Political

1. Meeting of the Heads of Government of the member states as and when necessary;
2. Signing of Treaty of Amity and Cooperation in Southeast Asia;
3. Settlement of intraregional disputes by peaceful means as soon as possible;
4. Immediate consideration of initial steps towards recognition of and respect for the Zone of Peace, Freedom and Neutrality wherever possible;
5. Improvement of ASEAN machinery to strengthen political cooperation;
6. Study on how to develop judicial cooperation including the possibility of an ASEAN Extradition Treaty;
7. Strengthening of political solidarity by promoting the harmonisation of views, coordinating positions and, where possible and desirable, taking common actions.

B. Economic

1. Cooperation on Basic Commodities, particularly Food and Energy

   i. Member states shall assist each other by according priority to the supply of the individual country's needs in critical circumstances, and priority to the acquisition of exports from member states, in respect to of basic commodities, particularly food and energy.

   ii. Member states shall also intensify cooperation in the production of basic commodities particularly food and energy in the individual member states of the region.

2. Industrial Cooperation

i. Member states shall cooperate to establish large scale ASEAN industrial plants, particularly to meet regional requirements of essential commodities.

ii. Priority shall be given to projects which utilise the available materials in the member states, contribute to the increase of food production, increase foreign exchange earnings or save foreign exchange, and create employment.

3. Cooperation in Trade

i. Member states shall cooperate in the fields of trade in order to promote development and growth of new production and trade and to improve the trade structures of individual states and among countries of ASEAN conducive to further development and to safeguard and increase their foreign exchange earnings and reserves.

ii. Member states shall progress towards the establishment of preferential trading arrangements as a long term objective on a basis deemed to be at any particular time appropriate, through rounds of negotiations subject to the unanimous agreement of member states.

iii. The expansion of trade among member states shall be facilitated through cooperation on basic commodities, particularly in food and energy, and through cooperation in ASEAN industrial projects.

iv. Member states shall accelerate joint efforts to improve access to markets outside ASEAN for their raw materials and finished products by seeking the elimination of all trade barriers in those markets, developing new usage for these products and in adopting common approaches and actions in dealing with regional groupings and individual economic powers.

v. Such efforts shall also lead to cooperation in the field of technology and production methods in order to increase the production and to improve the quality of export products, as well as to develop new export products with a view to diversifying exports.

4. Joint Approach to International Commodity Problems and Other World Economic Problems

i. The Principle of ASEAN cooperation on trade shall also be reflected on a priority basis in joint approaches to international commodity problems and other world economic problems such as the reform of international trading systems, the reform of international monetary system, and transfer of real resources, in the United Nations and other relevant multilateral fora, with a view to contributing to the establishment of the New International Economic Order.

ii. Member states shall give priority to the stabilisation and increase of export earnings of these commodities produced and exported by them through commodity agreements including bufferstock schemes and other means.

5. Machinery for Economic Cooperation

Ministerial meetings on economic matters shall be held regularly or as deemed necessary in order to:

i. Formulate recommendations for the consideration of Governments of member states for the strengthening of ASEAN economic cooperation;

    ii. Review the coordination and implementation of agreed ASEAN programs and projects on economic cooperation;

    iii. Exchange views and consult on national development plans and policies as a step towards harmonising regional development; and

    iv. Perform such other relevant functions as agreed upon by the member Governments.

C. Social

1. Cooperation in the field of social development, with emphasis on the well being of the low income groups and of the rural population, through the expansion of opportunities for productive employment with fair remuneration;

2. Support for the active involvement of all sectors and levels of the ASEAN communities, particularly the women and youth, in development efforts;

3. Intensification and expansion of existing cooperation in meeting the problems of population growth in ASEAN region, and where possible, formulation of new strategies in collaboration with appropriate international agencies;

4. Intensification of cooperation among member states as well as with the relevant international bodies in the prevention and eradication of the abuse of narcotics and the illegal trafficking of drugs.

D. Cultural and Information

1. Introduction of the study of ASEAN, its member states and their national languages as part of the curricula of schools and other institutions of learning in the member states;

2. Support of ASEAN scholars, writers, artists, and mass media representatives to enable them to play an active role in fostering a sense of regional identity and fellowship;

3. Promotion of Southeast Asian Studies through closer collaboration among national institutes.

E. Security

1. Continuation of cooperation on a non ASEAN basis between the member states in security matters in accordance with their mutual needs and interests.

F. Improvement of ASEAN Machinery

1. Signing of the Agreement on the Establishment of the ASEAN Secretariat;

2. Regular review of the ASEAN organisational structure with a view to improving its effectiveness;

3. Study of the desirability of a new constitutional framework for ASEAN.

DONE at Denpasar, Bali, this twenty fourth day of February in the year one thousand nine hundred and seventy six.

For the Republic of Indonesia
(Sgd.) SOEHARTO
President

For Malaysia
(Sgd.) DATUK HUSSEIN ONN
Prime Minister

For the Republic of the Philippines
(Sgd.) FERDINAND E. MARCOS
President

For the Republic of Singapore
(Sgd.) LEE KUAN YEW
Prime Minister

For the Kingdom of Thailand
(Sgd.) KUKRIT PRAMOJ
Prime Minister

Appendix D

The Agreement on ASEAN Preferential Trading Arrangements (1977)

THE GOVERNMENTS OF THE REPUBLIC OF INDONESIA, MALAYSIA, THE REPUBLIC OF THE PHILIPPINES, THE REPUBLIC OF SINGAPORE AND THE KINGDOM OF THAILAND:

(Note: The Agreement on ASEAN Preferential Trading Arrangements signed on 16 February 1977 is subject to ratification by the respective Governments.)

Recalling the Declaration of ASEAN Concord signed in Bali, Indonesia on 24 February 1976, which provides that Member States shall take cooperative action in their national and regional development programmes, utilising as far as possible the resources available in the ASEAN region to broaden the complementariness of their respective economies;

EMPHASISING that preferential trading arrangements among ASEAN Member States will act as a stimulus to the strengthening of national and ASEAN economic resilience and the development of the national economies of the Member States by expanding investment and production opportunities, trade and foreign exchange earnings;

NOTING that the International Community has fully recognised the importance of encouraging the establishment of preferences among developing countries at the international, regional and sub-regional levels, particularly through the resolution of the United Nations General Assembly establishing the International Development Strategy for the Second UN Development Decade and the Declaration on the Establishment of a New International Economic Order and the Programme of Action for the Establishment of a New International Economic Order, the Declaration of Trade Expansion, Economic Cooperation and Regional Integration Among Developing Countries adopted at UNCTAD II and Resolution 92(IV) of UNCTAD IV: as well as of the General Agreement of Tariffs and Trade, particularly Part IV, and decision made in pursuance thereof;

NOTING further that developed and developing countries have taken some decision to promote preferential arrangements among developing countries as well as between developed and developing countries in terms favorable to the latter;

HAVE AGREED to establish ASEAN Preferential Trading Arrangement as stipulated by the following provisions:

CHAPTER I
General Provisions
Article 1
1. The respective Governments of ASEAN Member States on whose behalf the present Agreement is accepted, hereinafter trade preferences to each other in accordance with the provisions of this Agreement and the rules, regulations and decisions agreed within its framework.
2. The Contracting States agree to establish Preferential Trading Arrangements among them through the adoption of instruments, as may be appropriate, for ASEAN trade expansion.
3. Upon entry into force of this Agreement, concessions on products originating from all Contracting States agreed upon among them through rounds of negotiations shall be implemented by them in accordance with the provisions of this Agreement and any other supplementary agreements and/or contracts which may be concluded within the context of the Preferential Trading Arrangements on the individual products or groups of products.
4. The Contracting States agree that the Preferential Trading Arrangements among them shall be implemented in the spirit of ASEAN cooperation and mutual benefits.

Article 2
Contracting States shall cooperate through mutual assistance in respect of basic commodities, particularly food and energy; provisions of market support of the products of the ASEAN industrial projects; expansion of intra ASEAN trade and increase in the utilisation of raw materials available in the Contracting States.

CHAPTER II
Instruments and Definition of Preferential Trading Arrangements
Article 3
The Contracting States agree to adopt the following Instruments for Preferential Trading Arrangements: long term quantity contracts; purchase finance support at preferential interest rates; preference in procurement by Government entities; extension of tariff preferences; liberalisation of non tariff measures on a preferential basis; and other measures.

Article 4
The Preferential Trading Arrangements shall be applied to Basic Commodities particularly rice and crude oil, products of the ASEAN industrial projects; products for the expansion of Intra-ASEAN trade; and other products of interest to Contracting States.

Article 5
Long Term Quantity Contracts shall apply to selected products subject to specific agreements negotiated among the Contracting States or their nominated agencies. Long term contracts shall be for a period of three years to five years depending on the products and quantities to be agreed upon subject to annual review where appropriate. However, this provision does not preclude contracts of less than three years as may be agreed upon by the Contracting States.

Article 6
Purchase finance support at preferential interest rates may be applied to either exports to or imports from Contracting States of selected products of ASEAN domestic origin to be covered by the Preferential Trading Arrangements.

Article 7
1. Pre-tender notices for international tenders in respect of procurement by Government entities should be sent to the Missions of the Contracting States in the relevant ASEAN capital.
2. Subject to such provisions as may be embodied in supplementary agreements on Government procurement and to the rules of origin to be subsequently decided, Contracting States shall accord each other to a preferential margin of 2½% which should not exceed US S40,000 worth of preferences per tender in respect of international tenders for Government procurement of goods and auxilliary services from untied loans submitted by ASEAN countries vis a vis non-ASEAN countries.
3. The preferential margin should be applied on the basis of the lowest evaluated and acceptable tender.

Article 8
1. An effective ASEAN margin of tariff preference should be accorded on a product by product basis.
2. Where tariff preferences have been negotiated on multilateral or bilateral basis, the concessions so agreed should be extended to all Contracting States on an ASEAN most favoured nation basis, except where special treatment is accorded to products of ASEAN industrial projects.
3. In the negotiations on tariff preferences, considerations for the balancing of preferences should take into account the possibility of using other instrument of preferential trading arrangements.
4. The effective ASEAN margin of tariff preferences to be accorded to the selected products should take into account existing levels of tariffs in the respective Contracting States.

Article 9
Without prejudice to the provision in Articles 5, 6, 7 and 8, the Contracting States may decide on other preferences as may be mutually agreed upon.

CHAPTER III
Preferential Treatment of the Products of ASEAN Industrial Projects
and Industrial Complementation Schemes
Article 10
1. Notwithstanding the provision of Articles 5, 6, 7, 8, 9 and 15 of
this Agreement, the Contracting States shall establish special preferential
trading arrangements in respect of products of ASEAN industrial
projects which shall be embodied in supplementary agreements. Such
supplementary agreements shall include the provisions that trade
preferences shall be extended exclusively to the products of the ASEAN
industrial projects within agreed time frames and subject to such other
conditions as may be set forth in the supplementary agreements.
2. The products of the ASEAN Industrial Complementation Projects
shall qualify for preferential trading arrangements, provided that
these individual industrial complementation schemes or projects fall
within the guidelines approved by competent Committees of ASEAN
Economic Ministers and that the specific schemes or projects are
approved by the Committee on Industry, Minerals and Energy.

CHAPTER IV
Maintenance of Concessions
Article 11
Contracting States shall not diminish or nullify any of the concessions
as agreed upon through the application of any new charge or measure
restricting trade, except in cases provided for in this Agreement.

CHAPTER V
Emergency Measures
Article 12
1. If, as a result of this Agreement, imports of a particular product
eligible for Preferential Trading Arrangements are increasing in such a
manner as to cause or threaten to cause serious injury to sectors producing like or similar products in the importing Contracting States,
the Importing Contracting States may suspend provisionally and
without discrimination the preferences included in this Agreement.
2. Without prejudice to existing international obligations, a Contracting State, which finds it necessary to institute or intensify quantitative restrictions or other measures limiting imports with a view to
forestalling the threat of or stopping a serious decline in its monetary
reserves or limiting exports due to serious decline in supplies shall
endeavour to do so in a manner which safeguards the value of the
concessions agreed upon.
3. Where, however, emergency measures are taken in pursuance to
this Article, immediate notice of such action must be given to the
Committee referred to in Article 13 and such action may be the subject
of consultations as provided for in Article 14.

CHAPTER VI
Institutional Arrangements
Article 13
The ASEAN Committee on Trade and Tourism (hereinafter referred to as THE COMMITTEE) is hereby directed and authorised to conduct trade negotiations within the framework of this Agreement and to review and supervise the implementation of the Agreement. In respect of all matters concerning the implementation of the Agreement, all decisions of the Committee shall be taken by consensus. The ASEAN Secretariat shall monitor the implementation of the Agreement pursuant to Article III.2.8 of the Agreement on the Establishment of the ASEAN Secretariat.

CHAPTER VII
Consultations
Article 14
1. Each Contracting State shall accord adequate opportunity for consultations regarding such representations as may be made by another Contracting State/States with respect to any affecting the implementation of this Agreement. The Committee may, at the request of the Contracting State/States in respect of any matter for which it has not been possible to find a satisfactory solution during previous consultations.
2. If any Contracting State should consider that any other Contracting State has not carried out its obligations under this Agreement so that it nullifies or impairs any benefit accruing to it, the affected Contracting State, with a view to the satisfactory adjustments of the matter, may make representations or proposals to the other Contracting State concerned which thus approached shall give due consideration to the proposals made to it.
3. If no satisfactory adjustment is affected between the Contracting States concerned within 60 days from the date on which such representation or request for consultation was made, the matter may be referred to the Committee who shall consult with the Contracting States concerned and arrive at a solution mutually acceptable to the States concerned. Where the circumstances are serious enough, a Contracting State may temporarily suspend the application of the concession to the Contracting State/States concerned until a mutually satisfactory solution is arrived at. A Contracting State suspending the concession shall give written notification to the other Contracting States within 30 days prior to such action.

CHAPTER VIII
Rules of Origin
Article 15
Products mentioned in Article 4 of this Agreement shall be eligible for preferential treatment if they satisfy the Rules of Origin set out in Annex 1 which is an integral part of this Agreement.

CHAPTER IX
General Exceptions
Article 16
Nothing in this Agreement shall prevent any Contracting State from taking action and adopting measures which it considers necessary for the protection of its national security, the protection of public morality, the protection of human, animal and plant life and health, and the protection of articles of artistic historic and archaological value.

CHAPTER X
Miscellaneous and Final Provisions
Article 17
1. This Agreement shall enter into force on the 30th day after the deposit of the Fifth Instrument of Ratification.
2. This Agreement may not be signed with reservation nor shall reservations be admitted at the time of ratification.
3. All Articles of this Agreement may be modified through amendments to this Agreement agreed upon by consensus. All amendments shall become effective upon acceptance by all Contracting States.
4. This Agreement shall be deposited with the Secretary-General of the ASEAN Secretariat who shall promptly furnish a certified copy thereof of each Contracting State.
5. Each Contracting State shall deposit its Instrument of Ratification with the Secretary-General of the ASEAN Secretariat who shall likewise promptly inform each Contracting State of such deposit.

IN WITNESS WHEREOF, the undersigned being duly authorised thereto by their respective Governments have signed this Agreement on ASEAN Preferential Trading Arrangements.

Done at   this day of
in a single copy in the English Language.
Initialled 16th February, 1977
For the Government of the Republic of Indonesia
For the Government of Malaysia
For the Government of the Republic of the Philippines
For the Government of the Republic of Singapore
For the Government of the Kingdom of Thailand

RULES OF ORIGIN FOR THE ASEAN PREFERENTIAL TRADING ARRANGEMENTS

For determining the origin of products eligible for preferential concessions under the Agreement on ASEAN Preferential Trading Arrangements, the following Rules shall be applied:

RULE 1. ORIGINATING PRODUCTS — Products covered by preferential trading arrangements within the framework of this Agreement, imported into the territory of a Contracting State from another Contracting State which are consigned directly within the meaning of

Rule 5 hereof, shall be eligible for preferential concessions if they conform to the origin requirement under any one of the following conditions:

(a) Products wholly produced or obtained in the exporting Contracting State as defined in Rule 2; or
(b) Products not wholly produced or obtained in the exporting Contracting State, provided that the said products are eligible under Rule 3 or Rule 4.

RULE 2. WHOLLY PRODUCED OR OBTAINED — Within the meaning of Rule 1(a), the following shall be considered as wholly produced or obtained in the exporting Contracting State:

(a) mineral products extracted from its soil, its water or its seabeds;
(b) agricultural products harvested there;
(c) animals born and raised there;
(d) products obtained from animals referred to in paragraph (c) above;
(e) products obtained by hunting or fishing conducted there;
(f) products of sea fishing and other marine products taken from the sea by its vessels; 1/3/
(g) products processed and/or made on board its factory ships 2/3/ exclusively from products referred to in paragraph (f) above;
(h) used articles collected there, fit only for the recovery of raw materials;
(i) waste and scrap resulting from manufacturing operations conducted there;
(j) goods produced there exclusively from the products referred to in paragraph (a) to (i) above.

1/ 'vessels' — shall refer to fishing vessels engaged in commercial fishing, registered in a Contracting State and operated by a citizen or citizens or government of such Contracting State, or partnership, corporation or association, duly registered in such Contracting State, at least 60% of the equity of which is owned by a citizen or citizens of such Contracting State or 75% by citizens or governments of the Contracting States, provided that the conduct of fishing activities or operations in the territorial waters of any of the Contracting States, shall be subject to the provisions of the constitution and existing laws of the respective Contracting States.

2/ 'factory ships' — shall refer to special types of vessels equipped with processing facilities and able to do processing operations offshore and in the high seas, registered in a Contracting State and operated by a citizen or citizens or government of such Contracting State, or partnership, corporation or association, duly registered in such Contracting State, at least 60% of the equity of which is owned by a citizen or citizens or government of such Contracting State, or 75% by citizens or governments of the Contracting States, provided that the conduct of fishing activities or operations in the territorial waters of any of the Contracting States, shall be subject to the provisions of the Constitution and existing laws of the respective Contracting States. 3/ In respect of vessels or factory ships operated by government agencies, the requirements of flying the flag of a Contracting State does not apply.

RULE 3.   NOT WHOLLY PRODUCED OR OBTAINED

(a) (i)   Subject to subparagraphs (ii) below, for the purpose of implementing the provisions of Rule 1(b) and subject to the provisions of Rule 4, products worked on and processed as a result of which the total value of the materials, parts or products originating from non-ASEAN countries or of undetermined origin used does not exceed 50% of the FOB value of the products produced or obtained and the final process of manufacture is performed within the territory of the exporting Contracting State.

(ii)   In respect of Indonesia, the percentage referred to in subparagraph (i) above is 40%. On certain categories of manufactured products to be agreed upon from time to time, the requirement of 50% of non-ASEAN content may apply.

(b) In respect of the ASEAN industrial projects, the percent criterion of Rule 3(a) may be waived.

(c) The value of the nonoriginating materials, parts or produce shall be:

(1) The CIF value at the time of importation of the products or importation can be proven; or

(2) The earliest ascertainable price paid for the products of undetermined origin in the territory of the Contracting State where the working or processing takes place.

RULE 4.   CUMULATIVE RULE OF ORIGIN – Products which comply with origin requirements provided for in Rule 1 and which are used in a Contracting State as inputs for a finished product eligible for preferential treatment in another Contracting State/States shall be considered as a product originating in the Contracting State where working or processing of the finished product has taken place provided that the aggregate ASEAN content of the final product is not less than 60%.

RULE 5.   DIRECT CONSIGNMENT – The following shall be considered as directly consigned from the exporting Contracting State to the importing Contracting State:

(a) if the products are transported without passing through the territory of any other non-ASEAN country;

(b) the products whose transport involves transit through one or more intermediate non-ASEAN countries with or without transhipment or temporary storage in such countries; provided that:

(1)   the transit entry is justified for geographical reason or by considerations related exclusively to transport requirements;

(2)   the products have not entered into trade or consumption there; and

(3)   the products have not undergone any operation there other than unloading and reloading or any operation required to keep them in good condition.

RULE 6.   TREATMENT OF PACKING

(a) Where for purposes of assessing customs duties a Contracting State treats products separately from their packing, it may also, in respect of its imports consigned from another Contracting State, determine separately the origin of such packing.

LATEST DEVELOPMENTS IN THE ASEAN PREFERENTIAL TRADING ARRANGEMENT

Approval of 71 Products
The approval of the 71 products for qualification under the ASEAN Preferential Trading Agreement was ASEAN's first concrete step towards regional integration. These 71 products are classified and enumerated as follows:

1. Products receiving concessions initially on a bilateral basis and subsequently multilateralised on a most favored nation basis —

Indonesia
certain tyres and tubes for off-road vehicles, calcium carbide, portland cement, certain parts for motorcycles and side cars, certain electrical measuring instruments

Malaysia
twine, cordage, rope and cable plaited or not of Manila hemp, portable electric typewriters, vermicelli and noodles made from rice

Philippines
paraffin wax, glass jars for baby food, portable electric typewriters, certain cast, rolled, drawn or blown glass

Singapore
kain lepas and kain sarong batik, shampoo, solid raw beet and cane sugar, certain handbags, purses, wallets, briefcases, portfolios and satchels

Thailand
quinine (including its salts), margarine, twine, cordage, ropes and cables plaited or not of Manila hemp, ball bearings

2. Products on which trade barriers to exports from the other ASEAN countries will be unilaterally reduced —

Indonesia
maize
canned vegetables
cutlery
jewelry
filter blocks
facial tissues
sanitary towels
sorghum
white rice flour
clinker

Malaysia
soda ash
live animals (cattle)
vegetables
potatoes and onions
extracts (concentrates of coffee)
rice
shark's fins
maize
certain raw sugar
certain salts
gypsum

Philippines
meat from offal or bovine cattle
maize
green and yellow monggo beans
crude and refined palm oil
crude gypsum
anthracite coal
graphite and carbon electrodes
tractor tyres
ball bearings

Singapore
undergarments (cotton, knitted or crocheted, not elastic)
undergarments (not wholly of cotton)
outergarments (other articles not knitted or crocheted, not elastic)
shirts (knitted, crocheted)
outergarments for men (excluding sarongs and dhoties)
outergarments for infants
shirts (not knitted or crocheted)
stockings, socks (knitted or crocheted, not elastic)

cotton handkerchiefs
brassieres

Thailand
sawn timber
other nonconiferous timber
certain vegetables (except garlic and onions)
insecticides
lead-base rod solder
nutmeg, not powdered
chili, not powdered
paraffin wax
certain chemicals for agricultural use

Appendix E

Kuala Lumpur Declaration (ZOPFAN Declaration, 1971)

We, the Foreign Ministers of
INDONESIA,
MALAYSIA,
THE PHILIPPINES,
SINGAPORE
and the Special
Envoy of the National
Executive Council of
THAILAND:

FIRMLY BELIEVING in the merits of regional cooperation which has drawn our countries to cooperate together in the economic, social and cultural fields in the Association of Southeast Asian Nations;

DESIROUS of bringing about a relaxation of international tension and of achieveing a lasting peace in Southeast Asia;

INSPIRED by the worthy aims and objectives of the United Nations, in particular by the principles of respect for the sovereignty and territorial integrity of all States, abstention from the threat or use of force, peaceful settlement of international disputes, equal rights and self-determination and non-interference in the internal affairs of States;

BELIEVING in the continuing validity of the 'Declaration on the Promotion of World Peace and Cooperation' of the Bandung Conference of 1955, which, among others, enunciates the principles by which States may coexist peacefully;

RECOGNISING the right of every state, large or small, to lead its national existence free from outside interference in its internal affairs as this interference will adversely affect its freedom, independence and integrity;

DEDICATED to the maintenance of peace, freedom and independence unimpaired;

BELIEVING in the need to meet present challenges and new developments by cooperating with all peace and freedom loving nations, both within and outside the region, in the furtherance of world peace, stability and harmony;

COGNIZANT of the significant trend towards establishing nuclear-free zones, as in the 'Treaty for the Prohibition of Nuclear Weapons in Latin America' and the Lusaka Declaration proclaiming Africa a nuclear-free zone, for the purpose of promoting world peace and security by reducing the areas of international conflicts and tensions;

REITERATING our commitment to the principle in the Bangkok Declaration which established ASEAN in 1967, 'that the countries of Southeast Asia share a primary responsibility for strengthening the economic and social stability of the region and ensuring their peaceful and progressive national development, and that they are determined to ensure their stability and security from external interference in any form or manifestation in order to preserve their national identities in accordance with the ideals and aspirations of their peoples';

AGREEING that the neutralisation of Southeast Asia is a desirable objective and that we should explore ways and means of bringing about its realisation, and

CONVINCED that the time is propitious for joint action to give effective expression to the deeply felt desire of the peoples of Southeast Asia to ensure the conditions of peace and stability indispensable to their independence and their economic and social well-being:

DO HEREBY STATE:

1. that Indonesia, Malaysia, the Philippines, Singapore and Thailand are determined to exert initially necessary efforts to secure the recognition of, and respect for, Southeast Asia as a Zone of Peace, Freedom and Neutrality, free from any form or manner of interference by outside Powers;

2. that Southeast Asian countries should make concerted efforts to broaden the areas of cooperation which would contribute to their strength, solidarity and closer relationship.

Done at Kuala Lumpur on Saturday, the 27th of November, 1971.

on behalf of the
REPUBLIC OF INDONESIA
(Adam Malik)
Minister of Foreign Affairs

on behalf of
MALAYSIA
(Tun Abdul Razak bin Dato Hussein)
Prime Minister and Minister of
Foreign Affairs

on behalf of the
REPUBLIC OF THE PHILIPPINES
(Carlos P. Romulo)
Secretary of Foreign Affairs

on behalf of the
REPUBLIC OF SINGAPORE
(S. Rajaratnam)
Minister of Foreign Affairs

on behalf of the
KINGDOM OF THAILAND
(Thanat Khoman)
Special Envoy of the National
Executive Council

Joint Press Communiqué

1. The President of the Republic of Indonesia, H.E. General Soeharto, the Prime Minister of Malaysia, H.E. Datuk Hussein Onn, the President of the Republic of the Philippines, H.E. Ferdinand E. Marcos, the Prime Minister of the Republic of Singapore, H.E. Lee Kuan Yew, the Prime Minister of the Kingdom of Thailand, H.E. Krukrit Pramoj, met in Denpasar, Bali on 23–24 February 1976.

2. The Meeting was held in the traditional ASEAN spirit of friendship and cordiality.

3. They reviewed the activities of ASEAN since its inception in 1967, and expressed satisfaction with its progress especially in fostering the spirit of cooperation and solidarity among the member states.

4. They discussed developments affecting the ASEAN region. They reaffirmed the determination of their respective Governments to continue to work for the promotion of peace, stability and progress in Southeast Asia, thus contributing towards world peace and international harmony. To this end they expressed their readiness to develop fruitful relation and mutually beneficial cooperation with other countries in the region. They expressed the hope that other powers would pursue policies which would contribute to the achievement of peace, stability and progress in Southeast Asia.

5. The Meeting discussed ways and means of strengthening cooperation among member states.They believed that it was essential for the member states to move to higher levels of cooperation, especially in the political, economic, social, cultural, scientific and technological fields.

6. On the Zone of Peace, Freedom and Neutrality the Heads of Government expressed their satisfaction with the progress made in the efforts to draw up initially necessary steps to secure the recognition of and respect for the Zone, They directed that these efforts should be continued in order to realise its early establishment.

7. The Heads of Government signed the Treaty of Amity and Cooperation in Southeast Asia.

8. They also signed the Declaration of ASEAN Concord.

9. In pursuance of their determination to forge closer economic cooperation among member states, they agreed that a meeting of Economic Ministers be convened in Kuala Lumpur on 8–9 March 1976 to consider measures to be taken towards implementing the decisions of the Meeting of ASEAN Heads of Government on matters of economic cooperation.

10. They also agreed that the Meeting of Economic Ministers would discuss particularly the following questions:

i. The mechanisms by which member States shall accord priority in critical circumstances, such as natural disasters, major calamities, and shortages due to artificial or natural causes, to supply of the individual country's needs in food and energy and priority to the acquisition of exports from member States.

ii. The measures to be taken for intensifying cooperation in the production of basic commodities particularly for food and energy.

iii. The formulation of appropriate measures for initiating cooperative action toward establishing ASEAN large scale industrial projects. Examples of some of the ASEAN industrial projects that could be considered by the Meeting of ASEAN economic Ministers are urea, super-phosphates, potash, petro-chemicals, steel, soda ash, news-print and rubber products. The Meeting will also give consideration to other projects.

iv. The instruments to be employed in preferential trading arrangements to facilitate the expansion of trade among ASEAN member states in basic commodities, particularly in food and energy and the products of ASEAN industrial projects.

These instruments will include, but not be limited to, the following:
  a. long-term quantity contracts,
  b. purchase finance support at preferential interest rates,
  c. preference in procurement by government entities,
  d. extension on tariff preferences, and
  e. Other measures agreed upon,

v. The formulation of joint approaches to international commodity and other economic problems, giving priority to stabilization and increase of export earnings of ASEAN commodities, through commodity agreements, including bufferstock schemes and other means.

11. The Foreign Ministers signed the Agreement on the Establishment of the ASEAN Secretariat. The Heads of Government took note of the nomination of Mr. Hartono Rekso Dharsono as Secretary-General of the ASEAN Secretariat.

12. The Heads of Government of Malaysia, the Philippines, Singapore, Thailand were warmly appreciative of the exemplary chairmanship of their Meeting by the President of the Republic of Indonesia and expressed their thanks for the traditional Indonesian hospitality extended to them and the excellent arrangements made for their Meeting.

Further Reading

Although books on the individual countries of ASEAN are numerous, and well enough known not to need listing here, few full-length studies have been written on ASEAN as a whole. Most material on the subject is in the form of articles, conference papers and Press reports and in ASEAN's official documents. Without attempting to account for the entire literature, we recommend as current sources the *Far Eastern Economic Review* and its annual *Yearbooks*, the *Asian Wall Street Journal*, *Asia Pacific Community*, *Asiaweek*, the occasional papers of the Institute of South East Asian Studies (ISEAS, Singapore), the relevant research papers of the Australia–Japan Economic Relations Research Project (AJERRP, Australian National University, Canberra), and those of the Centre for the Study of Australian–Asian Relations (CSAAR, Griffith University, Queensland). Other academic journals are mentioned below.

This list is selected from sources we have used, but also includes sources which provide other views of the issues discussed.

Chinese and Japanese names are shown with the family name first and given name second.

AIIA Canberra Branch, *Australia and ASEAN*, report by a study group of the Canberra Branch of the Australian Institute of International Affairs, by Dr Frank Frost, *Dyason House Papers*, 5, 1–6 September 1978 (Melbourne, 1978).

Albinski, Henry S., *Australian External Policy under Labour: Content, Process and the National Debate* (University of Queensland Press, 1977).

Allen, Thomas W., *The ASEAN Report* (2 vols.), ed. Barry Wain (Hong Kong: *The Asian Wall Street Journal*, 1979).

———, *The ASEAN Update* (Hong Kong: *The Asian Wall Street Journal*, 1980).

Ariff, K. A. M., 'ASEAN Economic Cooperation: The End of the Beginning', *Economic Bulletin*, 3, 5, August 1977, Kuala Lumpur.

Arndt, H. W., 'ASEAN Industrial Projects', *Asia Pacific Community*, 2, Fall 1978.

Arndt, H. W. and Garnaut, Ross, 'ASEAN and the Industrialisation of Southeast Asia', *Journal of Common Market Studies*, XVII, 3 March 1979.

ASEAN Central Secretariat, *10 Years ASEAN* (Jakarta, 1978).

Asian Development Bank, *Rural Asia: Challenge and Opportunity* (Kuala Lumpur: Federal Publications, 1977).

Boncan, Raul A., 'ASEAN, the Natural Community', *Asia Pacific Community*, 2, Fall 1978.

Booker, Malcolm, *The Last Domino: Aspects of Australia's Foreign Relations, 1976* (Melbourne: Collier, 1978).

Boyce, Peter (ed.), *Malaysia and Singapore in International Diplomacy: Documents and Commentaries* (Sydney University Press, 1968).

Brown, Bruce (ed.), *Asia and the Pacific in the 1970s* (Canberra: ANU Press, 1971).

Brown, Colin, *Australia–ASEAN Relations 1976–1979*, Asian Studies Association of Australia conference, Griffith University, Queensland, August 1980.

Camilleri, J. S., *An Introduction to Australian Foreign Policy* (Queensland: Jacaranda Press, 1976 & 1979).

Chee-Meow Seah, 'Major Powers and the Search for a New Equilibrium in Southeast Asia', *Asia Pacific Community*, 7, Winter 1980.

Cheh, Edward K. Y., *Hyper-growth in Asian Economies: A Comparative Study of Hong Kong, Japan, Korea, Singapore and Taiwan* (Macmillan, 1980).

Chia Siow Yue, 'ASEAN External Economic Relations with Australia and New Zealand', Fifth Conference of Federation of ASEAN Economic Association, Singapore, 30 October–1 November, 1980.

Clapham, Christopher (ed.), *Foreign Policy-Making in Developing States: A Comparative Approach* (Hampshire, UK: Saxon House, 1977).

Clark, Claire (ed.), *Australian Foreign Policy* (Melbourne: Cassell Australia, 1973).

Crouch, Harold, *The Army and Politics in Indonesia* (New York: Cornell, 1978).

Dahm, Bernard and Draguhn, Werner (eds.), *Politics, Society and Economy in the ASEAN States* (Weisbaden: Otto Harrassowitz, 1975).

Drysdale, Peter, *An Organisation for Pacific Trade, Aid and Development: Regional Arrangements and the Resource Trade*, AJERRP, research paper no. 49, ANU, Canberra, May 1978.

Drysdale, Peter and Patrick, Hugh, *Evaluation of a Proposed Asian-Pacific Regional Economic Organisation*, AJERRP, research paper no. 61, ANU, Canberra, 1979.

Drysdale, Peter and Rix, A., 'Australia's Economic Relations with Asia and the Pacific', *Current Affairs Bulletin*, 1 April 1979.

Edwards, Clive T., *ASEAN–Australia Trade Relations: A Survey of Current Issues* (Canberra: ANU Press, October 1978).

———, *Australia and Asia: Can Australia's Economic Myopia Continue?* (Canberra: ANU Press July 1979).

———, 'Australia and Asia: Opportunities Amidst Challenges', *Australian Economic Review*, 1st quarter, 1978.

———, *Australian Economic Priorities in the Context of a Changing International Economic Order*, Metal Trades Industry Association national affairs forum, Sydney, October 1978.

———, 'Perspectives of ASEAN', *Australian Industries Development Association Bulletin*, 303, December 1978.

———, 'Recent Economic Developments in Asia: Their Significance for Australia',

Dyason House Papers, 3 (2), October 1976.

———, 'Restructuring Australian Manufacturing Industry: Is Freer Trade the Only Answer?', *Australian Bulletin of Labour*, 4 (3), June 1978.

Eldridge, Philip J., *Emerging Issues in Australia–ASEAN Relations* (Tasmania: unpublished, May 1978).

Elphick, E. S., *Australia's Relations with Asia* (Sydney: Reed Education, 1975).

Fifield, Russell H., 'ASEAN: Image and Reality', *Asian Survey*, XIX, 12, December 1979.

———, *National and Regional Interests in ASEAN: Competition and Cooperation in International Politics* (Singapore: Institute of Southeast Asian Studies, 1979).

Frost, Frank, 'Political Issues in Australia–ASEAN Relations', *Asia Pacific Community*, no. 7, winter 1980.

———, 'The Origins and Evolution of ASEAN', *World Review*, University of Queensland Press, August 1980.

Garnaut, Ross (ed.), *ASEAN in a Changing Pacific and World Economy*, Proceedings of the Tenth Pacific Trade and Development conference, ANU, Canberra, March 1979 (Canberra: ANU Press, 1980).

Golay, Frank H. (ed.), *The United States and the Philippines* (New York: Prentice-Hall, 1966).

Gordon, Bernard K., *The Dimensions of Conflict in Southeast Asia* (New York: Prentice-Hall, 1966).

Grant, Bruce (ed.), *The Boat People* (Melbourne: Penguin Books Australia, 1979).

Ham, Angela, *A Guide to Sources on Australian–Asian Relations* (Queensland: CSAAR, Griffith University, February 1980).

Harries, O., *Australia and the Third World*, Report of the Committee on Australia's Relations with the Third World (Canberra: AGPS, 1979).

Healey, Derek T., *Australia, Japan and ASEAN: the Emerging Trade–Aid Relationship*, ASAA second national conference, University of New South Wales, May 1978.

———, *Integration Schemes Among Developing Countries: A Survey*, Sixth conference of Economists, Hobart, May 1977.

Hironon Ryokichi, 'Changing Patterns of Economic Interdependence in Asia', *The Developing Economies*, XI -4, December 1973, Tokyo.

———, *The US–Japan Relations in the Economic Development of Southeast Asia*, unpublished, for the Japan–US in Multilateral Diplomacy Project, Columbia University, New York, September 1978.

———, *The ASEAN and Economic Policies Toward Australia and Japan*, AJERRP, research paper no. 52, ANU, Canberra, September 1978.

———, 'Towards Increased Intra-ASEAN Economic Cooperation', *Asia Pacific Community*, 3, Winter 1978.

Hoadley, J. Stephen, 'New Zealand and ASEAN', *Indonesia Quarterly*, V, 2 April 1977.

Hyde, J., *Australia: The Asia Connection* (Melbourne: Kibble, 1978).

Ichimura Shin'ichi, 'Japan and Southeast Asia', *Asian Survey*, XX, 7, July 1980, University of California Press.

Indorff, H. H., *ASEAN: Problems and Prospects*, ISEAS, Singapore, occasional paper no. 38, December 1975.

ISEAS, *ASEAN and the Multinational Corporations* (Singapore, 1977).

Jansen, G. H., *Afro-Asia and Non-Alignment* (London: Faber and Faber, 1966).

Jorgensen-Dahl, Arnfinn, 'The Emerging External Policies of the Association of Southeast Asian Nations (ASEAN)', *Australian Journal of Politics and History*, XXIV, 1, April 1978, University of Queensland Press.

———, 'The Significance of ASEAN', *World Review,* University of Queensland Press, August 1980.

———, *Regional Organization and Order in South-East Asia* (London: Macmillan, forthcoming).

Kojima Kyoshi, *An Organisation for Pacific Trade. Aid an Development: A Proposal,* AJERRP, research paper no. 40, ANU, Canberra, September 1976.

Lamb, Alistair, *Asian Frontiers: Studies in a Continuing Problem* (New York: Praeger, 1968).

Lau Teik Soon, *New Directions in the International Relations of South East Asia* (Singapore University Press, 1973).

———, 'The Role of Singapore in Southeast Asia', *World Review,* 19, 3, August 1980, University of Queensland Press.

Lee, S. Y. and Booth, Anne, *Towards an Effective Programme for ASEAN Co-operation from 1978–1983,* Third conference of the Federation of ASEAN Economic Associations, Kuala Lumpur, 2–4 November 1978.

Leifer, Michael, 'The Paradox of ASEAN: A Security Organisation without the Structure of an Alliance', *Round Table,* 271, July 1978.

———, *The Philippine Claim to Sabah* (University of Hull, 1978).

———, 'The Foreign Relations of the New States', in Wang Gungwu and J. A. C. Mackie (eds.), *Studies in Contemporary Southeast Asia* (Longman Australia, 1973).

———, *Dilemmas of Statehood in Southeast Asia* (Vancouver: University of British Columbia Press, 1972).

Levi, Werner, *The Challenge of World Politics in South and Southeast Asia* (New York: Prentice-Hall, 1968).

Lim Chong-Yah, 'ASEAN's Package-Deal Industrial Projects', *Asia Pacific Community,* 2, Fall 1978.

Lim Joo Jock, *Geostrategy and the South China Sea Basin* (Singapore University Press, 1979).

Lim, Robyn Abell, 'The Philippines and the Formation of ASEAN', *Review of Indonesian and Malayan Affairs,* 7, January/June 1973.

———, *Thinking about ASEAN in Australia,* ASAA conference, Brisbane, August 1980.

———, 'Current Australian–ASEAN Relations', *Southeast Asian Affairs 1980,* Singapore, ISEAS, 1980.

Lyon, Peter, 'Regional Organisation in South East Asia, *Spectrum,* 4, 3, April–June 1976.

———, *War and Peace in South East Asia* (Oxford University Press, 1969).

Macapagal, Diosdado, *The Philippines Turns East* (Quezon City: Mac Publishing House, 1970).

Mackie, J. A. C., *Konfrontasi: The Indonesia–Malaysia Dispute 1963–1966* (Oxford University Press, 1974).

———, (ed.), *Australia in the New World Order: Foreign Policy in the 1970s* (Melbourne: Nelson in association with AIIA, 1976).

Malaysia, Ministry of Foreign Affairs, *Facts on ASEAN* (undated), (Kuala Lumpur, 1977).

McLeod, Kenneth J. and Utrecht, Ernst (eds.), *The ASEAN Papers,* papers and talks on Southeast Asia presented to the Transnational Cooperatives' ASEAN conference, Sydney 1977 (James Cook University of North Queensland, 1979).

Moertopo, Ali, 'Future Indonesian–US Relations: A View from Jakarta', *Asia Pacific Community,* 7, 4, July 1976.

Morrison, Charles E. and Suhrke, Astri, *Strategies of Survival: The Foriegn Policy Dilemmas of Smaller Asian States* (University of Queensland Press, 1978).

Mortimer, Rex (ed.), *Showcase State: The Illusion of Indonesia's Accelerated Modernisation* (Sydney: Angus and Robertson, 1978).

Naya Seiji, 'Japan's Role in ASEAN Economic Development', *Asia Pacific Community*, 1, Summer 1978.

Niksch, Larry A., *The Association of Southeast Asian Nations (ASEAN): An Emerging Challenge in US Policy Towards Asia*, US Congressional Research Service Report, np. 78–197 F, November 1978.

Noble, Lela Garner, *Philippine Policy Toward Sabah: A Claim to Independence* (University of Arizona Press, 1977).

Nuechterlein, Donald E., *Thailand and the Struggle for Southeast Asia* (Cornell University Press, 1965).

Okita Saburo and Crawford, Sir John, *Australia, Japan and the Western Pacific Economic Relations: A Report to the Governments of Australia and Japan* (Canberra: AGPS. 1978).

Osborn, George K., *Balances of Power in Southeast Asia, 1978*, ISEAS, Singapore, occasional paper no. 53.

Osborne, Milton, 'The Indochinese Refugees: Causes and Effect', *International Affairs*, January 1980, Royal Institute of International Affairs, London (Oxford University Press, 1980).

———, 'Kampuchea: The Crisis Continues', *Current Affairs Bulletin*, 57, 6, November 1980, University of Sydney.

Ott, Marvin C., *The Neutralization of Southeast Asia: An Analysis of the Malaysian/ASEAN Proposal* (Ohio University, 1974).

Pace, Barbara French *et al.*, *Regional Cooperation in Southeast Asia: The First Two Years of ASEAN, 1967–1969*, Research Analysis Corporation, RAC-R-98-2, October 1970.

Pangestu, Mari, 'The ASEAN Economies: A Comparative Assessment of the Pattern of Trade and Direct Foreign Investment and Implications for Economic Cooperation', *World Review*, 19, 3, August 1980, University of Queensland Press.

Pettman, Ralph, *Small Power Politics and International Relations in Southeast Asia* (Sydney: Holt, Rinehart and Winston, 1976).

Potterton, Jayashree, 'ASEAN, Kampuchea and the Superpowers', *Current Affairs Bulletin*, 57, 4, September 1980, University of Sydney.

Rajaratnam, Sinnathamby, 'New Cold War in the Pacific', *Asia Pacific Community*, 3, Winter 1978.

Renouf, A. R., *The Frightened Country* (Melbourne: Macmillan, 1979).

Sarasin Viraphol, Amphon Namantra and Shibusawa Masahide (eds.), *The ASEAN: Problems and Prospects in a Changing World*, Conference at Chulalongkorn University, Bangkok, December 1975.

Shand, R. T. and Richter, H. V. (eds.), *International Aid: Some Political, Administrative and Technical Realities*, Development Studies Centre monograph no. 16, ANU, Canberra, 1979.

Shawcross, William, *Sideshow: Kissinger, Nixon and the Destruction of Cambodia* (New York: Simon and Schuster, 1979).

Siddique, Sharon, 'Contemporary Islamic Developments in ASEAN', *Southeast Asian Affairs, 1980*, ISEAS, Singapore, 1980.

Sim, P. J. (Chairman), *Australia and ASEAN*, Report from the Senate Standing Committee on Foreign Affairs and Defence, Parliament of Australia, AGPS, 1980.

Singapore Airlines, *Highlights of the ASEAN Economy* (Singapore, 1977).

Solidum, Estrella D., *Towards a Southeast Asian Community* (University of the Philippines Press, 1974).

Somsakdi Xuto, *Regional Cooperation in Southeast Asia: Problems, Possibilities and Prospects* (Bangkok: Institute of Asian Studies, Chulalongkorn University, 1973).

Stargardt, A. W., *Australia's Asian Policies: A History of a Debate 1838–1972*, Institute of Asian Affairs (Weisbaden: Otto Harrassowitz, 1977).

Stifel, Laurence D., 'ASEAN Cooperation and Economic Growth in Southeast Asia', *Asia Pacific Community*, Spring/Early Summer 1979.

Sycip, Gorres, Velayo Inc., *ASEAN: An Economic Profile* (Manila, 1978).

Tan Sook Joo, *ASEAN: A Bibliography*, Library Bulletin no. 11, 1976, ISEAS, Singapore.

Teichmann, Max (ed.), *New Directions in Australian Foreign Policy* (Ringwood, Victoria: Penguin Books, 1969).

United Nations, *Economic Cooperation among Member Countries of the ASEAN*, Report of a United Nations Team, *Journal of Development Planning*, 7, New York, 1974.

Van der Kroef, J. M., 'ASEAN Security and Development: Some Paradoxes and Symbols', *Asian Affairs*, IX, part 2, 1978.

———, 'ASEAN in the 1980s' *World Review*, August 1980, University of Queensland Press.

Vasey, Lloyd R., *ASEAN and a Positive Strategy for Foreign Investment*, Report and papers of a private conference organised by the Pacific Forum, University Press, Hawaii, 1979.

Viviani, Nancy, *Australia and Japan: Approaches to Development Assistance Policy*, AJERRP, research paper no. 37, ANU, Canberra, March 1976.

———, 'Australia's Relations with ASEAN', *World Review*, August 1980, University of Queensland Press.

Wang Gungwu, 'ASEAN: A Sub-region Emerges', *Development News Digest*, August 1976.

Wells, R. J. G., 'ASEAN Intraregional Trading in Food and Agricultural Crops – the Way Ahead', *Asian Survey*, June 1980.

Whitlam, Hon. E. G., *Political Interdependence, Security and Economic Prospects in the Pacific Region*, Tokyo, the International Institute of Strategic Studies, and the Brookings Institution, 16 October 1978.

Williams, Charlotte, *The Pacific Community: A Modest Proposal*, AJERRP, research paper no. 55, ANU, Canberra, March 1979,

Wilson, David A., *The United States and the Future of Thailand* (New York: Praeger, 1970).

Wilson, Dick, *The Future Role of Singapore* (Oxford University Press, 1972).

———, *The Neutralization of Southeast Asia* (New York: Praeger, 1975).

Wong, John, *ASEAN Economies in Perspective: A Comparative Study of Indonesia, Malaysia, the Philippines, Singapore and Thailand* (Hong Kong: Macmillan, 1979).

Yeh, Stephen H. K. and Laquian, A. A. (eds.), *Housing Asia's Millions: Problems, Policies and Prospects for Low-Cost Housing in Southeast Asia* (Ottawa: International Development Research Centre, 1979).

Zacher, Mark W. and Milne, R. Stephen (eds.), *Conflict and Stability in Southeast Asia* (New York: Anchor Books, 1974).

Index